Go-to Girl

Go-to Girl
Digs, Dives, and a Golden Spike
Copyright © 2023 by J.J. Gearhart

Additional copies may be ordered from the publisher for educational,
business, promotional or premium use.
For information, contact ALIVE Book Publishing at:
alivebookpublishing.com, or call (925) 837-7303.

Book design by Alex P. Johnson

ISBN 13
978-1-63132-205-1

Library of Congress Control Number: 2023914260

Library of Congress Cataloging-in-Publication Data
is available upon request.

First Edition

Published in the United States of America by ALIVE Book Publishing
and ALIVE Publishing Group, imprints of Advanced Publishing LLC
3200 A Danville Blvd., Suite 204, Alamo, California 94507
alivebookpublishing.com

PRINTED IN THE UNITED STATES OF AMERICA

10 9 8 7 6 5 4 3 2 1

Go-to Girl

Digs, Dives,
and a Golden Spike

J.J. Gearhart

ABOOKS
Alive Book Publishing

I dedicate this book to my daughters
Audrey Jo and Lauren Mackenzie.

No matter how much I say I love you,
I love you more than that.

CONTENTS

PREGAME

Somebody once told me I was born with too much serotonin, that waking up with a smile on my face before I bounce out of bed is abnormal. Somebody else told me girls are not as competitive as boys, but I've never known anybody as thirsty to learn and hungry to win as I have been. Imagine what I was like in college when I woke up and realized "It's a GAME Day!" On those days, I couldn't stop smiling.

When I had arrived at The Farm in 1979, athletes had little cachè in the academic microwave: our energy on the courts and fields reflected off of our disinterested classmates, then returned and melted us from the inside out. By the time I was a junior, the status of women's sports at Stanford was quite positive and we performed better, knowing we had proved our relevance in the classroom and on the court. We were no longer part of the Association for Intercollegiate Athletics for Women (AIAW), but part of the NCAA. Still, many felt we didn't belong.

During my first two years in college, I hid the fact I was a scholarship athlete, changing from practice sweats into preppy plaid skirts and polo shirts before I went to class. On game days in 1981, however, I knew I wasn't the only Stanford student-athlete who felt excited to represent our school in competition. I wore my comfortable red sweats with "Stanford Volleyball" stenciled on the front and became a walking billboard for a home game that night in Maples

Pavilion. Many of my classmates asked who we'd be playing, and many students, faculty and staff filled the stands.

Before 1981, I was the queen of pre-game meltdowns, throwing up before every game my sophomore year. As a junior, I'd conquered my queasies and learned to transfer my excessive physical energy into a warrior mentality that scared me sometimes. From the outside, I appeared carefree as I cracked jokes and teased my teammates, but on the inside, my excitement and anxiety churned the acid in my intestines. It took two years to learn how to manage my mind and my body. When we were playing on the road, I really leaned on my pre-game routine to stay calm in the hostile environment of another team's gym. The taunts and the screams timed to distract me just as I was about to make a play. It was hard to ignore these, but I learned to embrace them, to make a play that would silence that noise. I can still remember that routine, decades after our epic match at UCLA in 1981.

* * *

I begin the rituals of volleyball warfare, starting with my hair. I untangle my curls, slant my part slightly off-center, and begin to French-braid a pigtail. I embed red and white ribbons into the three strands as I twist and flip them over and around, smoothing the ribbon so it lies flat on my carefully portioned hair. I twist the elastic three times so no hair will fall out. I then tackle the curls in the other pigtail. In previous matches, my separate, untethered pigtails swung around and thwacked me in the face after I spiked the ball. But not tonight. I attach the two pigtails together at the bottom with another hair band, which has a bow tied in double knots; my braids won't budge the whole match, for my mom has taught me well.

She's sick again, and unable to travel to the match at UCLA, and I can feel her pain from 400 miles away. She has good days and bad days and I don't know what today has been like for her, but I am floating above the end-of-season injuries and my own pain at this point. My excitement and my joy masks all pain; I'm so pumped up I can hardly breathe. We're going to be on TV. A woman's sporting event is going to be on TV! Title IX is working. So unreal.

Here come the queasies, but my stomach, my second brain, is strong as I breathe into my nose and exhale out of my mouth. I'm calm. Abiding. Present.

We wear my favorite uniform: white Adidas short-sleeved shirts with red stripes down the sleeves, and red Adidas shorts, which are much more flattering than bikini-like bun-huggers. They're especially comfortable during our periods, which we all have at the same time. Fortunately, the moon is waning so the red seas of Aunt Flo are dry tonight. These uniforms are on a winning streak, but the sweat stains under my armpits are still visible after multiple washings. I grab my teammate Grits' Shower to Shower powder and sprinkle some on my pits and the jersey. The white talc covers some of the stain. I tap some on the inside of my filthy, smelly knee pads. In service to my superstitions, I have not washed them since our winning streak started. Before I pull up my kneepads, I drop my shorts and powder my buns so sweat won't make my underwear stick. I won't be yanking my undies on national TV tonight. I give the powder to Boom-Boom, who tosses the bottle to DD, who sprinkles a bit on her hands, then passes it to Krush without closing the perforated top, so Krush gets a face full of powder. Such a freshman move. Bakes grabs the bottle, closes it, and tosses it to Kisi, whose reflexes are equally quick with her right or her left hand.

Checking myself in the mirror, I practice my armswing, see my biceps flex, lead with my elbow, snap over the top of an imaginary ball, feel the surge of adrenaline start between my collarbones and tingle down my arms as I let go of the tension and exhale a blast of "aargh!" A red flush covers my face. I'm pasty white and muscular compared to our opponents, who are tan and skinny. As I look at my butt, my broad shoulders, and flat-abbed waist in the mirror, I still look like a boy. At twenty. No one ever told me I threw like a girl, I remind myself as I jog out of the locker room, down the corridor and toward the plaques honoring UCLA's ten NCAA men's basketball championships. I stop in the hallway and look at this pyramid of success. Stanford has no trophies on display in our gym. *Not yet*, I think, as I smack a volleyball between my hands and wait for my teammates to finish getting dressed before we play in the first ever Women's NCAA Volleyball regional final.

As I wait for my teammates, I think about our rapid rise over the last three years. Those of us who are juniors – Kisi, Boom-Boom, and I – helped transform our program from an under-funded AIAW (Association of Intercollegiate Athletics for Women) losing team to a nationally-ranked squad in the NCAA (National Collegiate Athletic Association). We're going to anoint the brightly lit court of Pauley Pavilion with our female sweat. It is December 5, 1981, and UCLA stands between us and a chance at a national championship. Maybe today is the day I will be the go-to girl, and make the game-winning play that everyone remembers.

In the world of sport, making the big play is akin to writing a song which everyone recognizes after hearing just the first three notes (Queen's *Another One Bites the Dust*), or writing a poem with a famous first line (Wordsworth's "I wandered lonely as a cloud"). Recognition and anticipation build, and everyone is filled with the joy, knowing what's to come. I want that.

As I approach to spike the ball, I want to hear the gasp of the crowd as I leap three feet in the air, hear their collective silence as I swing, and hear their cheers as the ball hits the floor for a point. I close my eyes and visualize that moment as I stand in the hostile hallway. Will this be the night I hit that golden spike? I drift into the past. I think about my first foray into sports, ten years ago.

I started on the basketball, not volleyball, court, but spent most of my time dreaming about owning a horse farm as I shoveled the stalls at a local barn to pay for my 4-H horse project. I had no inkling The Farm of my future was Stanford, and dreamed only of an acre with my own red barn.

CHAPTER 1
Plucked From the Playground

When the elementary school basketball coach saw me shooting hoops on the playground during recess, wearing a dress that exposed my skinned knees as I practiced my backboard swishes, he asked if I wanted to play on the school team. No girl had ever played, but he thought I could compete with the boys.

At practice the next day, I was told to guard the boy at the top of the key. I adopted the defensive stance my dad had taught me the night before: angle my feet and put my arms up to make myself look bigger. When the boy dribbled right at me, I stayed low and tapped the ball from his grasp, held it, then gave it back to him.

"*Shieeeek!*" sounded the whistle. Coach screamed, "Jenyth, why did you give the ball back to him? When you steal it, dribble to the other end of the court and make a layup."

I shrugged my shoulders, for no one had ever yelled at me like that before. I didn't like it. I shrugged again and went back to my defensive stance, as obedient as one of the men my dad commanded.

Next possession, the boy dribbled the ball right at me again, but with an angry look on his face. This time, I reached out with my left hand, tapped the ball away from him and scurried up the court. Someone pushed me from behind before I could take the shot. I face-planted and lost the ball.

"*Shieeeek!*" sounded the whistle. "No fouling! Let's start again."

My chin hurt. As I breathed in dirt from the floor, I saw a drop of blood. I stifled a cry for I hated the sight of blood. But this tiny drop didn't make me faint. It made me mad. Then I remembered what Stan, my one and only brother, did when he was sacked at quarterback. I rolled over and popped up quickly.

When I looked around, everyone was looking at me. I'd grown up with these boys, who ripped off the legs of daddy longlegs and teased me for being a straight-A student. Were they wondering if I was tough enough? Filled with a fire I had never known, I resumed my defensive stance and waited. I would be like the black widow spider in the barn, and pounce.

When I saw fear in the point guard's eyes the third time he dribbled toward me, I let loose my new killer instinct. I imagined he was one point on the triangle, I was another, and the third spot was where he wanted to go. I predicted, then leaped to the space where he intended to dribble, stole the ball, and sprinted to the other end of the court for a layup. Backboard-rim-swish. I loved that sound, the three beats of a snare-drum rim shot: *ba-tum-dss.*

Coach yelled, "Great shot! Great shot!"

I was happy but confused. Why did the boy try the same thing three times in a row? Wasn't that the definition of insanity, repeating an unsuccessful attempt but expecting a different outcome? At least that's what Einstein thought, according to the *World Book Encyclopedia,* a 15-volume set I'd read cover to cover. As the other guys called the point guard a wuss and pushed him away, they didn't include me in their stinky boy-sweat huddle. I remembered the words of my dad, who told my brother, "Sometimes the best offense is great defense." Dad was right again. Looking back, I wonder if my steals had poked a hole in the "o" of their macho.

I savored my little victory as I walked out to the playground and started playing tether ball by myself, punching the yellow sphere with my fist until the rope strangled the pole, whiplashing the ball into reverse. Little did I know then that the tether ball and a volleyball were the same size, and hitting a volleyball would pay my way through college.

The clovers on the playground lawn beckoned, and that's where my dad found me, putting daisy chains of mostly white clover flowers around the neck of my plastic Breyer horse, Tarquin. I twirled one purple flower, engrossed in my fantasy of finding a four-leaf clover, before I felt my dad's tie tickling my neck as he bent over to help me up.

When I told him I made the team, he gave me a big hug and told me my Mama Jo was going to be so proud. I was more concerned with getting home and getting to the barn so I could have time for a quick ride on my horse Tyler, before I fed her and shoveled the stalls. At age eleven, I wanted to be a jockey or an Olympic equestrienne, and I wondered if this team was going to get in the way.

We jumped into our 1966 Pontiac Ventura and drove back to our Carmichael, CA, rental house. I usually rode the bus to and from school, but on this special tryout day, my dad had left McClellan Air Force Base early in order to pick me up. I changed very quickly, grabbed the leash for Clancy, our Irish setter, snapped it on his collar, and went into the kitchen to hug my mom. She looked tired, but expressed happiness at my basketball results. Then I hopped on my purple Schwinn Sting-Ray. I rode down the driveway, with Clancy at my side.

Mom waved from the kitchen window as she shaved the carrots she would cook for dinner. I had sneaked one into my pocket so I could feed it to Ms. JB Tyler (Ty-Ty, for short), my beautiful black Appaloosa horse, who loved them. Tyler was named for the president I'd researched in 4th grade, and when I added the "Ms." I remember wondering, when would a woman be president? On this day, I noticed Mom's wedding rings were on, which meant her hands weren't too swollen from the medication she had to take. That was my daily diagnosis of Mom's pain level: rings off meant she was sad or mad. Rings on meant she felt okay.

The barn was a ten-minute ride away, although I had done the ride in less time after someone at school called me "encyclopedia brain" and hurt my feelings. Currying a horse who listened to my woes helped me get through the bullying. Clancy and Tyler were critical components of my childhood. When showing love to my mother meant leaving her alone to rest, I unburdened myself of the bullying and teasing I experienced at school by speaking to the animals, who listened without judgment. My days began and ended with a bike ride from our house to the barn, my loyal dog running beside me, my horse whinnying when she saw me from across the field where I had grown my tomboy.

Outside the Hospital

On the south side of the field, the parking lot curbs at American River Hospital provided me with a perfect balance beam. In the summer my mother fell ill after an emergency hysterectomy, I performed cartwheel after cartwheel on this curb outside the window of her room, just like the Olympic gymnasts I'd seen on TV. I wasn't allowed inside and didn't know she had almost bled to death after surgery. She had the rare blood type A negative, and they had a hard time finding blood for a transfusion. After that, the doctors couldn't determine why she remained swollen with fluid, for her heart was perfect. Finally, they let her go home.

Life was very different after this. I knew Mom was struggling but didn't know why. Somehow, my parents continued to create the ideal childhood for my brother and me: sports, 4-H, summer camps, and an annual road trip to visit National Parks and Kansas in our black, unair-conditioned car. I had few worries, a happy exterior life, and an interior life as full of pure imagination as the psychedelic *Charlie and the Chocolate Factory*.

Summer Concussion

The leisurely summer days of my job cleaning horse stalls, reading books while sitting on hay bales, and riding on the local trails as I dreamed of being an Olympic equestrienne were ending. Summer sports camps would be taking all my time. In what seemed like a day but actually began in 1977 and spanned three years, I began to split my attention between training my dog and horse for 4-H shows and traveling for competitive sports. Everywhere I went, I had to find a ride from a friend, as we had only one car and Dad needed it to drive to the base. I yearned for independence but appreciated help from our neighbors, who knew my mom was battling a disease of unknown origin. Shuttling me allowed them to help her.

Playing college sports first entered my mind when Title IX was being debated in 1972 and mom was in the hospital. My brother and I made a vow: we wouldn't let our parents borrow money for our college educations, so they could use anything extra for Mom's waxing and waning health. Stan was an outstanding three-sport athlete—four if you counted the golf he played on the side—and by the time I was in eighth grade, I had realized I possessed similar gifts. A high school track coach lived down the street from us, and when he brought home the high-jump pit and hurdles for the summer, I competed with the boys.

Coach Palumbo told me, right in front of all the boys, that I was the best athlete he'd ever seen. I shrugged it off, not really believing him. But by the time I was approaching my junior year in high school, I was hearing this praise from many different sources. I started to believe I could succeed in sports.

I looked forward to the 4-H State Fair Horse Show in August, 1977, sensing this would be my last ride. I was sixteen and had to get serious about my future. I would be up against the thoroughbreds in equitation on the flat, hunter-jumper, and show jumping competitions. I knew we would enter the ring counterclockwise, and the judge would think Ty-Ty was a beautiful black thoroughbred since she had no spots on her left flank. Only when we reversed direction, and her frosted, freckled right hip was revealed, would the judge realize she was a "crappy Appy." If we made a strong first impression, her lineage wouldn't matter and we would get a ribbon, though we wouldn't take home the blue with purebreds in the ring. Except for the time when she bucked me off when I was eleven, resulting in my first concussion and a broken wrist, Ty-Ty was a completely reliable jumper.

All that changed on the day before the 4-H State Fair Horse Show in 1977, when we were practicing a jumping course that included a brick wall. If my parents had known my friends and I swam our horses in the river or jumped them over the park benches, we would have been in big trouble. The park benches were fixed objects, unlike a show jumping rail which would fall if a horse's hoof or leg barely touched it. If the horse dropped a leg over a park bench, the horse would flip or fall. Still, this was good preparation for when Tyler and I advanced to the show jumping course with a plywood brick wall that was 36 inches tall, about 16 feet wide, but 24 inches deep. This third dimension of depth added some complexity to my ride. I envisioned the take-off point would be like planting before the bench seat on a park picnic table, about a foot farther away from the wall, and that would create a long enough arc to clear the jump. This worked the times we tried it in practice. But on the day before the 4-H State Championships, my mental measure-ment did not jive with Tyler's, and she skidded to a halt in front of the wall. Her dropped shoulder tossed me skyward as she barreled into the wall, knocked it over, and landed on top of it and me.

When I woke up cold as a cadaver in the drawer of a morgue, God and I had been talking. Black and white speck-led star-like orbs floated through my head, then rotated around me as more passed through me. I looked into green and gold swirling vortices and felt their vacuum pull toward an infinity beyond mortal comprehension. Astronauts de-tached from their breathing tubes crossed my view, and I couldn't tell if they were waving or giving a frantic SOS.

When God began talking about why bad things happen to good people, He was talking about my mom. I wasn't the good one in the family.

I had a lot of questions for Him. "If You are a loving and merciful god, why are You making my mom suffer? Is this an equal rights thing? You had Job, now You want a Job-ette?"

"No, the nature of suffering and the experience of pain open doors to another dimension for humans."

"Why my mom? Did she have any choice to go through that door? What did she do to deserve this? She's walking the walk, except when she's in bed. She's in bed more and more now but never complains. She prays every night. Are You listening?"

"Yes, Mama Jo's faith brings me joy."

"Then why is she suffering? You could cure her if You wanted to."

"One day, you will understand her journey."

"My mom needs help now. Healing. Mercy. Please, God, it's so hard to watch her suffer, to see her do everything right and still swell up with fluid. Can't You do something?"

"I guide her life every day."

"That's not the answer I'm looking for."

"Jenyth Jo, the nature of good and of evil is not the same thing as who is in physical pain and who is not."

"Oh, God, why be oblique? Can You just give her pain to me?"

"There will be a time when you ask that of Me again, and you will know I have answered. But today is not that time. The miracle you seek for your mother is not the miracle she will receive."

"God, I can't believe in You if that's Your best answer."

"To those whom much is entrusted, much will be de-manded."

"Jesus effing Christ. Will You stop?!"

I opened my eyes and saw a witch flying, then hiding in a white corner. Another black-robed being leaned over me, the Grim Reaper. Then there were two reapers, without eyes or mouths but with scythes raised and ready. Something tickled my nose and scratched my eyebrows. The pulse in my head burned down my neck, and my whole body lurched, then the room spun through blinking machines and tubes. I heard beeps and whirrs. It was dark.

The black robe said, "You're awake."

I couldn't place the accent—maybe an Irish hell or a Welsh heaven floated throughout the room. I looked up at the ceiling, which had red digital numbers counting up and counting down and tracking sideways. Where was God? Where was I? Was that an angel walking through the door, backlit by heaven? Was I dead? Alive?

As my altered-consciousness faded, my whole body jerked. I heard my mother's voice and felt warmth, then shivers. A warm blanket arrived as her dry and cracked hands smoothed my hair away from my forehead. The matted and tangled strands pulled at my tender scalp. I tried to say something, but "argh" was the only sound I made.

"She's going to be very sensitive," a voice that was not God said on my right.

My beloved mother was on my left, somewhere. I couldn't turn my head. I tried to lift my arm to pull off something scratching my cheek, but I couldn't find my arm. Nothing came into focus. I knew I was in my body but I didn't know where my body was.

The voice, taking form as a white-coated doctor, jumped in: "It's very important that you not move, that you not get upset. Do you understand?"

I couldn't nod, but I blinked and hoped he knew that was a yes. When I tried to open my eyes, I caught a fleeting glimpse of the bat flying back into the room. I groaned.

I tried to sit up, but many hands restrained me.

I could see the black-robed being huddled in the corner, so I shut my eyes. Was she a witch disguised as a nun? With God, I wasn't scared. Now, tears formed under my shut lids.

The doctor told me to open them.

When I did, a white light supernova-ed, so I squeezed them shut again. I realized my head was locked up. I tried opening my eyes a bit longer and saw my mom with more frown lines than I remembered.

The doctor flashed the light in each eye as he held the lid open. "Hmm, the right pupil is quite enlarged. She might still have some brain inflammation. I'm going to order tests." Then he spoke to me directly: "I'm your neurologist and have been checking on you since you arrived. Welcome back."

As he left the room, I remembered that Tyler had fallen. Panic heated me up, and the thought my horse might be dead started the shivers, the shaking, the fear I would never be warm again.

"Do you remember what happened?" Mom asked, looking very anxious.

I could see the walls of the room turning blue, my mom in a white, crisply ironed button-down shirt, her aqua eyes staring at me. My own eyes were starting to focus as they locked with hers. But I was dislocated. Where am I? Why am I here? What day is it?

Mom said I'd been asleep for several days. I tried to process that, tried to remember, but nothing about what happened after Tyler's skid before refusing to jump came into my consciousness. I remembered that part, because she never refused a jump. It was 1977, and we were going to the 4-H State Championships. Again, I tried to shake my head but couldn't. The room began to turn, sharp corners becoming waves, flat ceiling to curving floor.

When the doctor returned, he handed a hammer, a wrench, and a Phillips screwdriver to the being who was creeping away from the corner. The doctor tapped something with the hammer, twisted a nut with the wrench, and unscrewed the rest of the contraption. In his hand was a wire cage I'd never seen before. It had been immobilizing my head and neck.

"Janice, can you turn your cheek to the left?" the doctor asked.

I sighed. Another person who couldn't say my name, Jenyth—the name my dad had given me so I could be unique. *I should just be JJ*, I thought. I moved my head. Barely. Jackhammers started behind my eyes.

"Great. How about to the right?"

I could turn more to that side. I saw a very young nun holding the contraption. Her flushed cheeks and the tight white wrap around her head and neck made me wonder about her head cage. I thought I would apologize as soon as the room stopped spinning, as soon as I found more thoughts to voice.

The doctor helped me tilt my head back just a bit, then leaned it forward. He told me it was time to sit up. He put his hand between my shoulder blades.

But I had no strength to sit. As soon as I was about seventy-five degrees vertical, I threw up all over his white lab coat.

He told me not to worry, that concussed people throw up all of the time. He shrugged out of the coat, rolled it up, handed it to the nun, and walked out.

I thought, *If I were a doctor, I'd want to be like him: in charge but not arrogant about it. Calm and precise, knowledgeable but not a show-off, not bothered by anything gross.*

A few hours later, I learned I had a grade 3 concussion, which meant no sports or any activity that raised my blood pressure for a month or more. My formerly 20-10 vision was terrible, especially in my nearly blind left eye. I had a cracked skull, a cyst forming in the crack, swelling on the brain, and dizziness. My arm was broken, my hip twisted, and my whiplashed neck would take a while to heal. I was told I should be able to make a full recovery, yet it would take a long time as this was my third concussion in five years. I was also told I'd be incredibly vulnerable to the psychoactive drugs dealt on a daily basis at my high school. How did this doctor know about that?

I felt as if some kind of hallucinogen were already in my system. My formerly racing mind seemed to have nothing in it, and this realization made me very confused. How could I have less noise in my mind? What if I had nothing left? I was scheduled to take the SAT soon, but when asked, I couldn't spell my first name. So much for being "encyclopedia brain." On the practice SAT, I had missed only one question, but in the hospital, I failed every memory test. What was going to happen when I went home?

On this first day back to consciousness, people were coming through the room in waves, but my mom stayed solid. She never left my side. Mom had been in and out of hospitals for several years by this time and knew how to handle nurses and doctors: with firm charm. She had just the right words and the right timing, but I hated going to the hospital to see her because I feared she wouldn't come out alive. I thanked God every day she was making breakfast when I woke up at home. At some point during my hospital stay, I wondered how much longer she'd be on this planet. What could I do to save her? Maybe I should be a doctor instead of an Olympian. What if I could be both?

Several thoughts began to take shape: would my brain heal so I could get a sports scholarship? Or would I begin at a junior college, like many of my high school classmates? My brother had just graduated with the Class of 1977 and was going to play three sports at the local JC, which had a great academic reputation.

A kind of happiness began to unfold as I realized that maybe I too could be normal. Maybe I could stop hiding behind my guise as class clown. Then I remembered: being a smart girl was social suicide. Being a smart athletic girl was worse. I would never be normal. Better to crack jokes, if only I could remember the punch lines.

CHAPTER 2
Recruiting Season

Sunday dinnertimes at the Gearhart household were must-attend occasions. It was a time to catch up after a jam-packed week of sports practice, games, meetings, and yardwork. During my senior year, dinner was usually interrupted by a phone call from a college coach. The same coaches called every week during the fall of 1978, and the list of them narrowed to an eclectic set. After I took my PSAT in tenth grade, I received a mountain of mail from selective schools. Mom made me establish a filing system so I could sort through all the academic and athletic schools. I hoped Title IX funding would help pay for my education at a top academic and athletic school.

My mother loved Oral Roberts University (ORU), a Christian college in Oklahoma near the family homestead we had occupied since the 1880's. She had heard Oral Roberts preach at a Chautauqua style event and thought I could benefit from some religious instruction. She also liked how the dorms were single sex and far apart. Perhaps she thought her boy-crazy daughter would be safe there. ORU offered me a full ride for undergrad and guaranteed admission to medical school. If I went there, in eight years, I would be a doctor focusing on my favorite patient: my mom.

My dad, the three-sport college athlete, liked Alabama, as Paul "Bear" Bryant was still coaching the football team there. However, he really hoped I would go to Louisiana

State University (LSU); he and my mother had seen its team play in the 1959 Sugar Bowl in New Orleans. LSU didn't have much of a volleyball team, and the basketball team was too good for me. But their band had an unbelievable horn section, which those of us in my high school's marching band envied.

My brother loved 'Bama as well, so when he spoke at dinner, it was often to chant the Alabama cheer we had known since birth: "Hail Mary full of grace, Notre Dame's in second place. Goooo 'Bama!" Stan was a fan of the houndstooth pattern on Bear Bryant's fedora, but that wasn't enough for me. Alabama's Coach Stephanie Schleuter was a legend of the game, and I liked the idea of playing for a woman head coach. What to do, what to do?

University of the Pacific (UOP) had one of the top programs in the country, always vying for number one but not quite making it. My parents could come to all the games, as Stockton was only forty-five miles from our home in Carmichael. If I had a career-ending injury, I would still have a full ride, the dean of admissions told me, for my scholarship would be academic. I hadn't thought about that before. Nevertheless, I thought I shouldn't go to UOP unless it was my number one. But what was my number one? It seemed to change week by week.

My high school coach had nicknamed me J.J. after O.J. Simpson, my favorite football player from the University of Southern California (USC). I just didn't see myself as a SoCal gal, but that Trojan mascot and the horse he rode into the Coliseum were so appealing. Like Alabama, USC had a decades-long football tradition and it would be so fun to be part of its Athletic Department. They didn't seem to be doing much to make way for female athletes, but I was assured that was going to happen during my time there. Coach Erbe was very blunt: I had a deadline, and if I didn't say yes early, he had many others in mind.

Based on the number of phone calls I was receiving, I started to discern who was really interested in me. Coach Schlueter from Alabama was persistent; Coach Chris Voelz from Oregon was chomping at the bit; Coach Erbe from USC was cooling off; and Coach Liskevich hoped to add me to his arsenal on the nation's number two UOP team on an academic, not athletic, scholarship. Then there was Coach Fred Sturm from Stanford, who would be elevated to head coach and did not have a full ride to offer, only the promise of one my sophomore year. The campus visit to interview with the Stanford dean of admissions and to practice with the team was not as pressure-filled as such a visit would be today. Their team wasn't very good in 1978, and 1979 would be anybody's guess.

Driving down University Avenue, it was hard not to notice the incredible century-old mansions on both sides of the street. Crossing El Camino Real, University Avenue's name changed to Palm Drive, and the drive up a gradual hill between hundred-year-old palm trees, with the huge Stanford Church ahead, was beautiful. The buildings reminded me of the Spanish style of the dozens of California missions we had toured as a family. I didn't understand the lack of landscaped grounds, until driving a lap around Campus Drive, when I saw how huge the campus was. Stanford felt like a large country club, complete with golf course, equestrian stables and arena, and running paths all around. The Athletic Department building was typical of the others: sandstone tan with a red tile roof. I didn't find a vine of ivy anywhere, which was a big bummer. The interior of the offices was pretty impressive, but not as nice as at Oregon or USC.

As we waited to go upstairs to the volleyball office, the football coaches came out of a meeting and stopped to say hello. That was different. Would USC's or Alabama's coaches pay attention to a female athlete? We walked upstairs to meet the department secretary, who was articulate and polished, like the UOP admissions dean I had spoken to. Then she pushed open the door and revealed the young volleyball coaches. I shook their hands and sat down, thrilled I was to call them Fred and John, not Coach Sturm and Coach Bekins.

Fred was visibly nervous as he started his speech. That gave me time to study them both. Fred was still tan from a summer playing pro beach volleyball. He had stood up when we entered, displaying manners that would please my mom. His eyes were so dark they were almost black. John was completely different: blond; curly hair; riveting blue eyes; a light madras plaid shirt with aqua and pink that accentuated his freckled, tan face. These two were the epitome of Southern California beach and country club cool, with high volleyball IQs. They had very specific aspirations for the program and I was impressed.

My mother was much more cautious, focusing on the financial aid part of the deal. Reassurances about a full tuition and books scholarship were made, leaving only food and housing unpaid, but I still had to be admitted to the university, like any other student. John said my grades and test scores were excellent and he didn't think there would be a problem, but sometimes Stanford made decisions the coaches didn't understand. He explained that he and Fred had submitted a list of players they wanted admitted, in ranked order, and I was near the top. Another player wasn't as academically prepared and needed to be number one to get in, he said. Still, there was no guarantee either of us would make it. Hearing that made me want to attend Stanford even more. Financially, it was the only offer that wasn't a full ride. But my high school counselor had told me I would be crazy not to go. I knew these two liked me, because I had popped a pun and John cracked up. Fred wasn't sure how to react as my mom presented a formidable presence in her blazer and blouse with a bowtie. I thought he was stifling a grin.

After the Athletic Department office meeting, I went to the dean's office and met the famous Dean Fred Hargadon. The interview was very stimulating, and I heard myself conversing at an intellectual level rarely practiced outside of my closest friend group. We got along well, and he even called my application essay "unforgettable." I wanted to ask if that meant I would get in but didn't have the courage. We shook hands, and I took a voucher to eat lunch at Tressider Union. Afterwards, it was time to meet and practice with the team.

Old Roble Gym was all ours because the basketball teams were still in season and practicing in the brand-new Maples Pavilion. Roble was a relic of the round-roofed gyms of the pre-Second World War era. Roble Gym formed part of a complex, with the dance studio parallel to the gym, and a beautiful fountain in a courtyard between. I loved the feel of the space, the brick paver patio, and arcade all the way around the courtyard. Here, the school felt as hallowed as the Ivy League schools, and the gym floor certainly had the same antique appearance. I put all my dress clothes and jewelry in a locker and put on some practice clothes, tying my shoes in the lucky way.

Walking into the gym, I noticed I was one of the taller ones in the room. Fred introduced me to everyone, and we started practice. It was weird not to touch a ball for the first half hour, as we spent time doing a variety of agility drills, conditioning sprints, and balance tests. All were easy for me, and I could see I was one of the better athletes in the gym. I had the highest vertical leap by far. Everyone was really nice to me, and setter Paula was especially encouraging. Most of the sophomores and juniors looked as if they had just come off the beach, and several were talking about playing on the sand courts at the Phi Delts after the practice. I did some setting and serving, but when setter Jan threw me a perfect quick set and I crushed the ball, everyone stopped for a moment. I was surprised as well. John asked me if I could do that one more time.

I jumped up again to crush Jan's perfect set. The connection was instant, and Jan had a huge grin on her face.

John told me they were thinking of running a 6–2 next year, which meant I could hit in the front row and set from the back row. Did I like the sound of that?

I looked at Paula's face and decided best to take the party line: "I'll play where the team needs me." And that was that.

I was the last person out of the gym. The coaches were effusive, telling me they had heard from Dean Fred, and I had a really good shot at getting in.

"If you get in, will you come?" asked Fred.

I knew my mother would not want to hear me say yes, so I just replied that I really liked the school and the team.

They left, and I returned to the locker room to change. Jan, Linda, and Paula were waiting for me. Jan spoke for the group: "J.J., you have to come here. We need you. You'll play a lot right away. We just want you to know that. Even though

Fred is a first-year coach, he knows a lot about the game. And Beeky is so fun in practice. You'll have a great time here."

I thanked them, then went to the sink to wash up. I left my locker door ajar as I rinsed off. When I returned, my clothes were inside, but the little zipped paisley bag with my graduation necklace, class president's ring, and garnet birthday earrings was gone. Panicked, I got on my hands and knees and looked everywhere. Linda, Jan and Paula looked too. My mom came in to ask what was taking so long, and we said we were looking for the jewelry bag. It was gone.

The girls apologized, but my mom was furious. We talked to the attendant at the entrance, but nobody had turned in anything. I couldn't replace any of it, especially the class president's ring, which had cost over a hundred dollars—the equivalent of shoveling two months' worth of horse poop.

As we walked to the car for the three-hour drive home, my mom started bashing everything about Stanford.

When she took a breath, I told her I thought the coaches knew a lot about volleyball. In one practice, I improved. Jan set me so well I was crushing the ball. I told her the girls on the team were really nice, and thought I could play as a freshman.

Mom disagreed, telling me that girls who steal jewelry are not nice. She thought I wanted to go to Stanford based on the appearances of the coaches. She told me it was time to grow up and see that Fred couldn't answer all of her questions, that he didn't know what he's doing. She didn't understand why I would pass up a free college offer. Then she dangled the carrot: she and Dad had promised to buy me a yellow Camaro if I went to Oregon. If I went to Stanford, they'd have to take out a loan.

I balked at that. I told her I'd take out the loan and sell my latest 4-H horse, who was worth at least eight hundred dollars. I had over a thousand in the bank. I would work all summer at sports camps and at the barn. I reminded her that I might not even get admitted to Stanford. Oregon was still my first choice, and USC second, I pledged.

As we pulled out of the parking lot, I saw Fred getting into a 1978 yellow Camaro SS. He waved as he drove out. I wondered, *Is this some kind of sign that I'm not going to have my own Camaro, but I am going to play for a coach with one?* The muffler's rumble drowned out my final thought as we left campus: *I just lied to Mom. Stanford is my number one.*

Oregon Road Trip, March 1979

Maybe I didn't lie to Mom, I thought as we prepared to drive for my official visit to Oregon. The glamour of the Stanford coaches had worn off as soon as the fact I would have to borrow money for school sank in. The Oregon coach had some unusual ways to teach setting, and I needed to practice them and see firsthand what she would ask me to change. I knew I could adapt and really wanted to improve, and Coach Voelz promised I would be an All-American by my junior year. Oregon could be my pathway to playing in the Olympics someday. I loved the Nike brand, the green and gold colors, and my parents' yellow Camaro promise. At the time, my brother was driving an old blue Plymouth "land yacht" from the late 1960s, and he really wanted me to get that Camaro. Everything seemed in place, so we decided one Sunday that if I liked the University of Oregon, I would sign on the spot. My mom and I would drive up the next Thursday, and I would practice with the team on Friday and possibly decide my future.

By 9:00 a.m., we were on the road to Oregon in our white two-door Chevy Monte Carlo with French blue seats. Mom and I had never driven so far on our own, but it was a straight shot up Highway 99 to Eugene. We knew the new Highway 5 would open in a few months, and we wondered how much of the old road paralleled it. The first several hundred miles revealed green fields, forests, and beautiful granite formations. Once we crossed the Oregon border, we saw snow fields, some grapes, and lots and lots of horse farms. I instantly fell in love and imagined going to the Oregon Medical College in Portland, where my favorite cousins lived, and owning a huge horse farm and driving the tractor during haying season—just as my uncle in Kansas had allowed me to do. By the time we turned off a new section of the I-5 freeway in Eugene, I was smitten.

Mom pulled into the Motel 6 parking lot, and I called Coach Chris Voelz to tell her we were in town. She asked us to drive to a burger joint near campus, where she wanted to buy us dinner.

Across the parking lot from the burger joint, I noticed a river with weeping willow trees. A young man was standing in a boat, poling his craft like a Venetian gondolier as his girlfriend giggled. Everything was so lush and green. It was March 29, and spring was gaining steam.

Coach Voelz was youngish, very friendly, and super excited to see me. She insisted I call her Chris. I knew I was her number one before she had finished one sentence, and I could tell my mom was warming up to her. About once an hour while we were driving, Mom had said, "This is so far away, Jenyth, it's so far away." But I felt at home with Chris, and I knew my mom was beginning to trust her. We made a plan for the next day, which included practicing with the team.

I was too excited to sleep much, but I did notice my nose was running a bit and my jaw was achy. I figured I was about to catch a cold but could make it through practice. I was rarely sick, so I ignored the symptoms. As I finally fell asleep, I had the sense of satisfaction that the wait to make a decision was going to be worth it. A yellow Camaro with a green "O" sticker on the bumper was within my grasp.

The morning meeting with the athletic director and the dean of admission went well. They weren't intimidating at all, and told me I was admitted into the Honors College, which was very exciting. I think my mom was right when she said all the years of 4-H Demonstration Day and public speaking contests helped me keep my poise.

At each college interview, I had listened to the speech patterns and diction of the people in the room. At UOP, some of the officials seemed a little pretentious, saying "UOP is the Ivy of the West." The USC people used Valley Girl speech, with an uptick at the end of each sentence, making me wonder if they were actually asking a question instead of making a comment. Stanford's dean spoke Princeton style: erudite and witty. The "y'alls" and "fixing tos" of Alabama and Oral Roberts reminded me of my favorite Midwest relatives. Chris Voelz's speech fell into a different realm: she was firm, approachable, and down to earth. There was no mistaking her intelligence and competitive fire, but she didn't show off or seem as if she had something to prove. I thought she would be a good leader. When she said I'd practice in the brand-new gym the girls would be sharing with the boys, I felt she must have taken a stand and demanded equal access to the facilities.

Mom and I decided to walk through campus to the gym after the meeting, and that proved incredibly important. We walked by the place where they rented gondolas, and my eyes started to water under the weeping willows. Mom handed me a Kleenex, and by the time we were near the gym, I was sneezing and coughing. She told me to wash up in the bathroom and said there must be pollen in the air. She could recognize signs of allergies, having taken my brother to the hospital many times in Alabama for asthma and allergy attacks. The washup seemed to help, and I went into the locker room and met the team.

We warmed up in the huge gym space, and I thought there was no chance of a volleyball hitting the ceiling—the roof was too high. We ran up the stadium stairs to the top so I could see the brand-new logo of the duck and the volleyball court outline permanently painted inside the basketball court outline. That was an important symbol to Coach Chris. She wanted me to see how she was succeeding in the struggle to implement Title IX. I loved it.

The rest of practice went well, except my eyes were itching. Coach Chris wanted to completely change my hand position to form a W. Good setters should be able to set forward or backward with the same hand position, but I couldn't do this with the W. Making this change would not be easy. I took a shower, said thanks to the team, and headed outside to have lunch with Chris and my mom.

Both of them looked at me and said, "What's wrong with your eyes?"

My eyes had been itchy, but now they were starting to swell up. We walked in another direction on campus, but by the time we got to the student union, the allergy attack was really kicking in. Coach insisted we go to the student health center. She left to order us some food to go, because we intended to leave campus by noon. I had hoped to stay to sign on, but now I literally couldn't see.

After an extensive exam and lots of questions about my preexisting allergies to trees and grasses—allergies I didn't know existed before, and which my mom didn't recognize—the doctor gave me a stern warning: "Oregon is not for everyone. If you have an allergy to mold, you will be very sick here."

My mom startled at this. "Jenyth is highly allergic to penicillin. Does that mean she's allergic to environmental mold as well?"

He nodded, adding that from the time the snow melted until about June 1, they measured and communicated the mold spore level to the general community. This day, it was very, very high.

I started to scratch my side, and he asked if I had any other itchy areas. I pulled up my gown, and my mom gasped. Welts the size of quarters were forming on my back, under my armpits, and on my chest.

The doctor insisted I get an antihistamine shot to knock down this reaction.

I closed my eyes so I wouldn't see the needle go in. It didn't hurt much.

Then the doctor told me to lie down and rest. He told my mom we couldn't leave until the reaction was under control.

As he left the room, my watering eyes began to fill with larger tears. "Mom, I can't go here, can I?" I started sobbing. My back was on fire, my sinuses were swelling, and my whole head was aching and pounding. I tried to pull it together, as my mom sat there in total shock. "I really wanted that yellow Camaro, Mom," I cried. "And Coach Chris is so nice. You like her, don't you?"

Mom nodded, saying she would be an excellent role model. She knew how to use her manners and how to get what she wanted. Mom told me to take a note of that.

I gave Mom the look I reserved for her half-teasing, half-serious criticism. When she criticized me, she always couched it in something to soften the blow, as a nod to my oversensitivity.

Mom told me I had to call Coach Chris and tell her what the doctor said. I was allergic to Oregon. Mom wanted to get out of here as quickly as possible, so we could get home before dark. We needed to leave within the hour.

The doctor walked in just then with another doctor who was the local expert in allergies. This second doctor was old and crusty. He kept shaking his head as he gently touched the oozing hives on my back. He thought I was allergic to a lot of things growing in Eugene. He said I could take a bunch of tests and see what exactly made me react, but clearly my symptoms were quite serious. He wouldn't recommend my playing sports for the University of Oregon.

The hammer had come down. I started whimpering again, trying hard not to burst into tears. It had taken so long to come to a decision, and now that I knew what I wanted, I couldn't have it.

He rubbed some calamine lotion on my back for the itching. Then they left, and I tried to put on my clothes, leaving the jeans unbuttoned and covering them with my plaid shirt. Mom agreed for once that I shouldn't tuck in my shirt. I wanted to ask her to call Coach Chris, but as we walked out of the student health center, the receptionist had a message for us: Coach had bag lunches for us waiting in her office. *O God*, I thought, *she probably has my letter of intent to sign as well.*

Dread and despair poured through me, but I came from a family of stoics and knew I needed to deal with it. The athletic director was at the office, and the papers were spread on the desk. I didn't sit down when they asked me to, and they appeared confused. In an ill-advised moment, I turned around and lifted my shirt so they could see the welts. When I turned to face them, the tears started flowing, but I didn't allow myself to blubber. I became very formal, leaning on my Southern manners: "I regret I cannot sign to play volleyball for you. The doctor says I am allergic to Oregon."

Before anyone could say anything else, I grabbed the sack lunches and ran out of the room. My mom probably thanked them for their time and the visit. I wished I had been stronger, but I just wanted to go home.

But the drive home revealed something even worse.

By the time we were three hours south of Eugene, the throbbing in my jaw had become excruciating. My mom's face was nearly on the steering wheel, and I knew she was nervous driving over the Cascade Range and the border as dusk was starting to darken the road. Rarely did she exceed the fifty-five m.p.h. Jimmy-Carter-installed speed limit, but we were going eighty.

Once we hit Yreka, on the California side, I asked her to pull over so I could go to the bathroom. "Mom, something's wrong with my jaw," I told her.

We went inside the Shell gas station bathroom while the car was filled up by the attendant, and my mom found a welt inside my mouth. "Jenyth, I don't think that's from the allergies. It's right by the tooth you knocked out last summer. Does this hurt?" She squeezed on the painful part, and some nasty-tasting pus oozed out. She thought my tooth was abscessing, and reminded me the dentist had told me it was dying, and someday I'd have to have a root canal. The throbbing matched my pulse.

The Shell station had a tiny convenience store. Fortunately, it sold aspirin. Mom bought the last remaining packages, with two pills each. I gulped the first two, thinking of my Uncle Bob who had taught me to swallow pills by thinking they were bits of steak, and tried to force them down before my gag reflex responded. We were back on the road as the sky turned bluish pink, and Mt. Shasta's glacier glowed in the setting sun.

Those last three hours were horrible. My mind turned over the allergies, the weird W hand position, the abscessing tooth that was oozing pus and making me nauseous, the weeping willow with the gondolier boy, the awesome burger joint, the doctors and my hives, and my lost yellow Camaro. By the time we drove into the driveway, I was essentially wordless. Dad and Stan were waiting up for us, as it was nearly midnight. When they saw Mom leading me into the house and heard her ask for her aloe vera plant, they knew something was horribly wrong.

The next day, I called up Coach Erbe from USC. I thought that was where I was supposed to be all along, even if I had to sit the bench for a few years. Coach Erbe didn't answer but called me back a few hours later. "Well, J.J., I don't have any money to offer you. I'd love to have you walk on."

Walk on to a private school team? I couldn't afford to do that. First Oregon, now USC. I stayed in bed the rest of the day, partly because the Benadryl and other antihistamines made me sleepy. Mostly, I stayed there to pout.

When Fred Sturm from Stanford called that evening for his weekly Sunday call, he had the good news I had been admitted. It was April 1, national signing day. Would I sign and play for The Farm? He sounded really excited.

I tried to match his enthusiasm as I made sure I still had a full tuition and books scholarship, then said yes, I would sign.

I was stuck with Stanford.

Elegy

April is the cruelest month for a high school senior who wants to go to college but can't afford the tuition. Financial aid offers were, or were not, coming in for my friends. Everyone felt the reality check. We couldn't figure out how to minimize the sense of being graded, judged, rewarded, and punished for all of our past actions. Most of my friend group were going to Stanford's rival, the University of California, but two of the smartest were left out due to Cal's quota system. The Board of Governors thought Cal should reflect the demography of California: if our state were seven percent Asian, then Cal should be too. But what about the merit argument for my deserving Asian friends who'd been left out? They felt affirmative action was to blame for their lack of success in the admissions cycle. Knowing Title IX had helped me gain admission to Stanford, I felt guilty that I had a full-tuition scholarship, especially as the May 1 decision day approached, and lack of financial aid kept some really intelligent friends from enrolling in four-year colleges.

Looking back, I believe Title IX was not just another government program designed to help a select few but a necessary move that would allow women to show what they could do in the classroom, in the world of intercollegiate sports, and in the realm of graduate school programs. I still struggle with definitions of "fairness" and "justice" in college admissions, notions magnified by the 2019 Varsity Blues scandal. In 1979, it never occurred to me that someone would pay half a million dollars to get their daughter into USC. College admissions and sports recruiting were much simpler back then.

For months, I had tried to be noticed. I had applied to every college scholarship available, written dozens of letters to coaches, talked on the phone, and navigated territory new to female athletes trying to be recruited. I had succeeded, and if the reactions of my principal and high school counselor were to be believed, going to Stanford was a big deal. I just didn't feel that way. I broke up with my boyfriend of three years and stopped socializing, which was strange for me, the senior class president who knew everybody. Graduation day pictures show me surrounded by my favorite high school friends, as if everything were normal. But I was far from myself.

My parents started asking what I was thinking about all the time, but what could I say? I was grateful my mom's health was steady, which meant I didn't have to worry about her as much. My dad had received another promotion at the Air Force base, which meant a raise and a little financial breathing room. I was going to play volleyball and basketball at Stanford, major in pre-medicine, and cure my mother. Why did I feel so terrible?

At the time, I didn't understand how stressful major life changes could be. I had no perspective on what I'd accomplished; I just knew I was sad that I had to sell my horse and leave my childhood behind. I wonder if, hidden somewhere in my undeveloped self-awareness, I knew that I was wholly unsuited to be a doctor. I had needle-phobia. An aversion to blood and gore. A squeamish stomach. Due to my history of concussions, I needed at least 8-9 hours of sleep a night. Instead of embracing and battling pain, as my mother did on a daily basis, I ran from pain.

How much longer could Mom keep fighting? Even when she exhibited no external symptoms like chunks of skin falling off, butterfly rashes on her face, and constant exhaustion, her organs could be inflamed, her liver cysts expanding, her lungs collapsing. She finally had a diagnosis my senior year: Systemic Lupus Erythematosus, Rheumatoid Arthritis, Eczema, and a clotting issue related to her autoimmune diseases. Reality suggested an early death, so nothing was as important to me as keeping my beloved mother alive.

When I went to the bank to take out a loan for my first-year living expenses, signing the stack of papers made going into debt another reality I couldn't avoid. No matter what happened at Stanford, I'd owe the bank twelve hundred dollars.

CHAPTER 3
Pepper on the Pillow Plot

Two weeks later, I was on a plane to Chicago's O'Hare Airport. We stopped at my aunt's new house on our way to Illinois Benedictine College (now Benedictine University) in Lisle, the site of the 1979 USA Volleyball Junior Olympics. Our team had a good shot at finishing high in the tournament.

Much to my surprise, my mom had come along on the trip and I worried the travel might make her sicker. She had made fast friends with my volleyball club's Coach Debbie and was acting as team mom for the week. Mom had arranged for the entire team to eat dinner at Aunt Jeanne's house, which had a circular driveway and a dining table for sixteen. I loved the gray stone façade and double doorway.

As we drove into Lisle, I felt like an expert on college campus architecture. This one looked exactly like a college was supposed to: red brick walls with ivy climbing on them, white ionic pillars with logos and emblems, flags on the buildings, a Herculaneum-like font on the building signs, beautiful green lawns crisscrossed with pathways, and a large church steeple. Unfortunately, the gym left much to be desired, as the ceilings barely made the regulation height of twenty-five feet. The high balls our setter delivered were not going to be easy to track with the single can lights hanging from the ceiling. As it turned out, she was blinded several times trying to set the ball. We were supposed to pass the serve to the middle of the court, and she would set the ball about 14 feet to the left or to the right side, or straight up in the middle. But the can light hung directly above the midpoint. It was much easier to interpret the arc of the set to the outside when I saw the setter as one point and the expected place where the ball would drop into a hittable zone as the other end point. Geometry was my favorite class in high school. It would be another year before I learned *I* was the vertex of the inscribed angle, and I needed to adjust my footwork according to the setter. I couldn't see this third dimension until my college coach explained it.

Meanwhile, I played in all the matches but not in the same position. Coach Debbie wasn't satisfied with the way we were playing and kept trying different lineup combinations. She told me, "You're smart enough to play anywhere. Don't worry, just play your game."

Debbie had noticed me in 7th grade P.E., then enlisted me to play on her club volleyball team, Club Sacramento. I was still in the throes of horse love, but attended a weekly practice and the occasional tournament. In junior high, we played each of the six rotations on the volleyball court. When I was supposed to line up in left front, I stayed in left front and played in left front. When we rotated to the next position, after winning a point and getting the opportunity to serve, I stayed in that new position. There was no position specialization at that time, but volleyball was evolving and our U.S. National Team was innovating. Their strategies were adopted by all of the coaches, for volleyball attracts students of the game. By the time I was a sophomore in high school, I might be in the left front position when the ball was served, but I'd switch to middle front where I'd control the defense like a linebacker on the football field. I had to remember where I was in the actual rotation each time the play ended, go back to that spot, then switch to my specialization.

When Coach Ted came to my high school my sophomore year, he told me the best athlete on the team had to be the setter, for that player would touch the ball every time it came over. I became a setter and liked the role as I viewed running the offense as an opportunity to make my teammates look good. Bump, set, spike: the three-beat rhythm of our offense. In addition, Ted wanted me to play middle blocker as I rotated across the front row, and also hit the sets from our other setter. When I rotated back to serve and play the back row, I became the setter. Front row: middle blocker. Back row: setter. I really had to focus to remember where I was on the court and what I was supposed to do. I didn't know any other player who had this much responsibility, but I loved the challenge on my high school team.

Junior Olympics June 1979

On the other hand, my club Coach Debbie liked to put her best athletes in the outside hitter position, and give them the primary responsibility for passing serves. A good pass meant we could run an offense with three hitters; a bad pass meant the ball would be launched to the outside hitter, who often had to make something out of nothing. At these Junior Olympics, Debbie played me in all three positions, knowing I would follow directions and work hard no matter where I was on the court. But I wasn't comfortable with the changes in our line-up. Just when I'd get into the rhythm of the game, she'd move me to another position so that I could block the best hitter, or face a weaker blocker, or serve to a weaker passer. She knew exactly what she was doing and I trusted her expertise. But it was hard, hard not knowing where I'd play until right before the game began. I needed to know, to plan, and to strategize. In hindsight, her confidence in my abilities was a huge compliment but at the time, having a blank next to my name made me crazy.

I wonder if Debbie knew about my anxiety. Did she sense what no one else, not even my own mother, understood? Was she trying to toughen my sensitive skin, to prepare me for life without my mother directing it? Maybe she thought I would be homesick for my mom's amazing cooking, or maybe she thought I was too immature to live on my own. Even though Mom was in remission for the early part of 1979, my nightmares were full of funerals. I didn't realize it at the time, but the fear I felt about my mom's life was never fully suppressed. My overly active mind stalled with a strange anxiety that became "analysis paralysis," a term I learned later. My antidote? Read a book alone.

After playing and eating as a team, I looked forward to curling up with a great book and reading for a few hours in my hotel room. A lot of the girls played Risk or Monopoly or Truth or Dare in one of the player's rooms, laughing and yelling so I could hear them. I wasn't feeling social.

The night after we won our preliminary pool play round, my mom tapped on my door and asked what I was doing.

"I'm reading *Gone With the Wind*, Mom. What's up?" Always annoyed when someone interrupted my time in the fantasy world of a story, I probably had a sour look on my face.

"Jenyth, everyone is in Lisa's room playing games. Why are you here on your own? You've already read that book dozens of times."

"I'm tired, Mom. I can't be 'on' all the time. You know how sore I get at these tournaments. I'm trying to rest." This was truly how I felt. I wanted to be out of physical and emotional pain and ready to kick butt the next day as we entered the second round of competition. I didn't know lactic acid needed movement to disperse it. By lying around all night, I was actually making the soreness worse.

Mom shrugged her shoulders, quietly shutting the door and leaving me alone.

I returned to the world of my book, where Scarlett's daughter fell off her horse and never regained consciousness.

Pepper on the Pillow Plot

Coach Debbie had decided to play me at middle blocker for the rest of the tournament, which meant I was at the mercy of the set. I had to jump, hang, and hit or sometimes hit the ball on the way up or tip it over the net when it was too low. This setter and I didn't have a great connection, and after a few games, my back was starting to hurt from arching as I landed. I tried to better each ball I was given, but it was exhausting.

Still, we were winning. By the time day three ended, we had positioned ourselves to be in the top four, and would be playing Orange County in the semifinals the next morning.

I watched their quarterfinal match. Their setter, nicknamed Krush, had been an All American at nationals before, was a junior, and launched the fastest set to the outside I had ever seen. Her hitters were so early they were able to face only a single blocker. It would be my job to close the hole and put up a double block. But she also set a quick backset, one I would have to move in the opposite direction to defend. The middle sets didn't bother me: I owned that part of the net real estate. But I knew enough of volleyball strategy to understand that once I stuffed her middle hitters, she would be running me back and forth across the net until her hitters saw a hole. I was going to need a good night's sleep.

Back at the hotel after dinner, and after we were all in our pj's, Coach Debbie knocked at my door, telling me to come to her room in the sternest voice I'd ever heard her use. Immediately I thought something was wrong with my mother.

When I entered her room, however, a sea of teammates' faces glared at me.

"Sit down, Jenyth," Debbie said. "Do you have pepper on your pillow?"

"What? I, uh, don't know. I just got out of the shower."

"Well, you don't have pepper on your pillow because *you* put pepper on all our pillows tonight for a joke. What do you have to say for yourself?"

"What are you talking about? Who has pepper on their pillows?" A chorus of "me" rang through the room. Even my mom had pepper on her pillow. "What's the point of that?" I wondered out loud.

"I have no idea. You'll carry the balls from now on and collect and count them after every warm-up and match. You won't be captain during the semis tomorrow," said Debbie.

I couldn't believe it. My face was redder than a Kansas radish. I looked at my mom, and she was looking at the ground instead of defending me. If Debbie had wanted to humiliate me, she had succeeded. My teammates' faces were against me.

I hadn't put pepper on anybody's pillow, but I did want

to go to sleep. So, I accepted the punishment and left the room.

I slept little, and during warm-ups, my teammates gave me weird looks. That made me totally fired up to take out my anger on the ball. This was so unfair. I knew I couldn't swing too hard, for if the set were off, I'd screw up my back. But I exploded when I could, and we took the first set.

Orange County roared back as their wily coach rotated his lineup so I would be in the back row when his best hitter was in the front row. I had done a better job blocking her than I thought possible, but our other middle was struggling. Krush was an incredible setter, and cross-footed me several times.

We were neck and neck in the third and deciding set, when I went to the back row to serve. On the next rotation, Krush ran our blockers all over the place, and they ended up defeating us. I had played well enough to be nominated to the All-American list, but I wasn't selected. Many college coaches came up to me after the match to congratulate me on my performance and ask me if I were playing setter or middle in college.

"Setter," I proudly said. "But this team needed my blocking and hitting."

A Special Kind of Loyalty

The pepper on the pillow incident forgotten, my teammates and I whooped it up during the finals, as Orange County crushed the team from Chicago. We had given them the better match, and the Orange County coach came up to me again after the finals to congratulate me on my blocking. "You had me scared, J.J. You were awesome."

There is a great tradition in the world of volleyball: after a match is over, everyone congratulates and compliments their opponents. We play hard against each other on the court but party together afterward. I loved this small world of volleyball, where everyone knew everyone else. Those of us who had just graduated from high school shared where we had signed to play college ball, although most of us knew where the superstars were going. It seemed all the top teams had players who had gotten a volleyball scholarship. Our Title IX timing was perfect.

In the afterglow of the match and the accolades of my club teammates, I left Illinois feeling I was ready for college. We had played so well, and we'd see each other on the college courts. I would play Karen's UOP team in a few months, and Kyra's Hawaii team too. All of us would be on opposite courts during the huge UC Davis women's tournament in early September. We parted on great terms, with bronze medals around our necks.

In 1981, Coach Debbie's Sacramento State team won the Division II national championship. Still, she managed to come and see me play and supported me in every way possible. Volleyball produces a special kind of loyalty.

Near the end of my mother's life, I heard many confessions. I was shocked to learn that she and Coach Debbie were so worried about my silence and low spirits that they concocted a scheme. Mom came up with the pepper on the pillow plot since she had peppered her softball team's pillows during the Kansas State Softball Championships many years before. Debbie did the actual peppering while we were at the team dinner. They wanted to distract me, to shake me up so I would compete hard against Orange County. It worked. I got mad, I got tougher, and I performed, without ever suspecting who had engineered the whole thing.

In the five weeks I had between volleyball Junior Olympics and the start of preseason volleyball at Stanford, I rode my blue Schwinn ten-speed to other people's barns, shoveled the stalls, and rode their horses while they vacationed.

Also, my brother encouraged me to take the weight-lifting class with him at American River Junior College, where I was the only girl in the weight room. The football coach welcomed me, taught me the correct form, had me lift free weights and work on overall sports strength, then had me run on the par course along the horse trails after each workout. After being treated like every other athlete in the gym, I was in the best physical condition of my life.

Then it was time to go to The Farm and see if I could live up to Stanford academic standards while playing a Division I sport. I expected to be successful without really knowing that I was a big fish in a small pond about to be thrown overboard into the Pacific.

CHAPTER 4
The Firsts

I didn't understand why I couldn't get my mom to leave after she had helped me unload my athletic gear into my dingy Stern Hall dorm until a few decades later, when I dropped off my own daughter on the East Coast for her pre-season volleyball training. Volleyball started many weeks before school, and after I had dumped my two brand-new suitcases on the bed, I wanted to start meeting people. The other bed in my room was empty, so Mom opened the blue Samsonite cases on that bed, while I looked down the hall.

At eighteen, I was five feet, nine and a half inches, and weighed 153 pounds. I had no fat and wore size medium in everything. I was dying to know how I would compare with everyone else.

I looked back in the room as my mom unloaded my perfectly ironed t-shirts, Levi's, hippie sundress, and workout clothes. She ran her finger across the top of the built-in desk and said, "We need to clean this place before we put away your clothes." She returned from the bathroom with some paper towels and wiped down every surface on that side of the room, then started loading clothes into drawers.

"Mom, let me do that. You have a long drive home, at least three hours."

My mom fought tears as she hugged me, and I waited awkwardly until she let go. We walked down to the parking lot and had one last hug. She was sweating heavily in the ninety-degree heat and I took one lingering look at her face. She slid into the front seat of the Monte Carlo and wiped her forehead with her little cotton embroidered handkerchief. As soon as she drove off, I was filled with so much excitement I had to run back to the dorm to see if anyone else had arrived. I tried not to think of her flushed face and her shallow breathing and vowed not to worry about her all of the time that I couldn't see her. She probably felt the same about me.

I found my teammate Jan, who told me freshies had to be at the gym by one o'clock for physicals. She pointed the way to Maples Pavilion.

My first encounter with the blond, blue-eyed, blue-chip athlete that was incoming freshman John Elway was in a line of first-year athletes. On that hot August afternoon, we were all herded into the gym for questionnaires and physicals. Elway was a coveted recruit in both football and baseball. I was a scholarship volleyball player who also hoped to make the basketball team. Everybody knew him and nobody knew me.

I wanted to meet a famous person, so I skipped up the line and introduced myself. "Hi, I'm J.J."

"Hi J.J. I'm John." John was completely normal, I thought. He looked like he had a good sense of humor. Other football players introduced themselves, and we laughed as we walked through the registration stations.

I felt a tap on my shoulder and turned to see a nurse with a needle gun. This was not my first negative encounter with an immunization, but my pediatrician knew to warn me before a shot. I fainted dead away at the sight of the three-inch needle and woke up smelling something sterile, with the doctor and everybody else staring at me.

Some guys picked me up and carried me into a side room away from the gym floor. I was dizzy and humiliated. What a way to impress the big man on campus. The doctor told me he had a cure for my needle phobia, and over the next four years, I donated two gallons of O+ blood, without ever seeing the needle enter my vein.

John wasn't laughing as he waved goodbye, and I couldn't tell if he was sympathetic or just sorry it had happened next to him.

Within a week, Elway and I were "hey" and wave buddies. I was competing for the starting setter position for our team, which is the volleyball version of a quarterback. He was hoping for any playing time at quarterback. I hoped we would both succeed.

First Practice

As I walked into Maples Pavilion for my first volleyball practice, Coach Fred asked us to introduce ourselves and give our hometowns. As I heard Redondo Beach, Manhattan Beach, Hermosa Beach, Imperial Beach, Pacific Palisades, West Los Angeles, Honolulu, and Del Mar, I realized nobody was from Northern California.

A talkative brunette named Tucker said, "Dallas," and I said, "Carmichael, near Sacramento."

A voice said, "We've got a valley girl!" Everyone laughed.

This wasn't the first time I had felt out of place, but I was surprised that nearly everyone was from a SoCal beach town. Tucker and I made eye contact and became friends immediately.

I also realized I looked very different from the thin and

tanned girls with sun streaks in their long hair, waxed legs and bikini lines, and track shorts in sunset-streaked colors, trimmed with white piping. I was the only one wearing bun-huggers—shorts that looked like a high-waisted bathing suit bottom and exposed my thunder thighs.

When all of us sat in a circle to stretch, the dissing began.

Tina had just returned from Italy and was interrogating everyone. She asked me why I was wearing bun-huggers and why my hair was so short.

I didn't want to get into trouble for talking during warm-ups, so I looked at the coaches, saw they weren't listening, and continued stretching as I answered. I told her the comfortable buns were from my Junior Olympic team, and I had Dorothy Hamill's haircut because she was my favorite athlete. I did gymnastics for years but really wanted to ice skate, I told her, showing off my flexibility with the splits and a flourishing arm wave and giggle.

A few of the older girls laughed, but not *at* me. Some other teammates nodded. I felt like some were with me, others neutral. If only I didn't have skin that burned and freckled.

Sherry, a senior middle blocker whose light brown hair was the same color as her tan limbs, asked me in a very friendly way what I had done for summer break.

I thought about Italy and beach clubs. And then I thought about riding my bike to my summer job shoveling shit and coaching sports camps at my high school. I took a big breath, and edited as I spoke, hoping to find a way to connect with the team. I mentioned Junior Olympics in Illinois, where we beat my new teammate Aly's Laguna Beach team in the quarters and lost in the semifinals to Orange County. Then I told her about my visit to the family farm in Kansas.

Aly from Del Mar looked surprised; she probably didn't remember our team. But I remembered her team's glamorous fuchsia uniform tops and sleek white Dolphin shorts.

Tina thought I was kidding about Kansas, then Paula told me I truly did have a Dorothy complex as she twirled her ponytail and winked at me. As the whole group laughed and began getting up and moving to get the volleyballs, Tina pulled me aside and asked me if I was one of the lesbos from Club Sacramento.

"Are you kidding?" I said, meaning, *Why should you be asking me this, and who cares?* She interpreted my answer as no way, but told me I had the ripped muscles of a buff dyke.

I saw her forehead had a bit of a widow's peak as she looked down her aristocratic nose at me. I stifled a comeback. *And you look like a witches' tit in winter*, I wanted to reply, *with your sun-shriveled face and long, pointy nose.* Instead, I said nothing, and realized I'd have to be very careful around her. While I didn't know the words to use, my actions could speak for me. I decided I'd be first in every wind sprint and every conditioning drill. Even after she took the time to teach me how to make perfect spaghetti carbonara at our team dinner the next evening, I knew Tina might become an enemy. I vowed to be the glue that kept the team together, not the selfish player who split the seams in the team foundation.

Boot Camp

Before school started, I learned many lessons from my teammates and from the soccer and water polo teams. First of all, the huge beer bellies proudly displayed by the polo guys were a necessary defense against preseason workouts and Hell Week.

Hell Week had nothing to do with hazing and everything to do with surviving double-day workouts. The water polo coach designed workouts so grueling that the average guy lost twenty pounds in the first week. Without their preseason blubber, they wouldn't survive. They all floated easily on day one, but by day five, they all sank, with no body fat left to serve as a flotation device.

Backgammon followed by a trip to Bud's Ice Cream was our evening ritual, until after day six, when everyone was too tired to do more than shower, eat, and watch a movie in the lounge. Our team was on the second floor, and on Saturday night after practice, I had trouble walking up the stairs. Going down was worse. I tried going sideways, holding onto the rail, backwards on my toes, but it wasn't working. If only we'd had ice baths and Jacuzzis back then. We didn't know how to take care of our bodies, didn't know the importance of rest, stretching, hydration, and diet. In 1979, we ate steak and potatoes. In 1980, lots and lots of carbs. I loved all food and didn't know then that my muscles responded differently to protein than to high glycemic index foods.

Late August through the middle of September was a glorious time. The freshies hung out with the water polo team and bet on backgammon games and ate gallons of Bud's ice cream, since we couldn't eat enough calories to keep up with the demands of double days. We assessed the upperclassmen in our positions and schemed how we could beat them out. It was clear we were a new breed of volleyball player: athletes first, volleyballers second.

Boom-Boom and I had never played beach volleyball, but

both of us were recruited for basketball and volleyball. Our classmate Kisi was an expert on the sand and had to adjust to the hard indoor court, like most of the upper class. She could have made the water polo team too, if we'd had a women's team. She did make the softball team. All three of us displayed a competitive mindset all the time. We soaked up the new techniques.

For the first six weeks, we had no classes but were in a kind of boot camp with physical and mental challenges. Since our volleyball coaches were professional beach volleyball players, they played in the scrimmages with us. As I sweated and scraped myself up off of the floor after diving after their incredible spikes, I started to anticipate, or read, their shot selection. They were amazing models of perfect technique, and I tried to imitate them.

After three weeks of camp, everyone's tan had faded a bit, but as a freckle-faced mesomorph, I still stood out. I refused to lose a single race. Everything was a competition to me—something in my genes that I couldn't control once sports became involved.

My older teammates had a leisurely approach to wind sprints. They had other interests outside volleyball and put academics before everything else. I was a hundred percent into volleyball, and some of the seniors told me to stop working so hard.

One day, our coaches wanted to show off our stamina, so they decided we would do our wind sprints on the football practice field. It was lined for the forty-yard dash, and we needed to do ten reps under a certain time as a team. The football coaches were watching us, so I asked one if he would throw me a pass after we were finished. My brother had been the high school quarterback, and I often ran his routes for him. The coach called a high post pattern, and I sprinted to the thirty-yard line and turned around to catch the ball with my left hand, never missing a stride. I wasn't quite in synch with our volleyball team in terms of the tempo and rhythm of our offense, but I could make plays due to sheer athleticism and stubbornness. The football coach gave me a high-five when I returned the ball to him. That was fun.

At a recent volleyball reunion, Boom-Boom and Kisi told me my athletic ability was out of control. "J.J., sometimes you jumped too high, were too quick," Boom-Boom said. "You got in the way!"

Kisi agreed, but threw a compliment my way: "J.J., sometimes you were too fast, but you never gave up on a ball. I loved that about your game."

At the time, I gloried in what my body could do and how all my anxieties disappeared after a hard-driven spike.

Rinconada

At eighteen, I was looking forward to freshman orientation weekend and meeting more people after our pre-season was over. I packed up my gear early in the morning so I could grab the bags and rush over to Rinconada—my new home for the year—between the last of our two-a-day practices. The university was conducting a housing experiment and had decided to put most of the premedical students into this dorm, with boys on the first and third floors and girls on the middle floor. It was a "sandwich dorm," we were told. I looked forward to meeting some other girls who wanted to be doctors.

I hopped up the stairs and ran down the hall, dragging

my suitcase behind me. Over the summer, I had saved up one hundred dollars just to buy matching comforters for me and my roommate, and any other supplies we would need to make our room special. I wondered if she would be from the East Coast and unfamiliar with California, what she would be interested in, and what she would look like. Would she like rhythm and blues, funk, soul, and Motown, like me, or would she be a classic rock and roller? What kind of medicine did she want to study? Would we be in all the same classes? Maybe we could be study buddies.

I didn't see my name on any of the doors, which had cute doorplates on them already. I found the resident assistant and asked who my roommate would be.

"You are so lucky. You have one of only four single rooms for freshies on campus."

"I have a single? I don't get a roommate?" I tried not to cry. I had been thinking about this girl all summer long, and she didn't exist.

"It's all very scientific. We looked at all the housing applications and school counselor recommendations and then put the shyer girls together in the middle of the hall, near the bathrooms. This will increase their interaction with others and make them feel part of things. The more extroverted the girl, the farther she is from the bathroom. Clearly you are one of the most outgoing people in the entire freshman class, so we put you in a single room at the far end of the hall."

What kind of a plan is that? I thought. It was weird that they knew all this stuff about me. I didn't know what to say, so I went back to my room and began unpacking. My parents would be arriving around 5:00, with my new trunk and some other things, after we finished our second practice. I couldn't wait to see them.

I was still excited about freshman orientation, even if I didn't have a roommate. After our last practice, because of my sweaty state, I did a quick rinse, ran down the hall in my towel, and changed into something fresh. When I reached the orientation, it was crawling with people. Each girl I met seemed so nervous. Since I'd been on campus for so long, I offered to help them find their way around. By the time my parents arrived with my stuff, I knew everyone's name, and they knew me as J.J., what I would be called in college. I suppose the housing staff was correct.

When my parents arrived, we discovered that the three of us couldn't fit inside my room, which looked like a converted storage closet. I had a built-in clothing rod and a desk with a chair that hit the bed when I pulled it back to put my suitcase on it. My mom felt bad I didn't have a roommate. My dad opened my window and said I could put a chair on the entrance awning for my own balcony. Later that weekend, I did.

After we had unpacked everything, and Mom wiped down the surfaces one more time, we left. We walked around downtown Palo Alto until we found a small restaurant with an affordable menu. I didn't think my mom would ever stop asking questions about volleyball. My parents dropped me off after dinner, and we hugged. I told them I couldn't wait to start school on Monday.

In the meantime, events for the weekend were beginning. Would my big hopes and dreams come true? Could I become an Olympic volleyball player? Could I make it into medical school and do a research project that would find a cure for my mother? Six weeks of preseason training had confirmed these goals would be difficult to achieve. I was physically and emotionally exhausted.

On Sunday evening, I shoved an old folding chair through my window and onto the awning, just as my dad had suggested, and enjoyed some private time outside after all of the parties had ended. I went back inside and sat on my narrow bed, wondering if this single room was really a blessing. Stanford was full of unique individuals, that I already knew. Everyone had passion, energy, and intelligence. Here, I would have no need to hide my love of learning. As I leaned against the wall, I understood mine was to be a solo journey. Yet, I felt very, very lucky. I had the freedom to create myself—as J.J. or Jenyth or someone in between.

CHAPTER 5
Stanford Women

As I thought about volleyball and school, I also worried about my mother's health. Being busy allowed me to not think about her pain. The pain I felt any time I thought of losing her scared me into thinking I couldn't handle falling in love and losing the boy of my dreams. It was clear to me I would not have time for a boyfriend in college anyway. However, when I learned about the tradition of becoming a Stanford Woman, I embraced it many times over.

One of the senior soccer players asked Tucker and me if we knew how to become a Stanford Woman. He explained that we had to kiss a senior in the middle of the Quad at midnight on a full moon. Tucker and I looked at each other and started laughing.

"J.J., I would be honored to make you a Stanford Woman," he said.

I was floored. I hadn't noticed this soccer player before, but he wanted to kiss me?

I didn't see much of him until September 5, when we walked from the athletic dorms to the Quad. There, we briefly kissed. We laughed at the other couples surrounding us in front of the church under the full moon spotlight, then trudged back to Stern Hall to make an early wake-up call to practice.

The next morning, Tucker and I were sitting with the

soccer guys again, when Dougie, a freshman geology major, dropped a bomb: "You guys know you aren't Stanford Women yet, right?"

"Yes, we are," we chimed in unison.

"Nope. I hate to tell you, but the moon was only ninety-seven percent full last night. It might have looked like a full moon, but tonight is the real thing. Those guys played a joke on you."

Doug and the other first-year soccer players laughed at us. Many offered to help out, but we reminded them we had to kiss a *senior*. Since so many people were in the Quad, were we really not Stanford Women? I couldn't believe it. Did I need a man to make me a woman? Hmm.

Hypnosis

My dad loved to fool my mother and make her laugh, as she was so gullible. When he fooled me or when I face-planted, I was the first to laugh at myself, for as high as I reached, I was still pretty down-to-earth.

As classes and volleyball ramped up in intensity, my physical tiredness made me battle to avoid nodding off in large lecture classes. My exhaustion dulled my appreciation of humor.

I made a huge effort not to be seen wearing my sweats to class. After the first week of school, it was clear other students looked at female athletes as people taking admissions spots from the real academics. I didn't want to hear "You're an athlete? Oh…" So, I rushed to shower and change my clothes.

But one day in early October, I needed to see the trainer, so I arrived in Dr. Zimbardo's famous Psychology 1 class in my warm and cozy red sweatshirt and sweatpants. Seven hundred and fifty freshies sat in theater-style seats arranged in a semicircle. Zimbardo was a cult favorite, because his Stanford prison experiment had revealed the base nature of humans, who, when randomly selected as prisoners or guards, became sadistic if they had guard positions. A brilliant lecturer, he had the flare of P. T. Barnum and a comedian's instant audience connection. I loved his textbook, his teaching style, and everything about his class.

On this particular day, in my warm sweats, I began to sink into my chair as he described the powers of hypnosis and susceptibility, and then began to make suggestions. I fell asleep. According to others, however, he had put me under his spell. I woke up to laughter, saw my arm waving in the air, and bolted upright.

Dr. Z. pointed at me. "You just did an amazing job. What's your name?"

A bunch of athletes were in the class, so they called out "J.J." Everyone laughed.

"Great. J.J. Come up on stage. You and you, join us as well."

Three of us, bemused and embarrassed, walked up the stairs and sat in chairs next to our hypnotist. As someone who didn't want others to know she was a jock, I was bummed. Half of the first-year class would now remember me as the easily hypnotizable volleyball player.

Dr. Z. led us through some simple relaxations and suggestions on stage. I didn't unwind much at first, but his sonorous voice and comforting suggestions were impossible to ignore. I guess I performed well.

After the class, Dr. Z. encouraged me to learn more about hypnosis and the power of positive suggestions. Around campus, my classmates enjoyed waving their arms at me as I rode by on my bike. Clearly, I was the dorkiest Stanford Woman ever.

When I told my mom about the hypnosis lecture and opportunity to participate in psychology studies for pay, she was silent for a minute. "Jenyth Jo, did you know I had you by hypnosis? When I had Stan, they put a gas mask over my face and I missed everything. Going through that much pain without feeling the success of the birth didn't seem right. So, I took hypnosis prenatal classes and had you without medication for pain."

"Really, Mom? What was it like?"

"Painful, but you were smaller than Stan, so it wasn't too bad. I saw your dark hair and eyelashes right away. I counted your fingers and toes. I'll never forget how perfect you looked. One's mind, one's memory, is a really powerful thing, you know. Once I saw you, I completely forgot the pain."

I thought my mom was just stubborn when it came to fighting her disease and her conflicting treatment plans. Now I realize her approach was what we might call mindful living or habits of mind today. She tried to avoid pain medications and just took anti-inflammatories and steroids for her autoimmune disease, while using meditation and prayer to deflect the pain. At the time, I wondered if I could train my mind to be as strong as hers.

Go-To Girl

The University of California Santa Barbara (USCB) campus is one of the most beautiful in the world. As our team van cruised down the coastal range and into Goleta, I saw an incredible beach reminiscent of Hanauma Bay in Oahu, with every shade of Pacific blue imaginable. Sand volleyball courts lined one area. As we drove by them, the high-rise freshman dorm perched like a high-end hotel above the bay. I couldn't believe I had never paid a campus visit.

Later that night, we battled the nationally ranked Gauchos. Three freshies were in the starting lineup: Boom-Boom, Kisi, and I. I shared the setting duties with sophomore Jan; sophomore Tina and senior Sherry were also on the court. We were playing in front of a large, beach-dressed crowd wearing Hawaiian shirts, flip-flops, and Ray-Bans.

UCSB beat us in the first game, but we came roaring back to win the second game. In this two-out-of-three match, taking the second set would be a victory for our first-year coach. I remember the time out during the third set as vividly as a movie scene.

FRED

Ref, ref, TIME OUT!

TINA

Omigod Fred, why did you call a time out? We got this.

BOOM-BOOM

You just hit the ball out. We can't have any more errors.

FRED

Okay, we have to figure out how to pass Iris's serve. I want to rotate you closer to the net, Tina, so Kisi and Boom-Boom can split the court and pass.

BOOM-BOOM

I'll take it.

TINA

Whaaaat? I'm the best passer on this team. You need to rotate the freshies over.

FRED

Tina, I'm trying to get Jan closer to the net so she doesn't have to run as far. If you two are at the net, she's ready as a target for the passer.

TINA

Jan, you better set me the ball.

SHERRY

Set me. They won't be expecting it. They'll be expecting you to backset to Tina.

JAN

Why don't you let me decide who I'm going to set? If I'm already at the net, I can see their block. You guys just have to pass me the damn ball.

BOOM-BOOM

You should set J.J. on the outside. She's unstoppable. J.J., move up and I'll pass for you.

J.J.

meets Boom-Boom's eyes and nods.

FRED

Jan, set Tina. Everybody, just play your regular positions and let me be the coach.

Everyone except Tina gives him a furious look. Fred turns his back to the huddle and starts writing on his clipboard.

JAN

We can do this, girls. With a good pass. Who's ready?

GROUP

We are!

JAN

Pulls J.J. aside and whispers to her
J.J., I don't care where the pass goes. It's on you. Be ready.
J.J. *nods.*

Funny how a spike that ends the point is called a "kill." I wanted to crush the ball to get the side-out point as much as I wanted to kill Tina. *As long as the set is in a hittable zone, this rally will be over,* I told myself. *We'll get the ball back and serve out the game.*

We three freshies looked at each other as Iris from UCSB went back to serve. I took a step up, then Kisi and Boom-Boom took one step toward the larger gap I left. The ball's topspin flight path was easy to read, for the ball would go on a straight line, then drop.

Boom-Boom stepped in front of Kisi, passed the ball slightly left of center on purpose, so Jan was forced to set me on the left side. I started a powerful approach from well off the court and saw Jan run forward to deliver a perfect set with a low arc. I planted my left foot, swung my right foot forward, and blasted off the ground, drifting forward with a force that would add to my arm swing, which was loose and fast and now aimed down the line—my favorite shot. The ball hit the ground in front of the defender before I returned to earth. I had only seen guys do this and I had never hit the ball so straight down in my life. I bounced off the ground again, nearly as high, in sheer joy.

SIDE-OUT *gestures the referee.*

In the swarm that was the beehive of our team, everyone high-fived me and screamed. Except for Tina. She grabbed the ball and headed back to serve, without looking for a serving signal from Fred. She launched the ball ten feet out, and we didn't earn a point after my powerful side-out. It was at this moment that we freshies knew we were some of the best players on the team. We knew Tina would lose the respect of our head coach. I knew Jan had faith in me. She had called my number and anointed me the go-to girl.

Even though we didn't beat Santa Barbara, we had an amazing performance against them and another national powerhouse, Cal Poly. The opposing coaches took notice of a new team in town. When I called my mom and told her what happened, she said she wished she could have seen everyone's faces. "Did you really hit the ball straight down, and land after it? That's so cool. I wish I could have seen it. What are Ray-Bans?"

I told her about the fancy sunglasses, secretly hoping some had fallen off of the bleach-blonde heads after my spike. "You'll get to see us play next week in Davis, Mom, I promise. I'll see if I can get that hit again. Jan is such a great setter and great teammate. I just don't think the seniors are as into volleyball as the freshies. We have our own little group of super-competitive people."

Buttermilk Brownies

The UC Davis tournament was a reunion of my high school club teammates and our parents. I was very familiar with the new Recreation Hall from coaching at the summer camp, but my mom was amazed at how state of the art it was. She arrived early, staked out a spot in one of the corners upstairs that had a full view of the courts below, and started arranging her spread of delicious homemade food. I knew she'd had a good week: her wedding rings were on. But her elbows were swollen and I wondered how much time she'd spent cooking.

I was drooling at 8:00 a.m., but we had a few matches to play before we could eat. I did stuff a blueberry muffin in my mouth right after I hugged her. "Mom, you've done it again! How did you have time to make all this stuff? I'd almost rather eat than play!"

She laughed.

A few parents of my club volleyball teammates walked over and poured themselves cups of coffee from the large machine my mom took to church events, as I headed for the stairwell. Her picnic spot was a hub of energy for the rest of the day.

I had former teammates who now played for Cal, Sac State, UC Davis, and UOP. One teammate was at the University of Hawaii, but her parents showed up to socialize in Davis even though her daughter's team hadn't made the trip. In a brief huddle with our club Coach Debbie, who was there with her Sac State team, we shared stories. I already knew my high school teammate, who played for Cal, didn't have any hot water in the locker room, and they didn't get to play their matches in the "boys' gym." The facilities at Davis were still segregated and very unequal, as the girls played in the old Hickey Gym, not the new Rec Hall.

I began to realize Stanford's Title IX effort to provide equal access for women with locker rooms, training facilities, and weight rooms was the exception, not the rule, in 1979. UOP had a lot of construction going on, so they would soon be able to fulfill their responsibility to provide equal participation, financial aid, and other benefits guaranteed by Title IX in a brand-new facility. It would be years before the University of California system and most of the other colleges complied.

When it was time to take a lunch break between matches, some of my teammates pulled out the little bag lunches we had brought along and ate them as we sat on the bench. I was so proud to invite them all upstairs and told them that my mom had a surprise waiting. Coaches Fred and Beeky went up the stairs like two middle school boys and stopped in their tracks when they saw my mom's folding card tables covered with homemade Stanford red-and-white checkered tablecloths. She'd put a small bouquet of sunflowers in the middle and created an indoor picnic scene. Everyone grabbed a paper plate and loaded up with German potato salad with homemade mustard, deviled eggs, fruit salad in a carved watermelon bowl, chicken salad spread between slices of homemade wheat bread, and blueberry muffins. Once everyone was standing around, eating with plastic forks and drinking Mom's sweet iced tea, she unveiled her coup de grâce: buttermilk brownies.

Fred took one bite—a bit of chocolate frosting dribbling down his chin—and rolled his eyes. "Joanne, I've never tasted anything like this," he exclaimed.

Each of us took a three-inch square and let the cake texture melt in our mouths like butter. That was the secret: lots and lots of real butter, on top of the buttermilk, in both the frosting and the brownie. Mom became everyone's favorite. She knew how to be a team mom, and I strutted a little, proud that everyone appreciated a bit of Mom's home cooking.

Before our last match, my teammates and I went up for another brownie. By the time that match was over, we weren't playing well. In 1979, an all-day tournament meant first whistle at 8:00 a.m. and last whistle at 8:00 p.m. It's really hard to sustain a quality level of play after six or eight hours, let alone twelve. When it ended, I went upstairs and overheard Fred talking to my mom.

"Joanne, I know you meant well when you made all this food. But too much sugar is bad for the girls' muscles. That's why we lost the last match. Don't bring any brownies to our tournaments again." I saw him put another brownie in his mouth, and he walked away with another.

My mom was shocked speechless, then turned to me. "What an ungrateful man! He didn't even say thank you! The school gave you a turkey sandwich and a bag of potato chips. What kind of food is that for an all-day tournament?"

As I started to help her pack up, I said, "Mom, the girls loved everything. Nobody cooks like you. Fred's just mad we ended on a loss, but I don't think our lineup was that great for the last game. It's not your fault."

Mom had a tear running out of one eye as she thumped the Tupperware containers on top of each other and stacked them into a bag. There was no food left; we had eaten every last bite. I knew the effort she'd made baking all week. She must have stayed up late on Friday night to finish everything, and I could see cracks in her cuticles. I don't know where she found the energy, and now she looked completely sapped. "Mom, thank you so much for bringing all my favorites. It's just like you always say, 'food is love.' We all felt it today."

"Well, humph. I'm not impressed with the coach and I'm not impressed with his manners. Your coach took the last brownie, and I told your brother I'd save him one." She looked at me, and we both started cracking up. "Your coach is just a twenty-seven-year-old teenager, Jenyth. He doesn't know what he's doing. His words don't match his actions. When we met him last spring, I knew he was inexperienced, but I didn't know he was rude."

The team started to leave, and Kisi called out for me to grab her another brownie.

I looked at my mom, who had her hands out in a what-am-I-supposed-to-do-now gesture. She'd made quite an impression: everyone on my team was calling her Mom by the end of the tournament.

Weak Ankles

A few weeks later, during a practice scrimmage, I landed on Linda's foot, spraining my ankle. The crack was so loud that everybody stopped, and I nearly went into shock.

Our trainer ran for a wheelchair and wheeled me across the street to the training room. Head trainer Scotty evaluated the injury and said it was a third-degree sprain.

A few minutes later, a screaming John Elway was wheeled into the training room, with his ankle wrapped up. Same diagnosis.

Scotty looked at both of us and said he was going to test

our manhood, our pain tolerance. I gave him The Look, and he said, "Sorry, J.J."

He filled two painter's buckets with ice and water, until the ratio was about seventy-five/twenty-five. Our trainer, Patty, unwrapped my ankle, and Scotty unwrapped John's, and the battle began. The first plunge into the ice wasn't that bad, but within five seconds we both pulled out our ankles. Elway cursed under his breath. I could barely breathe, but I took a big inhale and stuck my foot back in.

Over the next ten minutes, I finally became numb enough to keep my foot in the bucket, but John couldn't do it the first day. We went to the same X-ray facility, saw the same team doctor, received the same treatment, but I beat John Elway in the ice bucket challenge. The trainers loved it.

For the next month, John and I sat in the training room from one o'clock to two o'clock, watching *All My Children* and getting the same treatment: electronic stimulation patches on either side of our injured ankles, which were stuffed into an ice bucket; then heat packs, massage, and range of motion exercises. Patty and I had already bonded at a preseason pasta feed at her home in Mountain View, so spending more time with her was terrific. John was an all-around great guy, but so pigeon-toed. I made it my practice to try to beat him at every exercise we were given, but to be fair, he didn't know he was competing.

Instead of watching soap operas at lunch, I should have been studying. I didn't have an overwhelming academic schedule, but I now realize how much time I wasted. The study skills class showed me how to stay organized—which has been a lifelong issue as I am easily distracted and tend to leave piles of papers everywhere. As an athlete, I knew the value of extra practice and repetition, but as a student, I read everything once and expected to remember it. I didn't review. I'd never ever reviewed or studied in high school. While my ankle healed, I did the problem sets in calculus and chemistry, then limped down the hall to find someone to talk to. A lot of the girls on my floor were struggling with the same chemistry equations, but we ended up talking instead of working out the 3-D models.

When my first midterms were returned, I'd earned C's and B's. The shock put me in a tailspin for a while. Others who were as social as I had earned A's. They never seemed to study. Instead of changing my methods, I decided to do better next time. If I didn't know what my score would be when I turned in a test, I knew I didn't know the material.

When I returned to the team at full strength, I expected to either sit the bench or be put back into the lineup as setter. But Paula was playing really well, so I sat for most of the next match. However, our middle blocker, Sherry, contracted appendicitis. Fred remembered I had played middle blocker in the front row while setting from the back row in high school, so he threw me into some practice drills.

I hit well, but blocking middle was much harder against the faster collegiate offenses. On the one hand, I was happy to be playing again; on the other hand, I wanted to set. I ended the season with decent stats. I had no idea Fred had recruited Krush, the setter from Orange County who had driven me nuts at Junior Olympics last June. From this point on, he saw me only as a middle blocker. Beeky, our assistant coach who trained the setters, decided to focus on law school, leaving me with no advocate.

Boom-Boom and I switched from volleyball to basketball in a day. We hoped to make the team during a special tryout session. Boom-Boom rebounded really well and held her own underneath the basket. The coaches wanted to see me play point guard, my worst position. I did fine on defense but not so well on offense. I wanted to be on the wing, where I could go one-on-one with my defender, instead of being at the top of the key in a crowd.

When I learned that I'd made the travel team but would have to stay on campus during Christmas, I chose to go home and see my mom. I had already missed Thanksgiving and yearned to be home for Christmas.

On Thanksgiving, when my team had sat down at the opulent dining table for twenty-four in a gorgeous house in Atherton, all I could think of was Mom. I had never missed a family Thanksgiving at home. I missed the smells of her special turkey, roasting in a baking bag. I missed basting the turkey for her, squeezing juice all over the breast from the bulb of a baster. Mom's grip had slipped on the baster and the juices had burned her when I was about fifteen, so I had taken over this part of the cooking. I missed taking the foil off the bag for the last hour so the breast could brown, and missed stuffing the bird after the Stove-Top stuffing had cooked in a pot first. I missed looking at the turkey through the oven window, with the oven light on, waiting for the skin to be perfectly brown. Only Mom got to put in the meat thermometer near but not touching the thigh bone, as she looked not at the temperature but at the color of the turkey juices flooding the bottom of the bag. If they were pink, more time on the timer, but if the juices ran clear, she'd grab a soup spoon, put a bit of the juice in it, smell it, blow on it to cool it, then taste it. We'd call my dad, who would pull out the turkey and put him on the stove to cool. We always had a young Tom turkey.

Mom's hands betrayed her during the last years of her life. Some days, she could grip a brush and dry my hair for me. Most days, she needed help with zippers and buttons with small buttonholes. One of her shoulders was a bit frozen, so she had a hard time pulling small-necked sweatshirts off. She was too proud to ask Dad for help, so I usually helped her undress at night. How did she manage without me this fall?

Her Thanksgiving table would have a beautiful antique cornucopia she'd cleaned and spray-painted a pale bronze sitting as the centerpiece. Fresh mums and sunflowers would be arranged into an oasis to keep them hydrated, then stuffed inside the cornucopia so they spilled over in complete abundance. Dad had bought her an electric carving knife when her grip weakened, so she could still slice the bird. Having grown up at the Tindell Hatchery in Scranton, Kansas, she knew her way around any kind of poultry. She would arrange the dark and white meat in an artistic swirl, place the serving fork on the side, and ask Dad to carry it to the table to complete her spread. I didn't like turkey much, so I crowded the accompaniments onto my plate first: Uncle Bob's sweet potato casserole topped with mini-marshmallows, Aunt Louise's Watergate salad, Mom's carrots with honey glaze, Campbell soup green bean casserole, Mom's super-duper potatoes, Aunt Jeanne's cranberry-orange salad, Kansas twenty-four-hour salad with bacon and mayonnaise, and pies. Sometimes she made pumpkin pie for my brother, other times pecan pie for my dad. I loved apple pie, and she enjoyed her strawberry-rhubarb pie. Often our breakfast the next day would be a piece of pie with coffee or milk.

What I didn't miss? Her hands. She could never keep on

her wedding rings during the holiday season. She insisted on maintaining a certain standard of cooking, cleaning, and decorating, and after a few days, her left hand would be too swollen for the rings. We'd sit at the table and pass the food, and the heels of her hands would be cracked from swelling, her fingernails shredded from forgetting to put on her rubber gloves while she worked. For most of Thanksgiving week, we were kicked out of the kitchen so she could do her thing, but when we sat down to eat, I wondered whether her efforts were worth it. Once I suggested we buy the grocery store pre-made meal and just heat and eat it. I was trying to be considerate, but of course she was destroyed by the idea of not cooking. Stuffing ourselves, then stumbling into the family room to plop on the couch and watch the NFL with our eyes closed was not possible with store-bought food.

A wave of homesickness unlike anything I'd ever experienced urged me back to the Sacramento Valley. I missed my mom's hugs. I missed my dog's tail thumping whenever I walked into the room. I missed my brother's teasing. Also, I needed my dad's help with calculus, as the lecturer was hard to understand. I needed to review before the next quarter's differential equations class.

After I arrived home, I slept for the better part of the next day and woke to see my mom walking into my bedroom with my washed laundry, ironed or folded, ready to be put away in my room. I was so exhausted, but felt guilty.

"Oh Mom, you shouldn't have," I said, as she leaned over to push a curly bang from my forehead so she could plant a kiss.

"It's 11:00 a.m., Jenyth. Are you sick? You've never slept in so long."

"I pulled an all-nighter before my chemistry final and studied in the lounge at my dorm. Everyone was doing it." I sighed. "I'm worried about that grade. The first seven problems were fine, but he threw in some tricky ones at the end."

"I'm sure you did your best, and that's all that matters."

I expected Mom to ask when I'd get my grades—an old report card ritual that began in kindergarten when I was marked down for talking too much. But she and my dad never asked for them the entire time I was at Stanford. They thought I put too much pressure on myself, and wisely, they didn't want to add to it.

CHAPTER 6

Stanford Spring and Sacramento Summer

During spring quarter of my freshman year, in 1980, I was struggling with chemistry and calculus; acing English and Values, Technology, and Society; and enjoying windsurfing as my fun class. I was near Lake Lagunita when I had yet another "How did I get into this school?" moment. Rob, a freshman football player, came and sat next to me, and we watched as a frat boy took off on a slalom ski and began doing cuts in the lake behind a ski boat. I thought he was really good. Rob told me not to talk too loudly and pointed to the guy sitting next to me. Did I know who he was? I sneaked a glance to my left, then shook my head no. Rob informed me that he was the national junior slalom waterskiing champion.

I shook my head again. How many times in my freshman year had I been introduced to someone as the greatest virtuoso flautist in the country or the top fencer or Miss Alaska or a 1976 Olympic champion? Once again, I wondered how I had been admitted to this school with every kind of student—from socially established trust-fund babies to geniuses with incredible brains to world-class engineers who would fuel the dot-com boom of the 1980s. I knew I wasn't worthy. The term *imposter syndrome* had yet to be coined.

Since we had conditioning and workouts only four times a week, I explored as many opportunities as I could. Some of us were sitting in the dining hall, where I scooped ice cream for two hours in the early morning for extra money, when one of the guys looked at me. He declared I was too normal to rush a sorority. I was surprised at the negative judgment, as he'd gone through fraternity rush.

Tiny Jan, who lived near me on the second floor, wanted to know what was wrong with the Greek system. She was signed up to rush. A debate began about the value of social organizations, and a different guy challenged me, saying he knew I'd never rush. A perverse thought began to form, purely to oppose his assumptions.

"How do you know that? My mom was a Delta Gamma, and my dad was in the Delta Tau math frat." At my declaration, Tiny Jan begged me to rush, saying we'd have so much fun if we did it together. Then the dare came from a crazy premed from the first floor, saying I'd never rush. I have a hard time not taking a dare, so I told Jan I had the requisite white dress, and I would rush with her.

I went to the first meet-and-greet that night and had a blast. The girls on my team were one kind of female group, but the sorority girls were very, very different. I was surprised to learn about requirements to have a certain grade point average, and the fact there were no sorority houses on campus. The school had banned them during World War II, since girls were committing suicide when they didn't get bids to join their preferred sororities. Chapters met off-campus and functioned as study groups with social causes, such as fundraising for Stanford Children's Hospital and the Food Bank.

I continued the selection process, despite my parents telling me it wasn't in the budget. When Delta Gamma dropped me, my mom was furious. But I loved the girls in Kappa Alpha Theta, and my teammate Linda was a member.

When the bid to join arrived with a rose, I accepted. While I wasn't the most active member for the next three years, I truly enjoyed being around these young women and getting a glimpse of another type of student—girls who were serious pre-med and pre-law and pre-business. I studied every Monday, Tuesday, and Wednesday night, danced at frat parties on Thursday night, then studied all weekend, just like my sorority sisters.

Thursday night was the peak of my week. At a Phi Delt party, I met Marcus, a six-foot-five-inch member of the men's volleyball team who was also a great beach volleyball player. From LA, in a rock band, and a brilliant history and economics student, Marcus gave me a Long Island iced tea and advice: "Don't drink the jungle juice out of the garbage can. Never accept a drink from someone you don't know. For every drink you have, chase it with a full cup of water. You won't get dehydrated. You'll be able to play the next morning while everyone else is hungover." He was the first Stanford guy I met who took care of his body like a real athlete. I stopped drinking soda and started drinking a lot of water. When Mom called me to say she had to do some business at the Athletic Department next Friday, I was excited to introduce him.

Meanwhile, Marcus and I found out about some guys in his entrepreneur class who were starting the Big Way Yacht Club. For twenty dollars, one got a blue-and-yellow plastic blow-up raft, a paddle, and a pass enabling them to get a burger and a beer every Friday afternoon between 1 and 5 p.m. With eight Fridays to go, we joined. Marcus looked hilarious in the raft, as his long legs dangled over the edges. He had barely enough room for his water cannon. We pretended to be pirates and held up people for their beers, spraying them with water when they wouldn't give up their glasses. One time, Marcus actually grabbed one of the kegs, put it in a stolen raft, and tied that raft to his. As he power-paddled away from the dock, I couldn't stop laughing. On Lake Lagunita, I could finally relax.

My mom came down to do her business at the Athletic Department. I had arranged to meet her at two o'clock but figured I could get my burger and beer, paddle a lap around the lake, and still be on time back at my dorm. When I arrived, I introduced her to Marcus. She sized him up, and he politely left us to talk.

My mom made no comment about him but explained what she had been doing: "Do you remember how angry I was when your financial aid package came, and only the tuition scholarship was on it? Well, I took care of everything today."

"What do you mean, Mom? Coach told me he used the money for an incoming recruit."

"Right. But he promised us you would get the full ride for your last three years if you came to Stanford. He can't go back on that. It's not right. It's not fair. A deal's a deal."

I started getting scared. Did my mom confront my coach, a coach who thought I was awesome but a coach who told her no more brownies? I didn't want anyone to know how badly I needed the money. I figured I'd figure it out somehow. Mom, too familiar with my procrastination, had taken the matter into her own hands.

"The athletic director, Andy Geiger, is a good man," she continued. "I met him at parent orientation. He is going to guarantee your full ride for the rest of your career." She sat down on my tiny bed, a satisfied expression on her face. Then she sniffed. "Have you been drinking beer?"

I nodded, and proceeded to tell her about the Big Way Yacht Club, my new Greek friends, the sand volleyball court outside the Phi Delt fraternity, and everything exciting and fun—all in one breath.

She slowly nodded and said, "You're taking windsurfing? What's that?"

As I explained it to her, I slowed down. I stopped. I thought. I realized that while I had been playing at the lake, my mom had been fighting for me, for money, and for broken promises. I shook my head for a minute and came back down to earth.

After I showered, we went out for a quick bite. Then she drove home, over the Bay Bridge—she hated bridges—and in rush hour traffic, back to Sacramento.

I can't remember if I even thanked her. I do remember looking at her in her little suit, with matching shoes and bag, thinking she looked like she was about to go to church. Now I realize how much effort it must been for her to drop off my dad at the Air Force base, drive three hours to Stanford, argue for an hour about promises being broken, succeed in securing my financial freedom, then see me slightly high and giddy, say nothing about meeting my boyfriend, and hear that I was taking windsurfing—a class that had nothing to do with her world.

Old Town Job

Stanford's Career Planning and Placement Center (CPPC) had a board where employers posted summer jobs on three-by-five index cards. I took a job-readiness test, and the clerk told me my seventy-five word-per-minute typing skills would assure me employment.

I pulled a card that described a job in downtown Sacramento with a Stanford alum who owned a tent company. I sent Mr. Coleman a letter and was immediately hired.

After finals, my dad packed up my gear, and we headed home. Thus began one of the most difficult summers of my life.

To get to my job on time, I walked a mile to the bus stop and rode the bus down Fair Oaks Boulevard all the way to Old Town. It took seventy minutes. Then I walked back toward midtown to our office near Highway 50. My work functions included typing, filing, and reassembling rented tents that had been returned in disarray. I sewed up ripped seams, washed off the white canvas, and stuffed them back in their packaging on Monday mornings. They were ready to be rented for the next weekend.

During the week, I sat for eight hours a day in a windowless office without air conditioning. Sometimes I took a walk at lunch, but most of the time it was too hot by noon. In 1980, we had over thirty days of one-hundred-degree-plus heat, and I started drinking Dr. Pepper again. That "carbonated prune juice" had been my first experience with soda pop, and the caffeine in a lunchtime Dr. Pepper kept me going through the afternoon.

The hot walk back to Old Town usually left me covered in sweat. When the bus was late, I stood with a group of people trying to share a sliver of shade under a sycamore tree. Sitting on that bus for another hour—hopefully with a window seat, hopefully without anybody stinky next to me—is my main memory of that summer.

I started to gain weight, even though I did my summer workouts every day. My mom wouldn't leave me alone when I returned home. I didn't realize how lonely she was.

I just wanted some peace and quiet when I was done with my 7:00 p.m. workout and had to wake up early the next day to repeat the commute and job. Mom and Dad wanted me to watch TV with them, but I preferred to read novels. At the beginning of the summer, I read on the couch, next to my mom, while some game show played. But after the Fourth of July, I just headed to my room.

My volleyball teammates gathered for a beach tournament at Will Rogers State Beach in LA, but I didn't have the money to go. I imagined how different their summers were from mine. For example, arriving for an early morning run on the beach, before friends from high school got there. They'd set up mini-tournaments and play volleyball all day, stopping to reapply sunscreen and have a bite of lunch at the Beach Shack. I started feeling sorry for myself as I ate my peanut-butter-and-jelly sandwich and crunched on my apple-a-day. My high school friends and I couldn't find time to connect, and I missed the constant intellectual stimulation and social action of college.

One day, I met my best friends from 4-H. The twins and I had adopted each other as godbrothers and sister when we first met. I was eleven and they were ten. Their mom had been good to me, inviting me to go on trail rides, hiring me to take care of their house and barns when they went to their Lake Tahoe waterfront home, and including me on ski trips and society lunches. On a scorching day in the middle of that hot summer after my freshman year, I met the twins under the young oak tree at the picnic bench next to the elementary school, where I did my workouts.

My godbrothers revealed they had been sneaking out at night, driving to the bathhouses in San Francisco, and having sex until the early hours of the morning. With men.

When they told me they were gay, I asked how they knew. I thought they liked another set of twins we knew from 4-H. They agreed about the girls, but still said there was no doubt about their sexuality. I promised to keep their secret, hugging them both as we said good-bye. I promised to visit them and their parents that summer, but I never showed up to their house.

Everything about that summer was heavy. My grades arrived, and my non-science grades were my only A's. I needed to do better if I wanted to go to medical school and cure my mother. I worried about the twins, feeling the risks they were taking in driving to the big city at night were not worth it. None of us had any idea of the real risk then.

In August, I again had the good fortune to coach at the UC Davis volleyball camp, where USC's Chuck Erbe served as guest coach. After humiliating me in front of his team by saying, "J.J., you're goofy-footed!" he took it upon himself to improve my mechanics. I learned why his teams were so good. Their technique was consistent, and they had beaten UCLA and won the national championship last fall. He was an exacting coach who scared his team one moment and laughed with them the next. His ordered practices and repetitions weren't exactly a secret formula for success, but they were vastly different from our Stanford free-flowing workouts. In five days, Coach Erbe had made a few technical corrections that vastly improved my hitting.

Once my footwork motor pattern was in a groove, and I could aim anywhere on the court, I wondered if I should have paid to play there. He would have made me an incredible player, perhaps Olympic level. But I reminded myself that I didn't have the money to pay for a school like USC. I was surprised at his generosity and felt it was an example

of the volleyball communities' loyalty: we were all in it together. We wanted to take advantage of the boost that Title
IX had given women's sports and grow our game's popu-
larity.

Milk Farm Cow

After I had worked for the entire summer of 1980, Mom
and I were ready to drive back to the Bay Area for my sophomore year. I sat and ruminated as we drove by the playground and fields of Cameron Ranch Elementary, my free
high-performance gym. As my mom turned left toward the
freeway onramp, I looked out the window to see McClellan
Air Force Base, where my dad worked. Another ten miles
over the Yolo Causeway, I spotted the gym at UC Davis,
where I'd worked out the last two weeks at camp. These
thoughts gave way to anticipation about the courses I
needed to take. This fall was going to make or break my ability to get into medical school and cure my mother. I sighed
at the workload.

At my sigh, my mother said, "That's it." We were approaching the Pitt School Road exit, and she pulled over just
beneath the huge old Milk Farm cow sign near Dixon. We
usually stopped at Red Farm Road for a milkshake, but I
thought that maybe she wanted a vanilla malt from the Milk
Farm. Instead, she started crying.

"Mom, what's the matter? Are you in pain? Do we need
to call Dad?" I started panicking a little, as she had been
healthy all summer. Was this a quick onset flare up?

"No, Jenyth, it's you. I know we don't have a lot of
money. I'm sorry I couldn't buy you a plane ticket to fly to
LA so you could visit your teammates and play in the beach

tournament, but I will not tolerate your pouting any longer. It's time for you to grow up."

"Pouting? I wasn't pouting, Mom. I was just thinking about the courses I need to take."

"That's all you do: think about yourself. All summer long you've been sullen. You never visited the twins and their parents, after all they did for you. You barely left the house. And when you did borrow the car, you were gone for hours, without a thought that maybe somebody else needed it. And you never paid for gas. Do you know how much it costs to drive you to school today? Two tanks of gas. If you can't appreciate the home you have, don't bother coming back. Get a job and stay on campus next year. I don't care. I just can't stand being judged." She started the car and pulled back onto the freeway, tears streaming down her face. She grabbed the Kleenex box and blew her nose as she balanced the steering wheel between her knees, something she told me never to do. I had never seen her so angry.

I was in shock. Her attack had come from left field. I had conscientiously avoided complaining about my boring, repetitive job; the strangers who smelled and squeezed too close to me on the bus; the number of days when I was far away from the air conditioning vent in both the factory and the bus. But in her eyes, my silence must have felt like judgment, like disrespect. I had taken to heart her rule not to say anything if I couldn't say something nice. My silence must have seemed like a summer of negative grades. It was true: I had lost my happy-go-lucky ways as the responsibility of silence weighed me down.

I couldn't tell her any of that in the car. I couldn't tell her how cold I was in the winter when I scooped ice cream in the food service freezer for two hours, five days a week, so

I wouldn't have to ask her for spending money. So many of my concerns over the summer couldn't be shared with her: my head ached and my back hurt all the time; my ankle had lost some flexibility, so my jump wasn't as high. However, I should have done a better job of hiding my jealousy of teammates who played volleyball on the beach all day.

The world of Ray-Bans, Topsiders, windsurfing, and private beach clubs was inconceivable to my mom. The more I thought about what I didn't have, instead of thinking what I did have that summer, the quieter I became. I didn't want a different family; I wanted a different life for my family— one where my mom could play on a country club tennis team while my dad played for the golf club championship. Two great athletes, but lack of money kept them out of the games. Yet, money couldn't cure my mom: her illness was still undiagnosed and unpredictable. We knew she had eczema, rheumatoid arthritis, and lupus, but the lupus didn't behave as expected, and the doctors were looking for more. I should have vowed to be cheerful and appreciative of them that summer instead of feeling sorry for myself.

The huge difference between my parents' quiet lifestyles—Dad's dry sense of humor and Mom's day-to-day struggles—and the intellectual stimulation of Stanford was something I hadn't considered, though it should have been obvious, and I should have been more sensitive.

In the car, I felt unappreciated, misunderstood, and resentful. I loved Mom more than anything in the world, but I also hated her goodness. I could never be as brave as she was. I felt pity for her pain, and joy that I wouldn't have to watch her suffer every day. That I could leave her at all created more guilt. My mom and I had never fought like we did below the Milk Farm cow sign.

I had never considered how much she needed me, how my loving presence and cheerful attitude helped her cope every day. I didn't understand how much a mother could miss a beloved daughter and didn't comprehend the tediousness of her days. I was glad I'd kept the pact with my brother about earning our own spending money so Mom had extra money for alternative therapies not covered by health insurance. She was getting some relief from her chronic inflammation. As hard as it was to leave her to cope with her illness, she had hurt my feelings, and this made it easier, for some strange reason.

As tears continued to run down her face, I said, "I'm sorry, Mom." I meant I was sorry for her pain, sorry for my silence, but not sorry for escaping.

Only later, after she had died too young, did I understand the pain of loneliness. Every day I drove past that Milk Farm cow sign on my way to work at Vacaville High School, and for two years, I stopped to cry underneath that stupid cow jumping over the moon. My crying included much more than simply missing her. Mom was my strong and steadfast symbol of goodness and moral clarity. She had the ability to be fierce yet vulnerable, to nurture and to correct her children. Mom's example would be tough to follow, and without her presence in my life, I knew it would be nearly impossible to emulate her.

CHAPTER 7
Sophomore Slump

As I unpacked my trunk in the preseason dorm, I thought about my "self-absorbed silences" and saw them from Mom's perspective. We had such an open relationship before I went away to college, but she didn't know how my premedical and Olympic dreams were fading. Now, I couldn't share those fears with her. I was on my own and feared the dreaded "sophomore slump," a term in the athletics world for second-year athletes who don't live up to their first-year potential.

With ten extra pounds to carry around and a new assistant coach to impress, I was well aware that my volleyball career was at a crossroads. Would I be allowed to try setting again? How good were the incoming players? With a very heavy premed load, could I earn better grades that would help me get into med school? I'd heard stories of football players who were relegated to the bench when new coaches arrived. I was not going to ride the pine.

All summer, many of my junior and senior teammates had been rubbing elbows with our coaches, who were highly ranked players on the pro beach volleyball tour. We all knew head coach Fred was bringing Don Shaw from the Association of Volleyball Professionals (AVP) tour as our new assistant coach.

We sat in Jan's room. Now a junior, she was our setter and the de facto leader of the team. She had Fred's ear.

"Okay, girls, I saw Fred on the beach this summer, and rumor has it that he was dating one of the Pepperdine players. I couldn't get him to admit it. But, it's ammunition," she started.

Kisi howled with laughter. "Who is it?"

Jan replied, "It's a rumor I can't spread. But I can say our new assistant is in love with a beach player from Hawaii. And we're going to play them over there."

We all laughed, rolling on the floor and giggling.

We talked a little longer about the new coach, trying to guess what he would bring to our first practice that evening. The freshies sat and wondered with us, wide-eyed and a bit shocked by the way we talked. Only a few were beach club members, and I had the feeling Fred had recruited athletic ability first. The composition of the team was definitely changing.

I was really curious about our new coach Don (Big Daddy) Shaw. I had some terrific coaches to compare him with. My high school coach, Ted, had taught me to be hungry and intense on the attack. My club coach, Debbie, had preached consistency: tough serving and passing were boring but necessary skills to win a game. Possessed with a rapid-processing mind, I matched up with the demands of volleyball perfectly. As much as I loved basketball, this was the sport for me, as my quick reaction time and instinct often trumped my inconsistent technique. Coach Erbe had said as much when he fixed my footwork and boosted my confidence. Coach Fred had taught me many nuances of hitting, footwork, and advanced defensive technique. A data guy, he knew so much about positioning on the court and where to be before the opponent spiked the ball. He had learned defensive shifts from Stanford baseball coach Mark

Marquess and tried to show similar shifts to us, depending upon our opponent's hitting tendencies. We didn't have as much time to move as someone in the outfield, but he made sure we practiced the tennis hop-split-step so we were still when the ball came over. "Let's Do the Tennis Hop Again" was a song we sang to the tune of Rocky Horror's "Let's Do the Time Warp Again." We took a step to the right but never put our hands on our hips. We chanted a lot of ooh-aahs and laughed at ourselves. I wondered what the new coach would think of our singing.

At our first meeting, Coach Don took one look at my pale, muscular body, and I knew I had failed his assessment. "Aren't you too short to be a middle blocker?" he asked.

Why didn't I say, "But I'm really a setter, Don"? Too chicken.

Don was very different from Fred. He actually had a degree in coaching and was very organized and efficient. Fred delegated blocking and middle hitting to him, and Don's instructions were precise, intelligent, and effective. I tried hard to incorporate these techniques, and he drilled me and killed me with criticism. I tried to change everything about my blocking, but it was hard to change all my habits. Getting up to speed took on new meaning, as I needed to use my quickness and vertical leap to compensate for my lack of height.

It was clear to me that, with the new middle blocking techniques, my size was going to be a real hindrance. I begged to be allowed to do some setting drills, but after the first few practices, I was always in the middle hitting line. We learned transition hitting footwork, which meant after we closed the block, we had to get off the net in three steps. I could do that, but it was very difficult to reach the starting position for my spike approach because of my height. A longer-legged senior could do it, and so could Boom-Boom, but she refused to be a middle hitter.

Just as I had to explode off one foot to close the block on the strong side, I also had to explode off the net to get ready to hit, without knocking over the setter, who was crisscrossing in front of me. I visualized my angle of approach as the 3rd dimension of measuring the arc of the set, and my timing improved. I did knock down our freshman phenom, Krush, a few times, but Jan knew where I was going and avoided me. I realized I had to work twice as hard with these demands, but with Don's efficient steps, my spiking became very effective. Once again, in two weeks, the coaches had improved my game.

While I knew I was improving, the coaches only spoke to criticize me. I had lost a few pounds but was starving for praise. After three weeks of double-day practices, I was bordering on a breakdown, but there was absolutely no option to leave the team and just be a student. I had to have the scholarship money. My already sensitive nature became acutely aware of everything that could go wrong in practice, and my fear of making a mistake led to more mistakes. Nowadays, when a new coach arrives, players often leave teams or follow the coach who recruited them. I didn't have that option, so I forced myself to be positive, to be a good teammate, but inside I felt cheated. I could have been a setter at a number of other colleges. Once again, I felt stuck at Stanford.

I did find joy in playing defense. Don introduced the "pancake" in a defensive drill, which meant I had to put my hand on the floor before the ball hit. The ball would hit on top of my hand and pop up, keeping the play alive. A referee had a hard time telling if we actually succeeded, so we acted as if we had picked up the ball even when it bounced on the ground. I had learned to dive a bit as a freshman, but Jan's example of never hitting the floor unless absolutely necessary also made sense, especially for me, as I sweat like a draft horse. My jersey would be soaked by the second game and would leave sweat streaks on the floor, which was dangerous for my teammates. Also, it took too long to get back into a defensive ready position from being laid-out on the floor, but that's what Don wanted. He wanted to extend our range and create a defense we called "beat the ball to the floor." My high school coach had told us to play "defense from the floor up." My club team had perfected how to hit the floor, pop up the ball, then roll over our shoulders through the momentum and end up on our feet. Now we were rolling, diving, and pancaking for every ball. Soon we were covering every inch of the court. As much as I loved crushing the ball as a spiker, there was another kind of satisfaction in stealing a kill from an opponent. Instead of playing the ball, I took the space where the ball would land, and popped it back up, often shocking the hitter who was already starting to celebrate.

This did a number on my back. And I started getting debilitating headaches for the first time since my horrible concussion as a sixteen-year-old. This exhausting routine as a hitter and blocker in the front row and sprawling all over the backrow on defense left me battered, bruised, and dizzy. I didn't hit my head on the floor like my daughter Audrey did her senior year—necessitating an MRI and neck brace, now that we know about concussions. But my brain was shaken whenever I sprawled hard on the floor, and my ability to concentrate became affected. During preseason, I slept whenever I could, and when school started, things began to unravel, first on the court.

Every mistake I made resulted in coach eye rolls and teammate impatience. We had to start the drill over. This didn't happen that often in a single practice, but I felt my mistakes were magnified by the coaches' reactions. Others made similar mistakes but weren't called out. The old school philosophy of breaking down the ego of the player in order to build her back up is a model that rarely works and certainly didn't work for me. I'm not saying coaches should coddle their players, but they should treat them humanely. Hurt their pride, and players will perform more poorly. Criticism is so easy; catching a player doing something right and reinforcing that pattern takes much more time and effort. And when coaches recognize players' efforts, they build up the entire team instead of breaking it down. Everybody wins.

I'll never know if my coaches' criticism was an attempt to break my ego or a flex of their masculinity. USC's players never talked back to their coach. But us? We were Stanford Women: strong, outspoken, stubborn. I wonder if our boldly stated opinions antagonized Fred and Don. I really tried to listen, to be coachable, but in the end, all I can say is that too many women who play competitive sports are so broken down by their coaches that they never recover from the mental torment. Those harsh words echo in nightmares, invade consciousness upon waking up, and sit on the shoulders of an athlete during an entire practice. After they've been repeated a few times, they're embedded in the brain's right frontal lobe, an irritant that will grow into constant negative self-talk without some kind of intervention. But we didn't know that in 1980.

Sophomore Fall Quarter

The molecule manipulator I used for inorganic chemistry was supposed to reveal three dimensions, but I couldn't see that picture in my brain. Geometry and trigonometry were my favorite classes in high school, but I couldn't get the dimensionality in chemistry any more. What was a two-dimensional drawing on the page stayed flat instead of 3-D in my mind. I loved the *idea* of mirror-image stereoisomers, a non-superimposable set of two molecules that are mirror images of one another. I wanted to fold one on top of the other, but they had different 3-D orientations of their molecules in space and that made no sense to me. I couldn't visualize it, even though I knew what non-superimposable meant.

Strangely, I could trace the trajectory of a set volleyball and time my approach and takeoff as if I were the vertex. But when a volleyball was *served* straight at me, my depth perception failed. Sometimes I thought a ball was going to hit my chin when in fact it hit my foot. I learned to stand slightly to one side to gauge the ball's landing point, putting me off-balance but still able to make the play. I instinctively did this on the court, but hard as I tried in my classes, I couldn't figure out how to accommodate my gaps.

Inorganic chemistry was my early morning class, so half of the time, I just put on my volleyball sweats, mounted my old blue Schwinn ten-speed at the top of the Kairos House driveway, and lifted my feet off the ground to let gravity pull me down to the bump before the sidewalk. As I looked left and right, I hoped I wouldn't have to use my brakes. If no cars were coming, I adjusted my heavy backpack with a shrug of my shoulder and glided down to the intersection of Mayfield Drive and Campus Drive. Again, if I saw no cars on the left or the right, I continued down past the frat houses. I had to peddle past the music building, but I could drift past the post office and The Claw fountain and bookstore. As I turned left at the southeast corner of the Quad, behind the Memorial Church, I raised my hands off the handlebars in a salute to ugly architecture. Then I gripped the bars and peddled past the Geology Corner and down the lane to the yellow sandstone old chemistry building, where a Nobel Prize laureate faced the blackboard, hiding his calculations and muffling his lecture until the old white goat turned on his Bunsen burner.

My friend Arny sat next to me. A tall, blonde, blue-eyed full Swede, he was a main distraction in first-year chemistry, but as sophomores, we were close friends. I had taught him to play grass volleyball, and he held my hand in inorganic chemistry. Even Arny, a future statistics professor at the University of Kentucky, couldn't figure out how to help me remember formulas, and office hours were held during volleyball practice. Our professor talked into the blackboard, so nobody knew what was going on or could see his calculations until after class. As one week went by, then another, then another, and weeks turned into months, I couldn't score higher than a B- or C+ on any test. I could see my premedical dreams fading.

The intensity of the fall was as stifling as the late heat wave. My schedule—with an 8:00 a.m. inorganic chemistry class, followed by a 9 to 10:30 a.m. human biology (HumBio) core and an 11:00 a.m. abnormal psychology class—required incredible focus. About half of the premeds from my dorm Rinconada were in HumBio; the other half were straight biology majors, which was supposed to be more difficult. Yes, I'd chosen what was for me the easier, yet more interesting route, which was to focus on the intersection of biology on psychology. But this was not soft science, and the sheer amount of memorization and reading material was overwhelming. It didn't help that my headaches and need for at least eight hours of sleep were affecting what I could absorb.

Unfortunately, I would fall asleep even if I had studying to do. One evening, the night custodian in the library woke me up and sent me home at 2:00 a.m. After that, I studied in bed from 9 to 11 p.m., unless my roommate's noisy boyfriend was hanging around.

I loved living in Kairos House, a co-op housing unit with twenty-six rooms and about forty students. A Rinconada dorm friend and I put our lottery numbers together at the end of our first year, and she drew a great number. I slept in the main room, and she turned the walk-in closet into a lofted sleep arrangement. Both of us were happy. Food was cheap, as we could cook our own meals, and five weeknight dinners were provided. The open kitchen was great for traveling athletes. We had just a few premeds and a wide variety of people who loved our open kitchen and cheap fees.

Everybody seemed to have a job of some kind. My part-time job as Kairos food manager helped me start saving some money, but I still obsessed over being financially independent. Sometimes I wished I didn't have to play volleyball and dreamed of leaving the team and Don's criticism. I could just be a student. But this was not an option. And my mom's kidneys were malfunctioning. In and out of the hospital during September, she underplayed the seriousness, my dad refused to acknowledge it, and only my brother told me the truth.

I was so worried about my mom that the rest of my life started spinning out of control. I couldn't concentrate, sleep, or remember what my friends had just told me. Something was different about my body: sometimes my heart would race, and I'd start twitching all over; other times, I could sleep for hours and hours. My volleyball timing was off, and I started making mistakes I'd never made before: missed serves, net violations, forgotten shifts on defense, mental and physical errors. I kept my head down. I didn't want to call my mom with my woes; I didn't think she wanted to talk to me at all. We suffered separately.

When I returned to Kairos House in the evening, I tried to forget about the team as I joined others in the kitchen for our evening meal. I tried to concentrate on my studies, thinking I could figure everything out by myself. I was too proud to ask a classmate for help and too busy to attend office hours. I didn't believe I had any limitations I couldn't conquer, although I would soon learn what it was like to be at my limit, emotionally and physically. It didn't help that I had become Don's favorite target for yelling and disrespect. I knew enough about team dynamics to accept that our friction was affecting everyone, but I didn't know what to do about it. Trouble was brewing on the team, and I was in the middle of it.

I wish I would have turned to some of my volleyball teammates during this time. I had reframed my summer factory job as an internship, nobody knew about my mom's illness, and I was too reticent to ask the upper-class girls, many of whom were sitting on the bench behind me, to help me with my homework. I was completely, in my mind, alone.

Tina had returned from a summer of playing volleyball

in Italy, and she immediately displayed her accomplishments as a bully. After the first practice, she started complaining about my sets, and after that practice I never set her (or anybody else) again. After the second practice, Don wanted Krush to set her. When Tina didn't like Krush's set, she spiked the ball *in her face*, instead of over the net. We stopped in shock. Nobody stood up to her, not even our head coach, who was intimidated by her.

Lineups changed for no logical reason, and practices became unbearable. I was benched by the end of the first weekend road trip. These early road trips were the highlight of the year, for our academic studies hadn't yet begun. We could load into the van randomly, make up songs and sing them. Paula was the song leader, but Tina forced us underclassmen to the back of the van and yelled at us to shut up. She controlled the radio.

I was worried about Krush, whose talent and unselfishness made her an ideal teammate. She and Boom-Boom and I were the most competitive players on the team. Krush worked just as hard as I did in practice, and the upperclassmen no longer teased me about my work ethic. I had to make sure Krush knew I had her back, so I started high-fiving her every time she made a play. She had her own struggle, for the coaches wanted her to change the tempo of her sets. I could see her frustration, but as a freshie, she wisely didn't talk back. I loved her fast outside sets, but the coaches asked her to launch them higher and higher, the way Tina liked them.

In Santa Barbara, we stayed in a motel with exterior corridors: coaches on the first floor and players on the second floor. Birds of paradise divided the parking lot from the hallway, and thin doors with keylocks squeaked when they opened and closed. Night one, I heard the coaches sneak out about eleven o'clock, thirty minutes after they had checked us in. Our trainer Patty's light was on; she was probably finishing the novel she had told us about earlier. I tried to sleep, but Boom-Boom kept talking. She was always my roommate now and needed only about four hours of sleep a night. I needed eight. She was doing well in her premed studies and was studying when I fell asleep. I woke to hear the coaches' doors squeak at about 2 a.m., but she was asleep by then.

Night two was different. Head coach Fred left to meet the Santa Barbara coach, but Don stayed inside. Again, Boom-Boom was talking and talking and talking. I got up to stand and lean against the corridor railing for some fresh air and silence, but squealing and laughter emanated from below. Then Tina crashed naked through the succulents. I saw Don grab her arm, and laughing, they went back under the exterior hallway I was standing on. The door squeaked, and I was completely awake.

I asked Boom-Boom if she saw what I saw. She shook her head and I told her Tina just went into Don's room, naked. She wasn't surprised, and shook her head at my lack of comprehension. I mentioned the girl he loved in Hawaii. This made no sense. I tried to talk myself into understanding. "I think Tina is hitting on *him*. And he likes it," I replied.

Boom-Boom declared she knew this happened at other schools, but didn't believe it would happen at Stanford. At six-feet tall, nobody messed with her. She didn't care about team dynamics; she cared about playing time.

Decades later, I learned that Kisi had stolen Tina's bathing suit in the jacuzzi, and Don had merely thrown her a towel before he returned to his room alone. Then Kisi and Tina returned to their room. But my judgment was made, and this assumption aggravated my feelings of despair during the next few months.

Midterm Anxieties

On the long drive home, after beating UCSB but getting walloped by San Diego State, my mission to protect Krush started to take on a different meaning. The more I stood by her, the less chance I had to return to my coveted setter position. My dream of being an Olympian could only happen as a setter; I was too short to play middle blocker. But I had played both in high school, and my leaping ability and hitting percentage had earned me playing time as a middle blocker on this team.

At tournaments and matches, other coaches and former teammates starting asking me what was going on: Why wasn't I setting?

Constrained by a strange sense of loyalty to a team whose coaches had shoved me aside, I didn't say much. But I stewed in bitterness. No one else was criticized so mercilessly. Yells of "Oh my god, J.J." and "Jesus, J.J." and "Do it again, J.J., and do it right this time" circled through my mind instead of going in one ear and out the other, like my chemistry formulas. Any mistake I made in practice or a game became an opportunity for the coaches to replace me, yet I couldn't complain to my parents. I could only listen to my anxiety. Instead of studying, I worried about my mom, my playing time, my low inorganic chemistry and human biology grades.

By the middle of October, we were looking forward to a long road trip to UOP and Fresno State, one where my parents as well as my high school and club coaches would get to see me play. My mom's flares had gone into remission, and she would be at the UOP match. I was so excited to see her and show her I had attended to her criticism. I wanted a mom hug.

We had one more home match before the trip, with a start time an hour earlier than usual. We would play in the old Roble Gym instead of Maples Pavilion. I had a game plan: finish class, ride my bike to the training room, get taped, then ride across campus to gym.

In the ankle taping line, the football players kept cutting in front of me until it was finally my turn. But I was out in two minutes. Racing to my bike, I already had on my home white uniform top and sweatpants. If I hustled, I could be at Roble Gym on time. Red bag draped around my neck messenger style, I pumped and peddled. As I passed Memorial Auditorium, someone yelled to me, "Go J.J., go!"

I turned my head briefly, but it was long enough for me not to see a car backing out of a parking space.

The car hit my bike, and I went flying. Arms out, I instinctively prepared to catch myself—just like when I was diving for a ball on the court, just like when I had flown over the brick wall my horse refused to jump. I kept my head up as the asphalt and gravel ground up my hands, my sweatpants ripped, and I rolled through the momentum to crunch against the back car wheel just as the driver braked.

The guy in the car jumped out and yelled, "I didn't see you. I'm so sorry."

I said, "Can you drop me off at Roble? I'm going to be late." I threw my bent bike in the bushes and jumped into the stranger's car, brushing gravel out of my hair.

"Man, are you in a hurry!" the young professor-type said.

"Yes, I am on a short leash. If I do anything to screw up, the coaches are going to bench me again."

He nodded as his tires squealed and we rounded Memorial Church and cut through a little-known alley to the back of Roble.

With three minutes to spare, I ran into the gym.

I joined in the warmups, until Patty called me over. "J.J., are you bleeding?"

So much adrenaline was pumping through my body that I didn't feel my palms, which were bruising and bleeding. Fortunately, no blood got on my white jersey, but some was speckling my shoes. Patty wiped me off, taped my palms, and sent me back to warmups, making sure the coaches didn't notice anything amiss.

Things were fine until the middle of the second set, when the gym lights started looking blurry. I cross-stepped to the right to block the hitter, landed, then blacked out in a slow sink to the floor. Patty came running out on the court and helped me back to the bench. The coaches finally noticed that I was white and shaking.

"Oh my god, J.J., what's wrong now?" said Don.

I knew I was in for it, so I didn't bother telling him what happened. I really believed he didn't care. He sent me to the bench. I told Fred I'd been hit by a car, and he returned to coaching the match, without another question. I'll never forget waiting for either coach to say something encouraging after the match, but only Patty paid me any attention. Someone gave me a ride home.

The coaches called me in the morning and asked me to meet them in their office before we left on the road trip.

Don dropped the bomb: "J.J., this is harder on us than it is on you, but we've made a decision. We think you need to get your act together. You're not coming on the trip."

There I sat, with my bag packed, wearing my good luck plaid shirt, Levi's, and the Topsider yachting shoes I had bought with my summer earnings just a few days before. "I'm not going?"

"Yes. What exactly happened yesterday?" asked Fred.

"I got hit by a car on my way to the match."

"You what? Why weren't you paying attention? You're always in a hurry. You were going to be late again, weren't you? You're out of control," said Don.

Both of them looked at me accusingly, and I felt they were glad to have an opening, a reason to keep me off the court, even though I had earned a new starting position. I could have told them I'd never been late before. I could have explained that a friend distracted me with positive cheers, or that the professor was in a hurry and didn't look both ways. I could have told them my mom was finally out of the hospital and coming to see me play, but they didn't know anything about her condition in the first place. It was abundantly clear they thought they had finally found a rationale for keeping me off the court.

I knew the humiliation of calling up my former coaches and parents to tell them I wouldn't be making the trip would be a nightmare. As I walked toward the bush where I had stowed my bent bike the afternoon before, the irony rose in my mind. I wondered if a week without rushing from class to volleyball to class again might make me feel like a real Stanford student instead of "one who got in off the athletes' list."

For years, I had wanted coaches to notice me, to recruit me for basketball or volleyball so I could go to college. Now, I was doing everything in my power to avoid being noticed, both in the classroom and the gym. Knowing that my fellow students and professors would dismiss me as a dumb jock if I wore sweats to class, I was constantly changing clothes during the day. I morphed from a sweaty post-practice athlete to a sorority girl in a plaid skirt and loafers in about ninety seconds. It appeared I would soon be one of Stanford's many failed premeds, for no professor would write me a letter of recommendation with my grades. There was a rumor among the premeds that Stanford students' medical school admission rate was so high because only students with straight A's were recommended. I didn't stand a chance. And yet, I wasn't ready to quit.

If I could just remember something, just think straight, just hold onto my soul before it disappeared. Who was I, anyway? I did remember one thing, my last and best resource: the competitive fire that resided somewhere in my amygdala, where fear and anger also lived. I had two choices according to my psychology professor: flight or fight. Lifting up my deceased blue Schwinn ten-speed with ease, I tossed it into the Tressider dining hall dumpster. At least I didn't have to ask for money from my parents to buy a new bike. But I did have to get the nerve to call my mom and tell her about being left behind.

We weren't talking as often as we had last year, and she was very cool most of the time. When I checked in about her health, she was dismissive. This phone call was going to heat her up, that I knew.

What did she say? What did I say? I have no memory of the call, but I do recall the feeling of humiliation on my side and disappointment on hers. I suspect we both wanted to reconnect our mother-daughter bond, but that reconciliation would have to wait.

Voodoo

I had plenty of time on my hands now. Time to sleep. Time to eat, get a headache, then sleep some more. I probably should have checked in at the training room and told them about my bike crash, but my ally Patty was on the road with the team. I was too embarrassed to admit I got hit by a car on the way to a game. Instead, I wandered down the hill to the Stanford Bike Shop to see what they had for sale.

Most of the great bikes had been sold when school started, but an ancient black Sears three-speed with fenders and a basket caught my eye. No more trail of muddy tears would splatter up my butt on a rainy day, and the black-and-white triangle seat with springs was a throwback from the 1950s. Yet, the bike was in perfect running condition, with a polished chrome rack, sparkling spokes, and effortless gears. Best of all, it was in alignment, unlike my old ten-speed. But riding with no hands had to stop from this point on. The bike doc adjusted the seat and handlebars to the perfect height, and I was on my way to class for twenty dollars.

A question occurred to me as I rode: Did I run my life like a freight train without brakes so I could avoid thinking about my mom and how she felt…or how helpless I felt? I'd had a packed schedule since I was ten, between work, 4-H, my horse, and sports. I never had any homework, because I did it in class instead of listening to the teacher. I couldn't do that in college, and I had no study skills to speak of. The study skills class I was required to take first year was really a "how to organize your college life" class for athletes. No one taught me how to take notes, organize them, study them, review in groups, collaborate with classmates, or anything like that. My freshie premed dorm was so competitive and anxiety ridden that I couldn't concentrate there, even in a single room.

I'd found a place on the top floor of UGLY, the undergraduate library, where I could blow off steam by leaning over the rails and dropping paper wads on unsuspecting students in the book checkout line. This year, I staked out a cubicle by the third-floor occult section, thinking the vibes and luck might wear off on my chemistry studies. Nobody ever studied there, so every time I fell asleep while looking at the diagrams of molecular reactions, nobody disturbed me, except the occasional bat that lived in the top rafters. I kept Reginald Scot's 1587 book *The Discoverie of Witchcraft* nearby, thinking a magic spell might help my memory if I got desperate. Maybe the voodoo doll the rival high school girls poked pins into had really worked. Fortunately, I had stolen the doll during our last rival game and it was back in my Kairos House room, where my bed called me back to take another nap. A month later, before my second midterm, I opened the book to read it for fun, only to learn Scot's text didn't explain the discovery of magic but instead debunked witchcraft. No help there.

Many of the structured liberal education (SLE) students ended up in Kairos House, and these sophomores were brilliant. I had wanted to be in honors/SLE, but the Athletic Department forbade me to enroll in the rigorous program. I envied the living arrangements over in Gavilan, with SLE students living and taking seminars together. I envied their 3:00 a.m. talks while sitting on the floor of the dorm hallway. Unlike our freshie dorm, those in Gavilan discussed life, ideas, and the pursuit of something greater than themselves—pretty far away from the premed arguments over the rotations of chemical models in my dorm.

I was excited when they invited me to their ORGY, an Organized Reunion of Gavilan Youth, in their old dorm's dining hall. I loved dancing, and meeting more creative bright lights in one place would not have happened had I been on the volleyball road trip.

ORGY

On the afternoon of the Gavilan party, I had time to trim and polish my nails and shave the calluses between my toes and my rapidly forming bunions. All the jumping was spreading my feet, and I knew I had to take care of them. A little fire-engine red polish, my mom's favorite shade, and I was ready to go. The October Palo Alto sun had warmed up the day, and it was going to be a gorgeous summer-like night.

The party started at 8:00 p.m., but the Gavilan-Kairos group hung out in the pool table room of Kairos first. Gavilan never started their parties on time, I learned, and we decided to have a pre-party. We each had a beer, and then began to play a pool pocket game called Splash on Leland Stanford's second-best pool table. The table was in the former chapel room of Kairos, which had a dais for an altar. Some of us sat on the dais, waiting our turns, while the rest of us took shots at knocking balls into pockets with the white cue ball, without spilling any beer from our red Solo cups. Good Splash = ball in pocket. Bad Splash = spilling a drop of beer. It was a quick action game, with everyone jumping up for a turn. The old slate under the felt weighed over two tons, we had been told, so a rough game wasn't going to damage it. Lots of things happened on top of that pool table, but this night it was Splash action so loud other Kairosians came down to play.

We left them and walked to Gavilan. From a distance, we could see a disco light turning, rapid strobe lights flashing toward the ceiling of the old dining hall, and a bunch of people dancing. With the energy of high-level athletes who had missed a workout, some new friends and I ran all the way down the hill, into the dining hall, and onto the dance floor. The Cars' "My Best Friend's Girl" was just finishing, and the volleyball anthem "We Got the Beat," by the Gogos began. Someone had mixed a tape really well, for the beats never stopped and the tempo just increased.

"Vacation" was a favorite volleyball warmup song, and instead of missing the team, I started pogoing across the floor and slammed into a few people, who laughed and bumped me back. I was so happy to be moving and bouncing without any soreness in my ankles and knees. Four days without practice, and I was fired up. My head didn't hurt, my back was fine and after another beer, my ankle felt strong. Volleyball was far from my mind as I threw my head back and sang, knowing my voice would be drowned out by the noise outside my brain.

My week of freedom was soon forgotten, and my headaches returned, along with the realization that I didn't have time for the numerous opportunities that Stanford offered its non-athlete students. And social opportunities during volleyball season? It seemed I had to say no more and more to everything: no to planning the fall Kairos party; no to planning the fall Theta formal; no to anything but volleyball, class, and sleeping.

My housemates at Kairos were turning into close friends and partners in silliness. We were all creatives, in addition

to whatever we were majoring in, and a few of the girls were
in sororities. Many of my Kappa Alpha Theta sisters were
premeds, and they offered to share the study files with me.
I just didn't have time to meet my big sister to study.

Around this time, my mother had another episode and
had to be hospitalized for a serious case of pericarditis. I
heard about this from my dad, who wasn't one to speak
much. I couldn't go home to see her. The only treatment
they knew was the massive doses of prednisone she hated.
The steroids did stop the inflammation of the pericardium
and allowed her to breathe without too much pain. At the
same time she was recovering, I earned a D on the inorganic
chemistry midterm. I had to face reality: I might not be able
to save her life. I probably wouldn't get into medical school.
The premeds who were succeeding were only students, not
student-athletes (except for Boom-Boom), and not working
at jobs. They all were studying all the time.

Shank and Yank

After the volleyball team returned from the Central Valley, I had another shot at playing. My teammates told me
how happy they were that I was back in the starting lineup.
But the rules for my play had changed. Most of the time,
after blocking the three rotations across the front row, I was
allowed to serve and pass in the back row.

I had an effective serve, and I even obeyed the coaches'
target signal. I loved playing defense, doing the shifts I had
learned my first year, practicing the tennis hop to be
stopped when the ball was hit, then beating the ball to the
floor with a roll or pancake sprawl. I touched an amazing
number of balls. At our home games, a cameraman started

sitting near the baseline, putting his camera up when I was in the back row. The magazine he worked for had expanded from men's professional beach volleyball to include women's indoor volleyball, a move that pleased us. I hoped he would catch me digging to save a hard-driven spike. But if I didn't pass a serve perfectly, or shanked it off to the side—which usually happens when you're nervous and your forearms are as rigid as wooden beams—I was subbed out.

Paula came up with a term for my new torture: *shank and yank*. As soon as I missed a pass (shank), a substitute ran up to the sideline and pointed at me (yank). The more anxious I became, the worse I passed. My high school club coach, Debbie, would have been so disappointed, for passing serves was the highest priority for her. But I choked about twenty-five percent of the time. Shank and Yank.

Life on the bench with Paula became a subculture of the team. While Fred wanted to keep me in, Don would take me out. To avoid high-fiving him, I ran all the way to the end of the bench. Paula hadn't been given a real shot at the starting setter position, because Krush was a club All American, and Jan was Jan. So, we began making up songs. In the winter of my first year, Paula and I had rewritten the lyrics to "Get Me to the Church on Time." The revised version, called "Get Me to the Gym on Time," used "Bang, bang, the spittle's gonna fly" as revenge during our 6:00 a.m. winter workouts. Coach Fred would get so worked up that his spit would hang from the side of his mouth, and when he whipped his head around to try to hear us singing, drips would fall off. Many of us had been hit by flying spit.

Coach crush-fantasies—if any had existed before—disappeared during these brutal winter workouts. But rumors of what was happening on other college volleyball teams persisted. Some liaisons were player initiated, like the light flirting by a few seniors on our team during preseason of my freshie year. Once school started, however, my teammates were laser focused on grades and couldn't be bothered to think about our coaches after practice. Not so on other teams. We heard about one coach leaving his wife to marry his pregnant player. I have often wondered about players who were willing or were forced to have sex with a coach in order to play. Did they feel that was the only path to a starting position? Did such gatekeeping destroy them, or was it worth it to get playing time? How do they feel about it now?

It's hard to sit still on the bench. I had to stay warm, as I'd be going back into the front row in a few rotations, and I didn't want the shank and yank to include "miss the hit and you will sit." I started swearing around this time, creating myriad ways to use "fuck" in every grammatical context. Boom usually said, "Fuck me!" when she missed a hit, but I usually used the f-bomb as a gerund adjective: "get me the fucking ball," "make a fucking play," "get out of my fucking way." All of these were said under my breath, but I felt so much better for saying them. My freshie English teacher called them "oral fricatives," words that required an exhalation, and they did ease my frustration. I was working as hard as I could in everything, and nothing was really working. *Fuck it.*

Thus began our epic song, "Bench City." It began with this line: "People in the stands think we're shitty just cause we're (da da' da) Bench City." We had a chorus chant with "do do do'… do do do dodu'ty-too" in between each verse. Anyone could drop a line, and all of us would chant the chorus.

We added arm movements and leg crosses and caused quite a commotion as we laughed our heads off. The players closer to the coaches couldn't really chant or sing, but their feet did the tapping. Players on the court could hear us, and they'd tap their legs as they waited for the next play to begin, all of us keeping the beat.

Grits, a freshie with great hops, sat on one side of me, Paula on the other. They kept me pumped up, and made up another song to remind me how to block. To the tune of Paul McCartney's "Hands Across the Water," we sang "Hands Across the Net" to remember our new blocking technique. At times, we weren't paying attention to the game developments, but we were never bored. Volleyball was bearable, even fun, next to Grits and Paula on the bench. And I began to be put in the game for a three-rotation trip across the front row, blocking and hitting to the beat in my head.

CHAPTER 8
Coach's Mind

In 1980, points could only be scored by the serving team. We decided that if our opponent won the rally and got to serve, they would never be allowed to win a second rally in a row. This meant we would "side out" and get the ball back. One of Fred's favorite statistics compared the side outs versus points scored, and all of us realized we were not the biggest or the quickest team, but we could be the smartest and keep the ball in play. So, "rally ball" became our rallying cry. We kept the rally going until the other team made a mistake, which they often did out of frustration with our excellent defensive skills, or until one of our hitters terminated the play. In 1980, coaches were limited in the number of substitutions they could make, and that meant the longer the game went, the better chance I had to stay in the back row and dig.

It was on the bench with Grits and Paula that I realized I had a coach's mind. I recognized the different mindsets of players in the front and back rows. Stability and consistency as well as tenacity were needed to pass difficult serves. If you made a poor pass, you knew the server was going to serve you again, so the mental toughness required was important. All eyes were on the passer, for the serve could be the slowest ball to come over the net, or it could have tricky spin or incredible velocity. Once the ball was in play, vicious spikes and tantalizing tips had to be picked up by a defender with a different mindset: you must be ready for anything and must react quickly to the trick shots. While passing serves required a Zen-like concentration, digging spikes required a kamikaze's disregard for her body in order to pick up the shot. Within a point, then, the back row player is shifting positions physically and mentally in order to make the play.

When I rotated to the front row, another mindset must begin. While I couldn't understand the three dimensions of a chemical model, I could process the arc of the opponent's set; the directional approach of the spiker; the spiker's take-off point and potential landing; and her arm swing, contact point, and wrist snap. All this seeing and thinking occurred between 1.0- and 2.0-seconds' time. Even though I couldn't process everything, I knew the tendencies of my opponents even when I didn't understand the equilibrium of carbonic acid and carbon dioxide. Now, combustion was a different matter.

One of my freshie teammates sank under the pressure of Stanford academics and athletics. She didn't return for winter quarter and told me in a letter she was staying in SoCal for the winter. We had heard rumors of her crumbling during finals, and a non-volleyball player friend joked that Stanford allowed students to drop a class on the day of the final in order to keep the number of suicides down. Another student in the Wilbur complex was rumored to have committed suicide at the same time my teammate went downhill.

By the middle of sophomore year, I began to understand the despair of a suicidal person. October's fog and darkness descended and not even the occult section cheered me up. The rafter bats stopped flying. Perhaps I spent too much time looking for answers to my mother's ailments, answers that didn't exist. I switched from spells books to early alchemy papers by Isaac Newton. I began to understand herbal medicine. St. John's wort alleviated my mother's night sweats; however, knowing this didn't help my inorganic chemistry grade. I made sure I never missed a class and tried to get at least five hours of sleep, but I couldn't remember much. I did remember Hamlet's lines: "by a sleep to say we end / The heart-ache and the thousand natural shocks / that flesh is heir to," which became a recurring earworm when my alarm went off. I had never had a problem getting out of bed, but for a time around Halloween I didn't want to leave my cocoon. Still, I modeled my mother and put one foot in front of the other.

The second and third HumBio midterms did not go well, my mother wasn't telling the truth about how ill she was, and every volleyball practice and game was an exercise in walking on eggshells. How long before Don yelled at me? How long would I stay in the game before he yanked me out? By mid-October, I started throwing up in the locker room bathroom stall before every match, and had to arrive really early so no one would discover me. This meant I had to go to the training room even earlier to get my bad ankle taped, which cut into my studying time. Not that I could focus on anything but volleyball on a game day.

Waking up in the morning with a game in the evening used to be the happiest feeling I had. All day, I'd look forward to being in the locker room with my teammates, talking smack about our opponents, and battling on the court. I thought less about the number of kills or aces I would make and more about *the play*: could I make an incredible move I'd never made before? Could I hit a new shot, or pick up a hard-driven spike the hitter was sure would hit the floor, but I would keep alive? Perhaps if I'd thought more about consistency, I would have been more consistent, but I thought about making the play that shifted the momentum to our side during crunch time. I wanted to hit that golden spike and relish being the go-to girl again. Instead, I cleaned up the toilet seat where I'd driven the porcelain bus.

Be the Volleyball

Dr. Zimbardo, the extraordinary psychology professor, had invited me to learn more about hypnosis and the power of positive suggestions after my starring role in his hypnosis lecture first year. Following his lecture on cults, I visited the third-floor occult section in the library and learned a chant I did every time I went back to serve a volleyball: "Concentration will begin / keep the rhythm / step-toss-serve."

Over the next few years, I met many people in the psych department who were interested in my athletic performance. Once or twice a month, I'd get a phone call inviting me to participate in a study and earn a crisp twenty-dollar bill on a Friday or Saturday night. During these sessions, though I was always suspicious about what they were really studying, I dutifully filled out the forms and played my role.

During one of these Friday night psychology studies in my sophomore year, the graduate student researcher asked why I was so jittery.

I told him about volleyball and about the tension between me and my assistant coach.

He said, "Why don't you just let it go? He's a jerk. That's not your problem. You can't control that. What you can control is your response to him."

I was thinking about that and wondering how I might

stop barfing pre-match, when the researcher propositioned me. "Hey, want to have sex? You really need to relax. Nobody's here, and we could take our time in the lab."

Really? He had just offered me a way out of my mental stress, then offered me a way into physical stress. Like my body wasn't already wrung out? Jesus. I grabbed my twenty-dollar bill and climbed up the stairs from the psychology basement. I was too tired to ride my bike up the hill, so I walked it through the Quad; past the Claw fountain, which looked really spooky at night; past the music auditorium; and up Mayfield Avenue, where I probably forgot to lock it onto the bike rack at Kairos.

I was working myself into exhaustion, but then things started to click on the court. The coach's mind, along with my own improved instincts, allowed me to predict what others would do in a game time situation. I'd start in my defensive position, then read the action on the other side of the net and breathe, letting my body react to what my eyes saw. This zone was a place where my mind was finally empty, and I could just be. I could be the volleyball. I could be the floor. I could be the net. I could be the referee blowing the whistle to start the play. The ball slowed down, and I picked it up.

I learned to sweat out my stress. I tried to control what I could control and let the other stuff slide off my thin skin. If only I had thicker skin. I wanted to know how to turn off my emotions so they wouldn't take over. I wanted an off-switch for my racing thoughts. I wanted to stop running away from the pain. I wanted a quiet mind.

The Toe

By the time we returned from our last road trip, over

Veteran's Day weekend, we had qualified for our first National Championship Tournament. It would be the last one run by the Association of Intercollegiate Athletics for Women (AIAW) before women joined the National Collegiate Athletic Association (NCAA) and used the basketball play-off bracket.

Around this time, we started using "men's" and "women's" to describe a sport. As a result of Title IX, athletics departments were being combined under one set of administrators instead of colleges funding separate and unequal departments. Unfortunately, this streamlining meant a number of female athletic directors and head coaches were replaced by men, and sometimes the men knew nothing about the sport they took over.

Our team's record was solid, and we'd be going to UC Santa Barbara for the tournament with all the nationally ranked teams. It would be brutal. I had to take my first HumBio final, turn in a psychology paper, then drive down to Santa Barbara for the tournament. When I returned, I'd have to take the second HumBio final, take the inorganic chemistry final, and turn in another paper. I was so excited to play in the tournament that I couldn't sleep and couldn't concentrate that week. Once again, I was in the starting lineup.

The day before we left, I took my test in the morning, attended a rigorous practice in the afternoon, then wrote the psychology paper at night. It was my usual first-draft-is-final-draft effort, but I knew I'd hit all the important points and thrown in a few jokes for the tired professor to enjoy. I was pleased with it, and while I was typing, had actually made some notes for the second paper I'd write. A quarter of my brain was now free. *Maybe Boom-Boom and I can study inorganic together*, I thought as I collapsed into bed.

The smoke drifting under my mis-hung door didn't wake me up. The fire alarm didn't budge me, but the sirens from the fire trucks outside my window jolted me up. In a stupor, I opened the door to smoke, and instead of shutting it and crawling out the window, I yelled at my roommate Jen to get up. "Fire!" I shouted.

I turned and ran into hallway—right into the corner of the stair landing. I screamed and buckled over as the wood corner shattered the second toe on my right foot and its corresponding metatarsal.

The pain was excruciating, but Jen grabbed my arm, and we ran down the stairs and onto the front lawn in our old-lady Lanz nightgowns. The fire trucks were around the side of Kairos, and the fire was quickly extinguished. Someone had burned toast in the kitchen, setting off the fire alarms and causing a small appliance fire which burned the old varnished butcher block table. Everything else was fine.

Except my toe. By the time I went back upstairs, the throbbing was intense. It was 3:00 a.m., and I had to do something about my toe. We were scheduled to leave at 6:00 a.m. for the drive down. I knew from my ankle injury last year that I wouldn't be able to put my shoe on if my toe and foot swelled much more. After Jen went to bed, I looked at the toe under the light. It wasn't my big toe; it was the one next to it. How did that happen?

Fortunately, I had a stash of tape, Band-Aids, pre-wrap, sticky spray, and game socks from the training room. As the toenail had already turned purple, I knew it might come loose. I used Band-Aids to soak up the blood and keep it in place. I put too much antibiotic cream on the bleeding toe, so the Band-Aids wouldn't stick. I had the brilliant idea of placing the Band-Aids on, then wrapping my second toe to my third with tape, and taping over the Band-Aids to keep them in place. I stood up, tried to put weight on it, and felt a sharp pain up my foot. Fuck. I finished the taping the best I could, found a game sock, and put on my game shoes. I never wore them anywhere but on the court, as I wore out shoes quickly with my bad ankle and flat feet. However, that shoe stayed on from 3:30 a.m. Thursday until we won the consolation bracket final in the 11:00 a.m. match on Sunday.

I never told my coaches, never told my trainer Patty, never told my teammates. They probably wondered why I hid behind the wrestling mats during the ten laps of warmups, only to reemerge for the last lap. We beat the teams we should have beaten, and were ninth in the nation, after being unranked at the beginning of the year. We lost only to volleyball royalty: the fourth-place finisher UCLA, and then to fifth-place UC Santa Barbara by a tight score of 16-14 in the last set.

Photographers from *Volleyball Magazine* had showed up and pointed their cameras at the end line to capture one of our spectacular defensive plays. For once, I was glad to come out after my serve, but to see my sprawls and dives in a photo would have made my efforts more real. I wanted to be noticed, but I didn't want to be yanked. Ugh.

The coaches from UOP, University of Washington, and Cal Poly were fans of mine and made a point of stopping by our court in between matches. At different times that weekend, each had complimented my play and told me I'd had a great year. I didn't believe them: they didn't know about my barfing, about being benched, about never being allowed to set again, about my broken toe. Their kindness soothed some of my bitterness, however. It was nice to be noticed in such a positive way.

Chris Marlowe, the future (1984) US Olympic captain who did the radio play-by-play commentary, congratulated me in person as soon as we shook our opponents' hands at the net. I felt vindicated in my resentment after Chris and those coaches talked to me, but I had to let it go. I had new problems to solve.

I limped down to the end of the bench, the first limping steps I had allowed myself to take all weekend. What did my toe look like? I looked around the court, and nobody was watching. The smell of my kneepads was nothing like the smell of my sock once I took off my shoe. New blood was on top of the blood that had crusted around the toe of the sock, and I felt for my toenail. Ouch. It was still there. I gingerly unrolled the sock and saw how well my tape job had held up. Patty was looking at me, so I said, "Please don't say anything to Fred and Don." They were being interviewed by *Volleyball Magazine* on another side court.

"What happened, J.J.?" she asked, with her customary concern. Thank God for compassionate Patty. I felt so lucky she was on my side.

"We had a fire in the dorm Wednesday night and I think I broke my toe. I taped it up."

"Wednesday night? It's Sunday! Why didn't you, never mind. Let's take a look." She took some surgical scissors and carefully cut off the tape. The entire top of my foot was a big bruise, but the metatarsal was where it was supposed to be. My broken toe was blistered by friction and oozing like a sausage on the grill. The smell was terrible. Patty coated my whole foot with hydrogen peroxide and stuck the foot in a bucket of ice, right before the coaches came over to see what was the matter.

"What is it now, J.J.?" asked Don, with an eye roll.

"End of the season aches and pains, Don," I said, winking at Patty.

"J.J., you played really well during this tournament. Everyone is impressed by your efforts. Great job!" said Fred as he high-fived me. The challenge of keeping my foot in the ice bucket was one I had hoped to never repeat, but as the icy fingers gripped my broken bone, new thoughts invaded my mind. Volleyball was over, but inorganic chemistry was looming. Chris Marlowe walked by, and stopped when he saw my face. He wanted to know what I was worrying about, and when I told him I had an inorganic chemistry final at 8:00 a.m. on Monday, he sympathized. Then he told me something I hadn't thought about yet: our team was going to be really good next year. Coming from a broadcaster who had seen countless games that season, his appraisal really resonated. Fans, coaches and opponents were talking about how exciting we were to watch, how our defense was so good that the rally looked as if it were over, but Stanford might make another incredible dig to keep the ball alive.

We sat in the stands and watched USC shellac UOP in the championship match. We knew USC would win the whole thing, so no one objected when Fred said we were driving home after the first set instead of staying for the whole match. Patty found me some crutches, and I iced off and on the long drive home. I thought about the top two teams' offense. We had the best defense in the country, but we didn't have their offensive weapons. I felt we could have been more effective if Krush had been allowed to zip her sets outside so the hitter would face only one blocker, but there was no way I could suggest this to the coaches.

When we got back to campus, I walked straight into the

kitchen of Kairos at 1:00 a.m., looking for something to eat. A few housemates were there, eating ice cream on top of the charred table. Everyone was still talking about who had burned the toast last week. The school was trying to find the culprit. When I asked them why they were still awake, they told me they'd participated in the Princeton scream at midnight. Everything stopped in the undergraduate library, and students screamed for a few minutes to destress. I was sorry I'd missed it. We hugged after digging out all the fudge ribbons in the five-gallon tub, and I went back to my room.

Thirty-nine years later, an orthopedic surgeon broke two bones in my foot so he could realign and pin the metatarsals and roto-root the arthritis that had developed after I injured the toe in the fire. I spent three months getting around on a knee scooter and couldn't drive. It was then I learned who burned the toast that night. Her secret is safe, for now.

Do Not Grade

By 7:00 a.m., after reviewing every note I took and practice test I'd completed, I realized I was in big trouble. If I got a C, I'd never get into medical school. If I dropped inorganic, I'd have to retake it. I didn't even know how to drop a class. I never quit—not now, not ever. Then I realized I would have to ride my bike down the hill while carrying my crutches and my backpack. I was starving again. There was no toaster to make toast.

Gimping down the stairs, I bumped into the incredibly creative computer science boy who had a beard like a gnome and lived under the stairs in an illegal room. "J.J.!" he cried, giving me a hug. He asked about nationals, my foot, my tests that day, then offered to make me a Denver omelet. As I ate this awesome creation, I felt less like a zombie and more like a prepared student. *Maybe I'll do okay on the test.* I asked him if he had ever dropped a class on the day of the final. He told me about a difficult quarter freshie year where he carried twenty units. He dropped a class that wasn't important for his major, writing, "Do not grade. Drop me" on the final. That option made me feel better. As I left to take the dreaded inorganic chemistry final, he wished me luck.

I couldn't understand why some of my housemates called him the troll of the kitchen. He was the nicest guy around, if you could get past his shaggy hair, massive beard, and a grunge look before grunge existed. And I knew he was wicked smart. Dan would rise to the top ranks of a tech company, retiring for a time at the age of thirty. Upon his return to work, he invented and patented dozens of technology tools.

After a treacherous bike ride, I sat down to take the test. I completed two of the first ten inorganic chemistry problems, before the words started swimming on the page. Fatigue, pain, and tears are not a good lens through which to view a complicated subject, and I was getting madder at myself by the minute. I had worked as hard as I could with the time I had. I had never slept in and missed a class. I had a study buddy. I had not missed a due date or asked for an extension on anything, but I couldn't remember how to apply common formulas. The equations looked familiar, which was worse. This meant I had done the problems for practice but couldn't solve them when it counted. I didn't need luck for this test, I needed more mastery of the concepts. Doing a problem correctly one time was not enough when it came to crunch time.

I was the go-to girl: set me the ball, and I will end the point. But now I was choking, about to fold under pressure. Doctors say you shouldn't make big decisions when you're not feeling well. Pain meds for my broken toe, physical exhaustion from nationals, no sleep for two days—yet I was about to make a big decision. I knew I had eighteen units; if I dropped inorganic, I'd still have fourteen. I hoped I was buying time instead of ending a dream when I wrote, "Do not grade. Drop me" on my final, set it on the teaching assistant's desk, and limped out of the classroom. Shank and yank.

Mother-Daughter Talk

All fall I had tried to keep myself busy so I wouldn't be haunted by my mom's kidney issues and pericarditis, and by the two girls from first year who were no longer on campus. One night when I wasn't busy, I tried to remember who had not returned for second year, and that made me start thinking about my own time at Stanford. I was beginning to believe that every day I played volleyball was a day I decreased the number of pain-free steps I'd have in my future. I was looking for answers, for incantations to avoid the mental pain of failure and the physical pain of my injuries. If I kept busy, I wouldn't wonder whether I'd be able to hike with my own kids someday, or if my mom would live long enough to be a grandmother. In every spare minute, I waffled between a doom-and-gloom view and the desire to be fighting something. I hadn't spent any time at home in the fall—we'd had a road trip over Thanksgiving—and as if my list of anxieties weren't long enough already, I worried about how my mom would treat me when I arrived home for the holidays.

As I drove home with my dad the Saturday after finals, I studied this quiet man. With his military bearing and appearance of gravitas, Dad intimidated many people. They assumed his frown meant he was unhappy about something. In fact, Dad and I both frowned when we were simply thinking. Dad's leadership skills were enhanced by his goofy nature, and those who worked for him at the Air Force base adored his sense of humor. He never had to raise his voice to get them to comply with orders.

Dad did have one vulnerability: Mom. When I asked him about Mom's condition, he simply said she was looking forward to my homecoming. His strong hands gripped the wheel at ten and four o'clock, just as he had taught me to do, but I noticed his fingers tightened when I asked this question. His wedding ring, with waves engraved in white gold, glowed on his reddening ring finger. I could tell he was upset. Would he tell me why? And, how would my mom act toward me?

"You know how much your mom misses you, Jenyth. Some days, she walks down the driveway to go check the mailbox four or five times to see if you sent another letter."

"Dad, you said everything was fine. Is she in remission or is she still sick?"

My dry-witted dad, the man who had written a silly poem or limerick on my childhood birthday cards for years, was serious for once. "I'm glad you wrote the letters. Your mom is really sad."

That was it: my mom was really sad. I grilled Dad on the medical issues, but he said her blood work and other tests were much better. Still, I could tell he was worried. I was worried too. Since my mom had dropped me off in August, we had only had a few phone conversations. Sometimes, I couldn't find a pay phone when we were traveling, but most of the time I was avoiding another confrontation. I started writing letters to give her news, but they became a way of venting. Mom wrote back, asking questions about my studies, my new housemates, my new friends. Writing two or three letters a week, I began to bring in more drama and humor than actually existed. I imagined her laughing at me instead of yelling, so I embellished my self-effacing silliness.

When I walked through the front door with a few bags of musty laundry, Mom was in the kitchen. The smell of buttermilk brownies, Crock-Pot stew, and fresh coffee greeted me before I was in her arms. Mom didn't feel as bony as I had expected. She gripped me firmly. Four inches taller than she was, I rested my chin on her head, wisps of her thinning, hair-sprayed hair sticking to my chin. I felt her heart thumping and didn't want to let her go.

She leaned back and looked me right in the eye and said, "Did you get any sleep last night?"

I didn't want to tell her I had starting drinking at noon, so I said, "I slept fine." Marcus's trick of drinking a glass of water for every pint of beer had worked. "You've been busy, Mom. Can I have a brownie before dinner or do I have to wait?"

She grinned, cut a piece from the end where extra frosting had set, and handed it to me on a paper towel. "Let's get started on your laundry. Please tell me you don't have a dirty uniform."

"Mom, remember? The athletic department washes our uniforms now, just like they do for the men's basketball team. No more pink underwear!" I dragged my bags into the garage, found the one with sorted whites, and started dropping underwear into the washer.

"Let me do that," said Mom, gently shoving me aside.

Back in the family room, Dad had turned on a college football game. "Jenyth, we can watch the second half of the Alabama game. Can you grab the Chex party mix from the kitchen? Mom made a batch for you."

Settling down on the plaid sofa next to my dad in his recliner, I started to relax. Mom was buzzing around as if she felt great, touching my hair or my arm every time she walked into and out of the family room. She was smiling broadly. I thought about all times we had watched a game as a family, with my brother Stan on the sofa next to me. He had moved out in September when he transferred from community college to Sacramento State. I realized Mom must miss him too.

Being in this family room—with its trophy wall, disco ball light, homemade treats, and loving parents—contrasted greatly with being in the company of the brilliant students at Stanford, who were always wound up. Immersed in our studies and aware that we were competing for grades with every kid in the room, many of us lacked any kind of healthy balance. We never relaxed. Licking a little rice Chex crumb off of my lips, I started to nod off as 'Bama scored again.

After a huge dinner, which made me even sleepier, Dad and I rinsed the dishes, while Mom went back to her room. Dad loved to watch TV at night, but my mom preferred a book. I remembered a time when I was twelve, when I left my room, where I was reading Jane Austen, to peek into Mom's room. She was in bed, reading, with layers of toilet paper wrapping her beehive hairdo in place. I walked in, flopped on the edge of the king-sized bed, and shut my book.

She shut hers and said, "What's up, Jenyth Jo?" I liked the way she said my name.

"Mom, I have a question. When am I going to get my period? Everyone has hair under their arms and down there but me." Thus began a weekly ritual of my asking my mom about everything, explaining what was happening at school, then hearing what she had to say about it. Half of the time she confirmed what I thought she'd say; other times she'd offer insights that had never occurred to me.

My first night home, I peeked into her room and saw she was reading a Modern Library book, not a Harlequin Romance. I didn't dare interrupt her journeys into fantasy land, but I hoped Mom wouldn't mind a break from the literary stuff. "Mom, I have a question," I began, waiting to see if she'd shut her book. When she did, I settled into my favorite prone position: head resting on my hands, feet crisscrossing in constant movement. "Do you think I'll ever understand inorganic chemistry?"

She said, "How hard is it?"

"I didn't do well on the final, so I dropped it."

"You *dropped* a class? Do you have enough units to stay eligible?"

"Yes, I do. I can retake the class in the spring. I just kept forgetting the formulas."

"Well, you were probably tired. You don't think as well when you're tired. I'm glad you're going to try again. How are your other classes?"

"I love HumBio. It's the core series that includes psychology. You were a biology major, right?"

"Yes, I wanted to be a nurse, but I met your dad, and you know the rest of that story. But I did have a class that nearly killed me: college algebra. It was the only class I ever took in which I didn't understand a thing. The teacher took pity on me and gave me a C. Straight A's on my transcript, but that C. It still makes me mad."

"But Mom, you went to college when you were sixteen. How did you do that?"

"I applied," she said, with a wink.

"Argh, Maamaa," I said in my southern twang to make her laugh.

She got serious. "I wish I had graduated, Jenyth. I wish I could go back to school with you and learn all the subjects you're taking. I was a semester short of graduating when your dad and I moved up our wedding date from June to November. So close, but so it goes. Then we were transferred to Alabama."

"Could you go back to school? Would American River College have those courses?"

"Maybe I could. I haven't thought about it for a long time. Washburn College might let me do that. In the meantime, what about Stanford? Are you happy there?"

"Mom, it isn't a matter of being happy. When I'm with my teammates battling in a match, I'm beyond happy. Studying, not so much. The memorization part of biology is so boring, even though I like the systems."

"I never found it boring, but I like memorization and organization and everything adding up. You're different."

"What do you mean, Mom?"

"You've always walked to the beat of your own drum. I don't know what you hear, but since you were a toddler, you've had your own little world. If everyone went left, you went right, gazing at the stars and moon along the way."

"You mean like when Stan says I'm a space cadet or an airhead?"

"He's joking, but he has a point. You drift into your own thoughts, don't let us in. I'm always wondering what you're thinking. And, you're *always* thinking. I miss your silly puns. When's the last time you had a good laugh? I could use one." She paused, took a deep breath, met my eyes, and said, "Has it ever occurred to you that Stanford might not be the best school for you?"

"Huh? What do you mean?" Mom hadn't wanted me to enroll there, but I thought that conversation was long over.

"I mean, you're not stuck there. You're bright, you love to learn, but if you're not learning chemistry, it could be the fault of the teachers. Do they even know how to teach?"

I thought of my professor who talked into the blackboard instead of facing the class, and started laughing. "Maamaa, it's one of the top schools in the country. The professors have Nobel Prizes and publications and oodles of awards."

"That doesn't mean they know how to teach."

My God, Mom had a point. Maybe my failure wasn't entirely the fault of all-nighters and anxiety. Maybe I could get an A and get into medical school with a better teacher.

"You could transfer to UC Davis. You have a lot of friends there, and I'm sure the 4-H Extension leaders would give you a job. You could easily make the team if you wanted to play. It's closer to home too. We could watch all your games."

"Transfer to Davis? Transfer?" Stunned with the idea, I stared at my mom. "I'll think about it."

Part of me was ready to pack up and go. The intensity of the fall had drained all my energy, and as I drifted off to sleep, I wondered if there was an easier way to become a doctor. Maybe I could have a horse at Davis, or at least groom and ride other people's horses. The act of brushing a horse was the most relaxing thing I knew. I would definitely calm down. If I only had a barn.

But Davis was too familiar. I'd spent part of every summer there for 4-H events, worked at the volleyball camps, and while I loved the campus and my friends there, it wasn't Stanford. And my high school ex went to Davis. That thought made me pause. Maybe my infatuations with Stanford boys were what Zimbardo called *defense mechanisms*—ways to distract myself so I didn't get depressed about my academic failures. Maybe I wasn't a space cadet or an airhead; maybe I was a simple head case.

At Stanford, there was always something new to warp my brain. Full of everything bright and innovative, Stanford felt like the stage of an Emmy-winning musical, with a colorful cast of talented players who could create magic with a Bunsen burner, tragedy with a toaster, comedy with a toga party. The thought of missing our first Kairos Feast of Dionysus—complete with togas, grape peeling, and carafes of Mateus Rosé—was a thought I couldn't accept. Besides, the party was my idea. I had a lot to plan during the upcoming winter quarter to pull off this event in the spring. I didn't want to transfer.

The next morning, Mom laid a pile of papers next to my breakfast plate.

"What's this?" I asked.

"I wrote Davis a few weeks ago, and they sent me the transfer application. You don't have to decide today if you want to transfer, but if you send these in, you'll make the financial aid deadline. Even though Davis is much less expensive than Stanford, you won't get a full ride. But you will qualify for a Cal grant, and that will pay for most of your tuition. We'll have to borrow the rest."

I stared at my mom. All fall, I'd thought she hated me, and here was evidence she had researched an alternative path for my success. She thought I needed an escape. Was she right?

"Mom, it's Sunday morning. I have to go Christmas shopping. Can this wait?" I begged.

"Sure. If you fill them out tomorrow, and we mail them by Tuesday, you'll be a week ahead of the financial aid deadline."

"Okay. I'll do it tomorrow." Why not? I had nothing to lose except the ten-dollar fee, and a backup plan felt like a good idea. However, there was no way I would let my parents borrow any money for my education. I'd have to get a really good job. I could shovel shit at the polo barns, but that was pretty far from the glamor of volleyball.

Just thinking about leaving Stanford and my friends there choked me up. I started missing my roommate Jen, and even her boyfriend a bit. I thought of the guys in the upstairs quad suite, the ones who had been in the SLE dorm freshman year and introduced me to my peeps. Looking at the course catalog, I realized what an advantage I had as an athlete: I enrolled before the rest of the student body and always got into the classes I wanted. My winter term was going to be really interesting: the eight-unit human biology core, developmental psychology for four units, anatomy and physiology lab for two units, and a slot in the upper division neuroscience four-unit seminar. A quarter without chemistry would be great. I had loved my high school course, but our teacher was more a master showman than a calculator. He was an early version of the science geek, with a terrific personality and a clear lesson plan, so chemistry was easy with him.

After a trip to the mall, I returned to find my mom checking on the roast in the oven. "Mom, I told you I'd help you cook, but you've done everything already. I didn't have any luck finding a ball gown for my Theta formal."

"You can clean up the kitchen. I'm starting to get tired. Would you like a cup of Whole Earth cinnamon tea? The water's hot. I still think you should wear your mauve Grecian gown from senior ball."

"That dress is bad luck. Don't you remember what happened? I missed the whole dance. Is Stan coming home for dinner?" I hoped.

"Yes, he's on his way right now."

We sat at the kitchen table, set for four, and sipped our tea. I sneaked another brownie. Mom looked serenely happy: both of her kids would be home for dinner for the first time in months. I thought about that as she flipped through the Sunday ads.

Mom loved being a mom. What had it been like when Stan moved out? I'd been away from home for a couple of years, but she cooked for him, cleaned his room, and did his laundry after I left. Then he left, and she didn't have as much to do. She became really sick again, recovered with Dad's TLC, tried to come to a volleyball match or two. She wrote long, newsy letters to me. That, and having to take our Irish setter Clancy to be euthanized, was the entirety of her life this fall. What did she have to look forward to? How did she keep a positive attitude?

As much as she loved being a mom, I loved being a spoiled daughter. I knew if I gave in to the urge to sleep before dinner, Mom would do all my laundry and make all my favorite food, and I would wake up refreshed. I was so tired, but I fought the urge. I would try to help more this vacation, instead of sleeping all the time. "Mom, you haven't asked to see my toe. It's killing me. I'm going to change the bandages."

"Do you have to do it in the kitchen? Let's go into the

bathroom." She became my nurse, gently unpeeling layers of gauze, cleaning away the dried blood, administering the Neosporin, and rewrapping it after the goop dried. "Your toenails are really short. Do you do that for volleyball?"

"Yes. Like football players, we get turf toe if we jam the toes of our shoes into the floor. Short nails make it less likely." She began to massage my toes and sore heels and I made a little groaning noise. "Ahh, Mom, that feels so good! Are your hands feeling stronger?" Her flares usually produced swollen hands and flaky skin, but her hands were smooth and moisturized.

"I'm feeling great," she said, wiping the antibiotic ointment off of her hands with a towel.

Maybe what my mom needed more than my becoming a doctor, I thought as I watched her primp in front of the mirror and stick her tongue out at me, was time with the children she loved. If I went to medical school, I wouldn't see much of her for eight of the next ten years. What if she didn't live long enough for me to save her? That thought stopped me. Davis was twenty-five minutes from home. I should transfer.

As I filled out the Davis transfer form, I decided to change majors at Stanford. I could switch from chemistry to a HumBio major and still have a chance to get into medical school. On the transfer form, I selected psychobiology as my major. I loved the way the mind and body interacted, so this sounded perfect. The University of California would give me credit for one year of chemistry for every two quarters I'd taken at Stanford, which confirmed my suspicion: we went really fast in science classes. In three quarters, we completed the equivalent of a year and a half of chemistry or biology at other strong schools. No wonder I'd struggled. Maybe the rumor was true: premedical studies were less about teaching students the material and more about weeding them out from the program. Maybe this little weed could go to seed and grow elsewhere.

CHAPTER 9
Biofeedback

In the Roble studio, I was taking a dance class that combined ballet and stretching, with hopes my foot and ankle would become stronger. I pretended I was Cynthia Gregory of the American Ballet Theater, who at five feet, seven inches, was my height *en pointe*. I tried to channel her elegance and grace. I held my relevé a little longer, as music flowed through my limbs to rest in fingertips and toes, especially the broken toe, which was almost healed. We pliéd as a corps de ballet, and our piano player clapped for us. I sighed, relaxed and happy as I walked out with the other dancers. Here in the studio, I didn't need to compare my body to anybody's. I knew everyone else was shorter, thinner, and more feminine than I was, but it didn't matter when I heard a tune. I let the music control my body; I forgot everything else and unburied my soul. It was only in the dance studio that I could keep an empty mind.

At nineteen, I had the first massive period of my life. Like most women of my era, I felt I had to cover up my body when it was doing its bodily thing. After dance, I would rush to the restroom across the courtyard, hoping. Because I could never get a tampon to stay in during volleyball practice, I once bled through while wearing white shorts. In dance, I had to double up in order to dam the flow, for we still wore black leotards, pink tights and shoes. It was a relief to pull on my baggy red sweatpants and walk into the courtyard. Preparations for the Viennese ball were underway, and I peeked in at the fountain.

Viennese Ball #1

The Viennese ball is one of Stanford's strangest rituals. Begun in 1978 by students who returned from Stanford's program in Vienna, the event is held during Fasching, Austria's celebratory weeks between New Year's Eve and Lent. In 1981, the committee had rented potted plants from a local nursery and transformed the courtyard between the dance studio and Roble Gym into a formal European garden. Pink and white camellias adorned the side arcades, and beautiful ivy was strung above the round fountain in the middle of the courtyard.

In my best Frank Sinatra croon, I sang the beginning to "Three Coins in the Fountain," while wishing I could find a date as gorgeous as Louis Jourdan. I knew how to waltz and polka from taking dance classes in my high school's performing arts program. I had my high school senior ball dress ready, but no date.

I stopped by the student store on my way back to Kairos House and picked up a box of extra-long, extra-duty, mattress-sized pads. Stay-Frees weren't packaged in a squishy plastic bag in the 1980s, and the box didn't fit into my backpack. I stuffed it under my sweatshirt and laughed at my baby bump.

At dinner, I mentioned my lack of a Viennese ball date to some Kairos friends, most of whom had never heard about the ball and had no interest in changing out of their camo pants and tie-dye shirts. But one spoke up: "I have a friend in an engineering class who was just telling me he wanted to go. Let me call him."

We agreed to go on this blind date, and I hoped he could dance.

When I slid the mauve pink Grecian one shoulder-strap dress over my head the next evening, I sighed. Two years of volleyball training had made me flatter than ever. I didn't own a padded push-up bra, so I looked around the bathroom for something I could stuff into my strapless bra. I remembered my box of maxi-pads, and a light bulb popped. I cut a napkin in two, peeled off the adhesive guard, and stuck them to the inside of my dress, tossing the bra aside. With a little maneuvering and trimming, they increased my bust to a respectable size.

A tall, ginger-haired boy with acne on his cheeks, named Kurt, picked me up on time, and we did a quick practice waltz and turn in the Kairos lobby. Wow! Could this boy dance!

Hours later, lost in the music, as my date and I waltzed for the hundredth time around the Roble dance studio, he slipped on something. We stopped, and he pulled half a napkin from his shoe and dropped it on the floor. I looked down at my chest, saw a lopsided bump, and pointed to the floor.

"Eww! What's that?" I said to distract him, terrified he'd figure out what it was and where it came from.

We steered away, one-two-three. I made a quick bathroom run to take out the other side and check my tampon. I asked the attendant for two Band-Aids, covered my nipples, and didn't look in the mirror to check my makeup. One humiliation a night was enough.

The sanitary napkin stayed stuck to the floor, and every couple who went by it laughed or grimaced. I wanted to pick it up, throw it into the garbage can, and run back to my dorm. Or better, run to the red hut, where other women on the rag were sitting, huddling around the flames like Camp Fire girls. My mom had told me about wearing her E-Z belt sanitary diapers when she was young, and my grandma said rags that were no good for quilts were used to stop the flow. Now we buy "feminine hygiene," as if our periods were a virus to avoid, a disease we carried, a curse we earned.

The days when our cycles synchronized with lunar phases and we were deemed "hysterical" are long gone. We are far beyond the influence of male doctors who said women who play sports will have fertility issues. Run that one by Kerri Walsh Jennings, who won Olympic beach volleyball gold as the mother of two and pregnant with number three. But for female athletes, including ballet dancers, who are forced to wear sexualized uniforms, O woe when it's that time of the month.

Biofeedback

Winter quarter was unusually wet, but that meant Lake Lagunita would be ready for boating during the spring, I told myself as I trudged up the stairs to anatomy lab. I had to practice the power of positive thinking because the HumBio core was tough, abnormal psych led me to diagnose myself with every strange syndrome, and I was about to meet our group's cadaver for the first time. I was pretty nervous, as I'd never seen a dead body before.

When our professor unveiled Leon, I took one whiff of the formaldehyde and viewed his incredibly bushy grandpa eyebrows... and that was it. I guess I dropped on the spot. A few people dragged me outside to the warmer hallway until I came to, covered in sweat.

When I told the professor there was no way I could scalpel into the old man, he told me to drop anatomy. Still, I wanted to be a doctor.

My neuroscience seminar had four grad students and one senior, plus me. Professor Paul Pribram had recently published his endorphin/enkephalin research on the body's ability to create its own painkillers. Instead of writing about these endogenous opiates, I wrote my term paper about the pain gateway theory, so I could learn something to help my mom. The professor thought, off the record, that acupuncture might be an effective pain reliever, and my mom found a graduate of the London School of Acupuncture to help her inflammation.

One of Pribram's graduate students, Chip, was interested in my injuries, my pain management, my volleyball experience, and me. To put him off, I told him I wasn't a star, that I threw up before most games, and my play had started becoming worse instead of improving last fall.

He and Professor Pribram sat up when I said this, and looked at each other. "J.J.," the professor said, "would you be interested in learning biofeedback? Chip has developed a computer model that measures respiration, blood pressure, pulse rate, and brain waves. We believe humans have some ability to control these vitals if they learn Transcendental Meditation and other techniques. Would you like to try it out and see if you can relax and reduce your performance anxiety?"

I agreed to try one time, but ended up doing a series of five or six visits because the results were instantly visible. Lowering my pulse from 75 to 62 in one minute made me feel in control of my body at a time when I wasn't in control of anything else. Unfortunately, we had no neuroscience undergraduate major at Stanford then.

This success reignited my premed dreams at the beginning of spring quarter. However, to balance the repeat of inorganic chemistry and the memorization load of HumBio, I decided to take another dance class as well as introduction to aeronautics (aero-astro, for dummies), a class where my Air Force-inspired paper airplanes earned top scores. I never scored above a B on any science test, but I earned an A in dance.

At the end of April, as I was test flying a dad-designed airplane off of the third-floor balcony of Kairos, I realized I should be hearing from UC Davis that day. I jumped on my bike, sped down to the post office, and saw a letter angled inside my box. I was in, but Davis's financial aid package left a twenty-five hundred dollar per year gap in funding. I could be a psychobiology major there, something I now knew I loved, but I would graduate with at least a sixty-two-hundred-dollar debt once I added the twelve hundred dollars I borrowed to get through my freshman year. If I stayed at Stanford, I wouldn't have to borrow any more money. In fact, I had been chosen to be the Kairos food manager for the next two years, and would make extra money I could save.

I declined their enrollment offer before I discussed it with my mom, before she could convince me to move closer to home.

I still believed I could make it into medical school and cure my mother. So, I applied for a summer internship through the CPPC, just as I had my first year. Telling my teammates I had an internship then had been my way of elevating a manual labor job. Now, the CPPC counselor was thrilled I had skills.

"You can type seventy-five words a minute with great accuracy!" she cheered. "Most Stanford sophomores know nothing. Here are a few positions at the medical center for you to look at. Let me know if you need help applying."

I read through them, applied for all, and waited for a message to arrive. When I was accepted and told my mom I wouldn't be coming home until August, she was sad but proud. At last, somebody was going to give me a chance to become a doctor.

CHAPTER 10
Weighing In

My six-week internship in the summer of 1981 began with a tour of the hospital and an explanation of the various opportunities for us. I wasn't qualified to work in a research lab and had hoped at a minimum I could write up research reports, but the boys got those jobs. I shadowed a very young female doc the second day, and during grand rounds at a large table, an older white male doctor asked her to make coffee. She was furious, but made the coffee for the group. When she returned to the table, she sat with her head down. I thought she was taking notes. But then I saw she had a lump of Silly Putty in her lap, and she was working it and working it.

On the third day, I still didn't have a real job. I was wandering through the halls, trying to find the office where I was supposed to report, when I bumped through some double doors into a dark corridor. I heard a woman's voice screech, "Get off me!" Then I saw her emerge from behind a white curtain, trying to shake off a large middle-aged man. They saw me, and he straightened up his coat and walked the other way. She looked at me, and I saw tears streaking her makeup, her dress scrunched up above her knees, and her coat hanging off one shoulder.

"Help me with this, won't you?" she said.

I helped her put her white coat back on. Her name badge

was askew, and I pointed that out. It said "resident" under her name.

"Thank God you walked in," she said, "Who are you?"

"I'm a summer intern, looking for this office." I showed her a slip of paper.

"Well, you found the overnight call wing, where we sleep. Do you want to be a doctor?" She looked completely put back together, focused, and determined.

"Yes. I want to be an immunologist so I can cure my mom's autoimmune disease."

"That's a really interesting field, but it's full of men. As you just saw, men dominate this profession. You have to be better than they at everything to get any kind of chance. This hospital is the worst. I thought it was the best match, but Stanford is full of predators. Be careful while you're here." A nurse down the hall waved at her to take a phone call, but before she turned to go, she said, "OB-GYN is safe. Pediatrics okay. Stay away from anesthesiologists. They're all drug addicts." And off she went, leaving me terrified, without directions for finding the office.

I wandered back through the maze to the information desk, and a volunteer walked me to the office I hadn't been able to find for half an hour.

Inside, the hospital manager told me there were two positions left. I took the job outside the hospital building, and spent the next several weeks in the Office of Development, processing donations to various research arms of the hospital. Who would want to be a doctor after what I'd seen? Why should I work so hard in school if it was just to live like those poor female docs? Yet, I admired their strength and tenacity.

Questions like these raged through my mind as I rode

my bike back and forth from my summer room with Kisi in the Manzanita Trailer Park to the Stanford Hospital. Both Kisi and I had passed the lifeguarding course in Roble pool, and Kisi had been hired to teach swimming for the summer. We worked out in the weight room with the football team, swam in the fifty-meter pool, and lived on broccoli and Top Ramen. I lost weight and felt physically strong.

My doctor dreams, however, were just about over by the time I finished my internship in the Office of Development. Instead of reading research and writing white papers, I wrote thank-you letters to donors of money, property, organs, and other body parts. I couldn't forget the disturbing image of the male doctors who sat around a mahogany conference table at Stanford Hospital, while one of the chiefs ordered the female doctor to make coffee during their meeting. How could the rest of them sit there and let him bully her? Why did she sit down with clamped lips and crossed arms instead of calling them out? After all the memorizing she had to do to get into medical school, and after all the tests and all-nighters during school, why did she stay? Was she as powerless as that scene suggested?

And there was the resident I had inadvertently rescued while wandering about the hospital's call room. Did she have to work with that guy? Act like nothing happened so he would write her a good recommendation? Over the next decade, numerous sexual harassment and discrimination lawsuits were filed against the hospital. These cases shocked many people. Some plaintiffs remained anonymous, but still won many of their cases. I wondered if the resident received some kind of compensation.

Generous Coaches

Why would I, who was barely getting through the premed curriculum, choose to spend my twenties in that kind of environment? I struggled with these images as my mom picked me up at the trailers and drove me to UC Davis, where I would direct the volleyball camp again. I needed to discuss this with my elder volleyball mentors. I looked forward to philosophizing with them every summer. This was my fifth year working at the camp and my second year directing, thanks to my club coach, Debbie.

The previous year, Coach Erbe had changed my footwork. This year, we hired Marlene Piper, the Canadian-born future head women's coach at Cal. Her energy and enthusiasm for the game were infectious, and she was the lowest-maintenance guest coach we'd had. Each of my influential coaches had ingrained important ideas in me: my high school Coach Ted, the tenacity on defense; club Coach Debbie, the need for repetition in serving and serve receive; USC's Coach Erbe on footwork and technique; Coach Fred on overall strength, balance, and injury prevention; Coach Don on blocking footwork and transition technique. I didn't expect there was much left to learn from this five-foot-one-inch fireball, but Marlene preached conditioning and nutrition.

I heard a rumor she was fifty and determined to make Cal comply with Title IX equity in women's volleyball. Incredibly fit, she buzzed around the courts, yelling encouragement and talking about "bettering the ball, bettering your teammates." Marlene made conditioning sound like fun. "Extra suicide liners for anyone who wants to run one more." We all accepted her invitation. While Ted loved torturing us, and we loved him back for the high bar he set, Marlene made us love the work. Love the work and the work becomes fun. By the time the two weeks of camps finished, I was in remarkable shape from doing every extra sprint.

Besides meeting Marlene during summer camp, I met her friend Ken Preston, the men's volleyball coach at UCSB. He was a great setter, and we had a lot of fun playing while the campers were eating lunch. Ken invited me to work at his camp after UCD, and I had just enough time to do it before reporting back to Stanford for preseason training.

My first impression of Goleta Beach during my freshman year was that I'd stumbled onto paradise. Before the storm of 1998, the beach extended from the freshie dorms, around a cove, to another peninsula. The gorgeous sand was home to a dozen permanent courts, with poles made from the same railroad ties we had used back in the 4-H barn. I realized I would not graduate if I attended UCSB. I'd be out swimming, playing ball, and watching sunsets.

Isla Vista was a raucous party village, and this summer, I slept on the living room couch of one of the players. Our house was on the cliff side of Isla Vista, and our beer pong games lasted long into the night. The players were so friendly to me, and I couldn't wait to train with them on the sand. My hostess Iris (and her vaunted topspin serve) was tough to beat indoors, and she was a terrific player outdoors.

Nothing could have prepared me for meeting Kathy Gregory, the UCSB coach who had lightly recruited me by mail. She was a AAA-rated beach player in her late thirties, which meant she might not be as strong and quick as the other players, but she was clearly very crafty. We met during the morning session, and she said, "J.J., we are going to make you a beach player."

I showed up in the afternoon wearing shorts and a t-shirt, which was my first mistake. Everyone else wore string bikinis and looked great. While I did have mine on under my shorts, I wasn't going to get a sunburn on day one.

Kathy told me to play with her. I would play right side, as my hitting and blocking would dominate, and I had to pass two-thirds of the court, because she wasn't going to move.

I took that assignment as a compliment, but quickly learned I could not move on the sand. Every time I tried to push off, I sank deeper. I tried to get a big jump and got nothing. My timing was all off, and the ball was heavier so the wind couldn't carry it away. My serving needed adjustment, and I was terrible. Too proud to admit I was miserable, I kept playing and trying to improve.

Kathy's analysis was succinct: "You move like a freighter, and when you hit the sand, you appear to be a beached whale. You gotta get your sand legs, J.J."

Whatever that meant, I did not have them. I enjoyed the repartee and trash talk of the games, however. Kathy could swear up a storm and had a string of one-liners that were hilarious. If I hit a shot done the line, she'd yell, "Tubular." And if I hit a hard cross-court shot, she'd say, "Cut, cut, cut." She taught me different spin serves and showed me what to do to use the wind and the sun to my advantage. "That's a gnarly sidespin serve ya got now, J.J."

We never advanced from the lower courts to the upper courts, a ritual on the sand scene. Everyone wanted to hold onto the number one court—to be king or queen of the court—until some other team beat them and sent them back down to the lowest court.

During our games, Kathy never stopped talking, and her motor-mouth play-by-play was incredibly instructive. Her own players did a lot of eye-rolling, but to me, she was part cheerleader, part coach, part taunter. I dug it. When she asked me why I wasn't setting any more, I shrugged my shoulders. Hearing her say I was misused in the lineup and that I could set for her any time was balm on the blister of being out of my best position.

Weighing In

After a brief weekend home, where I enjoyed some mom spoiling, Mom drove me back to the Stanford campus.

I rode in the team van down to Lake Arrowhead for pre-season training camp. Krush's family owned a ranch—Hoss Ranch—near the lake, and her dad had arranged for us to train at Rim of the World High School nearby. It was a good thing I was in shape, since we trained at the altitude of 5,758 feet, enough to make us suck air during conditioning drills.

Once again, Krush and I led the way during wind sprints. We had a number of new recruits, and it was a lot of fun getting to know them when we weren't on the court. Krush's dad took us waterskiing, and it was no surprise Krush was an amazing water-skier. He also let me ride his horses. Bobbie and I owned the tennis court, easily beating Fred and Don in doubles. Bobbie had gorgeous ground strokes; in fact, she seemed more comfortable on the tennis court than on the volleyball court. Even so, a few years later, she became an All-American middle blocker. Krush's mom, Pam, cooked gourmet burgers, set up a Pac-Man game, and made us all feel welcome and important.

Our rivals, the UCLA team, were highly ranked.

We heard about their Hell Week from Boom-Boom's younger sister, Michele, who was competing for the starting setter spot. They had daily weigh-ins, and if anyone didn't make weight, their coach made them run the mile up the hill from Pauley Pavilion to the arboretum. When they heard this, Don and Fred had the brilliant idea of making us weigh in on the second morning of preseason. They didn't threaten us with hills, but we wondered about that as we looked at the tops of the San Bernardino mountains.

Patty was in charge of weighing and recording our weight. Despite having no body fat and sinking like a brick in water, I weighed in at 155, my perfect playing weight. When Fred saw that number, he freaked out. "J.J., you've got to lose some weight!" he said.

I had never, ever been obese; when I was 163 the previous year, I was still less than twenty percent body fat. At 155, the calipers had nothing to pinch.

The other girls heard his voice, and a few new players were given the same speech.

Tina, who was by far the skinniest on our team, started a whisper while she waited in line. "Just like with those white bun-huggers, we're not going to put up with this insult. I'm going to refuse to get on the scale." And she did, much to our joy. "It's none of your business how much I weigh," she said as she walked past the scale and sat down.

We figured we'd be ringside for a boxing match, but instead Fred backed down when Jan also refused. Don was upset and tried to reason with them, but we were done. The scale went back into Patty's bag and was never mentioned again.

Tina's protest shifted my view of her. Before, I thought her shrewish behavior fit in with the "bitch mode" often ascribed to opinionated women, but in this instance, I realized she had the strength of a true leader. I may not have liked her manner, but I had to respect her team-benefiting gesture. Everyone was relieved, yet some were even more intimidated by her.

Patty and I did one experiment with the scale that year, however. During my entire athletic career, I sweated an enormous amount. I was always thirsty during the long tournament days, and she was concerned about hydration. So, one day at Arrowhead, I weighed in before breakfast, then again before dinner. The two practices at altitude had wrung me dry, and I'd lost five pounds in a day. At that point, Patty encouraged me to drink Gatorade and to drink a lot of water before I went to bed. Despite my on-again-off-again troubles with Don, I knew Patty had my back and was really rooting for my success—and for everyone else's, too. We know so much more about physical recovery after a strenuous workout today, but just knowing Patty was watching our health more than our play back then was enormously soothing. She was such an important team member.

After ten days of workouts and team bonding, we were ready to hit the road. We blew through teams during preseason and started getting some media attention. Stanford was ranked in the top 10 for the first time, and Boom-Boom, Jan, and Krush were on the watch list for post-season awards. And I was in the starting line-up again.

CHAPTER 11
Crowns

When we traveled down to UCSB and Cal Poly to play that fall, I wondered what Coach Kathy would be like on the bench. I suspected she would be a yeller, and she was. It became clear only a mentally tough player could handle her stream-of-consciousness critique, but to me, everything she said made sense and was accurate. Fred rarely raised his voice and sometimes came up with wild notions we couldn't execute, but he never crossed the line with name-calling criticism. We laughed as he chewed up pen after pen as we played, but perhaps that prevented him from saying what he really thought. Don didn't filter, but his coaching tips were very specific—for example, "That hitter has a fast arm. You need to jump with her, not after her."

Our match with UCSB wasn't much of a match, as Boom-Boom and I were on fire. We passed their serves with precision, and our side-outs were simply pass; set Boom-Boom, or me, or another hitter; get the kill; get the ball back. They didn't score a lot of points this time, and Kathy was very frustrated with her team, who couldn't get past our incredible defense.

Iris from UCSB looked destroyed after the game, as her deadly topspin serve wasn't working as well as usual. We found out later that she didn't play much the rest of the season, after we beat them, and I felt bad about that. We had become friends during the Isla Vista week, and she was very philosophical and thoughtful. Yelling wouldn't be the best way to coach her, I felt. It must be horrible to be all-everything one year, then on the bench the next. I made a mental note to ensure that any player on a team I coached would feel I wanted them to succeed.

For the first time, we beat Cal Poly. Their coach praised me after the match: "J.J., I can't believe how much you've improved as a middle. I still think you should be setting, but wow! We couldn't stop you."

After that match, a new sense of my playing self emerged. My own coaches might be unreasonably hard, or totally negative, but other coaches recognized my efforts. They were studying me, and they respected my abilities. It wasn't until years later that I realized I really was out of position, that I was too short to hit and block in the middle. Fortunately, I ignored this fact during my college years when I fought doggedly to stay on the court.

When I started coaching, I realized two main points. First, good setters didn't sweat as much as I did. I would double hit a ball or two every match just because my hands were soaking wet. Setters need to be more reliable and consistent. Second, while I was too short to be an Olympic-caliber middle blocker, I could be a very effective middle hitter due to my quickness and tenacity. *Middle-blocker mentality* meant a middle blocker could make a timing error or misjudge a block, but if she kept her head in the play, she could keep the rally going and help her team. That's why I continued to start on Stanford's team. I never gave up. If I made an error, I reset to focus on the next play. I took a deep breath when the other team went back to serve, and exhaled as the play began. I was more mindful on a volleyball court than any other place, an irony I recognized quite recently.

At Long Beach State, I overheard the coach telling his team before the match, "J.J. can't hit to the right. All she does is cut back to the left. If you stay in your position, you'll dig her every time."

Hmm, I thought. *They are going to shift their block to the left, and I will have more angles into the court. Chuck Erbe, thank you for fixing my footwork; this one is for you.* Every time I got a good set, I hit it straight down to the right, in front of Beach's defender. If the set was off, I tipped in front of her instead. According to my own statistical calculations, all six of my first hitting attempts were to the right.

The Long Beach coach went ballistic. Every time I went up in the air, arm ready to swing before the ball was set, he'd scream, "Watch the shot monger! Watch the shot monger!"

If his intention was to tick me off with name-calling, this wasn't the right approach. I was having my best hitting percentage ever in a match. A few points before we would take the final game, Jan placed a perfect vertical set. This meant I got to choose where to hit instead of being led to one side or another. Already up in the air, I saw the ball's trajectory, saw the middle blocker in front of me start to jump and knew she would be too late, did not see the defender step forward in position, and I swung as hard as I could. The ball hit the defender in the face before she could get her hands up. I saw blood. By the time I landed, I felt terrible.

Everyone knows you stay back if there's a hole in the block, and for some reason, she moved forward into the hole. For a millisecond, I felt conflicted as she put her face in a towel and went to the end of the bench for some ice. I didn't look at my bench, which had exploded with "Oh my God!" And "Yes!" chants. Without looking, I knew our freshies were jumping up and down and hooting, thinking I had six-packed the player on purpose. Everyone had heard the taunts of the coach, and everyone thought I had answered him with playground rules.

I walked back to the middle of the net, stood with my hands in ready position above my head, and waited for Boom-Boom to serve. Through the net, I saw the Long Beach coach staring at me. I kept a poker face. If they thought I was an assassin now, let them. I knew I couldn't have hit that girl in the face if I'd wanted to; I wasn't made that way. I would have let up my swing if I had seen her keep moving forward, but I didn't. I took what the defense gave me, nothing more, nothing less.

On match point, a spinless ball was set to me, and I saw everyone back on their heels, expecting me to crush it again. The double block jumped with me, reaching for the sky to form a wall, which I saw in time to stop my arm mid-swing and tip the ball cobra-style—a shot Coach Kathy had taught me on the beach. The ball changed direction by ninety degrees and softly hit the floor behind the block and in front of the ten-foot line. Game and match.

As we shook our opponents' hands when we crossed under the net, the Long Beach coach grabbed mine and turned it palm side up. "Where did you get that black magic, J.J.?" he asked, as he read my palm.

I kept my mouth shut, for once, and shrugged my shoulders.

Don tapped me on the back, and when I turned around, he had his hands on his hips. "That, J.J., is what I want to see all the time," he said. He was smiling, truly happy for me. At last, I'd earned his respect. I never thought I would.

Fred followed up with, "Best shot selection ever, J.J."

I thought of Coach Kathy trying to school me on the beach and instilling in me the knowledge that there was always an open spot on the court. I just had to find it, just had to test the defense to see what they could and couldn't do. Of course in doubles, there's more open court, but the concept is the same indoors: a good hitter knows which shot to hit and where to place it. Finally, I could access some hidden aggression when I went up to hit in the middle.

I thought, *Where else can a woman go around and hit objects at other people with impunity?* I didn't mean to hit that girl, but knowing I could gave me more power than my elementary school basketball enforcer's stance. Instead of worrying about my mom, worrying about my major, worrying about everything, I embraced my role on the court. Instead of letting volleyball be the cause of my frustration in life, the game was going to be my outlet for it. Who knew how far volleyball could take me?

Creative Writing

At the start of the quarter, I faced some academic challenges. I needed to change majors. Again. Chemistry to Human Biology to Psychology. I loved all my classes but couldn't decide what to study. Here I was, twenty years old, with six quarters' tuition left from my volleyball scholarship, and I had no clue. I did know I did not want to be a doctor. Instead of turning to physical therapy, which would have made sense since I lived in the athletic training room, or to veterinary medicine, which would have been logical with my 4-H experiences, I turned away from science. I would still participate in Psych Department studies, but I missed reading. History was my favorite class in high school, but I didn't want to major in it because reading history books was something I could do after college. Besides, I couldn't finish in the time left. I could major in English, my least favorite class in high school, and finish in seven quarters.

Then, in the fine print, I saw "Creative Writing." I counted the number of classes required for the major. I wouldn't have to take as much German, and if I were admitted, I could finish on time. It would mean a few quarters of twenty-plus units, but they were literature courses, and I loved to read. I signed up for the Introduction to Fiction Writing class and started thinking about how I could get admitted to the tiny department. I could wear my preppy clothes before practice, as the class started at 10:00 a.m. and pretend to be a writer. Maybe I could "fake it until you make it."

When I walked into the Building 40 seminar classroom, wearing a skirt and two polo shirts with the collars turned up, seven other students filed in with me. Two wore camo pants and black turtlenecks; one young man wore jeans, a plaid shirt, and a jean jacket; and another woman wore a maxi dress. We sat at an old oval oak table grooved with pen scars, but our required composition books had enough padding to prevent the ridges from distorting our handwriting. Our teacher, Michael Koch, had been a Stegner fellow and stayed on to serve as a Jones Fellow, teaching undergraduate creative writing. He walked in slowly, with his old leather messenger bag clutched cross-body, as he squeezed in behind us. His other hand held a coffee mug that smelled of my favorite Peruvian blend from the campus Coffee House.

There we were: nine bodies in a little room lined with books, old windows looking toward the church, and a creative writing tradition eight of us didn't know about. We were premeds and history majors and engineers and economists. In ninety minutes, Michael learned our names, told me he preferred Jenyth over J.J., and said I "could write a sentence." I knew everyone's name and major, and thought this class was unlike anything I'd had at Stanford. We talked about ideas, we wrote about ourselves, and we shared some secrets. Michael assigned a short story to read and a guided writing assignment to be done before Thursday. We walked out of the room, new companions in thoughts and dreams.

As I walked downstairs, past the secretary's desk, and into the Quad, I felt like I had just arrived at Stanford. I spun 360 degrees—from the church to the religious studies corner, to the arcades near the history corner, and to the comparative literature and foreign language corner. I loved having a class in the old liberal arts part of school instead of the industrially designed lecture halls and labs.

The church beckoned, so I walked into the lobby and through the side door to the chapel. Ostentatious and out of balance, the nave's stained-glass windows hid little Leland Stanford, Jr., as Jesus in the cradle. Mrs. Stanford's image was an angel looking over him. I giggled. What would she say if she could see this institution now? If she could elevate her son to godly status, maybe there was hope for me.

I walked to the front pew, slid down the seat so my head rested on the back of the pew, and gazed skyward through the window at the top of the cupola. The ribs of the dome seemed to point to the English Department building. Maybe this was some kind of sign. Whatever it meant, nobody else was inside, and I had a few minutes of absolute quiet while I gazed at the galleries of stained glass. I breathed deeply, in through my nose for seven seconds, out through my mouth for ten, as if I were running wind sprints. Instead, I fell into meditative calm.

Later, I walked outside, past the German building, to my parked bike and rode back up the hill to the auditorium for Developmental Psychology, where four hundred students pushed into theater-style chairs to watch a lecture.

Every Tuesday and Thursday morning that fall, I switched from thinking about "13 Ways of Looking at a Blackbird" to memorizing Erik Erikson's eight stages of psychosocial development. I gave thanks in the church after every writing class, and once again loved learning.

I had no clue what I was doing, but Michael Koch was a terrific teacher. We talked a little about craft and a little about storytelling, and instead of making up stuff, I started living as the star of my own fiction. I'd always had a flair for the dramatic, but no singing or acting talent, so this was turning into a great way to act out for "research purposes." The English Department and Creative Writing teachers were very social, very encouraging, and very fun. I met Katy, a transfer from Wellesley, who was in two of my literature classes. Katy saw my plaid skirts and loafers and thought I was from the East Coast. She didn't know I was an athlete, and it was a joy to talk about books and stories with her. She was brilliant and funny. Her literary analysis was already beyond undergraduate level, but she listened to my ideas with interest.

Within a week of school starting, I knew I had made the right choice. I couldn't wait to turn twenty-one in January and join the Creative Writing Department for their weekly Tuesday night beer fests at Antonio's Nut House. Meanwhile, Michael encouraged me to major in creative writing, and I turned in my application and hoped.

Burger King

Home matches were becoming a scene. With new lighting in our gym, I felt like I was stepping on stage when the
match began. We were drawing hundreds of people in
Maples Pavilion, compared with the dozens of parents and
former coaches who attended matches my first year. Now,
the bottom side section was always full, and the football
team, who typically sat above the home bench in the second
tier, sometimes had to move their kegs of beer so fans could
sit down. The guys were loud and supportive, giving us a
home-court advantage when they groaned approval of our
opponents' errors.

Two boys, nicknamed the Sweat Wipes, sat behind the
end lines and were called out to mop our sweat from the
floor at the end of a rally. On their hands and knees, they
wiped wherever we pointed. I wondered if one reason I was
subbed out in the back row was due to the sweat streaks I
made while diving on defense. The sweat wipes had to
come on the court after every play I hit the floor. Teammates
slipped, and Fred would say, "That was almost an ACL tear
there." Saying Kisi did a terrific job in the backcourt would
have been a better explanation.

We were in peak condition when we played UOP in late
September on the road. Fred marked up a map, and we took
what seemed to be the longest route to Stockton in order to
avoid rush hour traffic. We passed by Casa de Fruita, in between Morgan Hill and Los Banos, and were starving by the
time we hit Highway 99 in Turlock. Fred pulled our van over
at the Burger King.

I ate a whole Whopper, and the rest of the team pigged

out. Kisi and I grabbed a pile of Burger King crowns, and the whole team assembled them and crowned each other. Our photographer, Jim "Spiro" Spirakis, encouraged a silly pose, and the resulting image is by far my favorite team picture. Not a volleyball in sight, but all of us wore our crowns with pride.

We walked into UOP's roller rink of a gym for the last time, as they had broken ground on the new Alex Spanos Pavilion. UOP would host our NCAA volleyball championships the following year. Some of us remembered the grapefruits they had worn during warmups my freshman year, and we started getting up a head of steam to give them a whoopin. Our white jerseys were going to be filthy by the time we finished, for our floor defense was amazing.

UOP was still very, very good, and ranked higher than we were, but without their All-American middle, they were not as dominant. Our hitters disrupted their timing on the block, and Krush had a terrific serving game. Jan set me vertical sets so I could crush the ball either right or left, and we were level after two sets. As the match wore on, they started to tire, and we started to smell fear. Kisi got a read on their outside hitter's bread-and-butter shot and started digging her every time.

After four sets, we were the winners.

None of us felt tired. None of us wanted to shower or anything. We wanted to get out of Stockton and get home to celebrate. We all knew this was our breakthrough match. We had arrived on the national scene, and now we belonged in the conversation for volleyball's NCAA first national championships, complete with a Final Four championship round, just like the men's basketball tournament.

We took a different way back, and Fred found a Straw

Hat pizza parlor that was totally empty. He was stoked and ordered himself and Don a beer. Watching our coaches celebrate at the end of the picnic table made our party spirits even higher. Pizza was not on our training table regimen, but who cared? We ate about a pizza each, baskets of bread sticks, and after an hour of singing, celebrating, and joking around with our Burger King crowns, Jan pointed out that she had an economics test in the morning. We got back into the van.

Don outstripped us, while Fred drove on the windy roads, talking over every play with Jan, who was shotgun, and me, who was sitting behind him. It was amazing how he remembered every serve, every good play, every mistake. If I'd had a memory like that, I'd be a doctor.

Fred had been admitted to medical school but didn't want to be a doctor like his psychiatrist dad. He loved coaching. The windy road was making a few of the girls queasy in the back row seats, so Fred slowed down. It was a good move, for a mile or so later, we saw the flashing lights of a CHP cruiser. Fred pulled over.

We all sat up, our uniforms grimy from the dirty old UOP floor, and pulled out a few books to read in the dark. The cop asked Fred for his license, took a look at it, then a look at us. "Where are you going?" he asked.

Jan spoke up, as Fred wisely kept his mouth shut. "Officer, we just finished a volleyball match and are driving back to campus." Nothing about Stanford was said.

"Sir, you'll have to get out of the van. I can smell beer on you. Please step in front of the van and leave your lights on."

Fred crawled out of the front seat, jumped down in a very athletic move, and walked in front of the van wearing his Burger King crown.

As if viewing a drive-in movie, we leaned forward in our seats and tried to hear what the cop was saying, while we watched Fred in the headlights.

Just as we did in the gym during warmups, Fred was walking the line. Not a wobble. Then he stood on one foot, touched his nose with each hand. Not a wobble. He switched feet, and did another balance drill he made us do in every practice warmup. Leaning forward, he kept his weight on one foot, touched the ground with his fingertips as his other leg stretched back. Not a wobble. Standing up straight again, he looked at the cop for instructions.

In the days before breathalyzers, this was the common field sobriety test. Did we do these moves every day in practice for volleyball or for a moment like this? If we hadn't been in such serious trouble, I would have laughed out loud. Was our glorious victory about to become a DUI suspension?

The cop walked back to the van, saying, "I think you're fine but just tired after your big win. Is anyone here twenty-one?"

Jan raised her hand.

"Okay, you drive."

Jan moved over to the driver's seat, and Fred slid into shotgun. The cop handed his license across Jan, who held onto it for a moment, trying to get Fred to laugh. He was silent. She started the car, and off we drove, under the speed limit. The CHP car followed us until we hit 101, then pulled a U-turn to cruise by Casa de Fruita again.

Nobody said a word until we were about two miles away from campus, heading down Embarcadero Drive. "Guys, guys!" called out Kisi. "Turn left here. I gotta pee. I can't wait."

Jan stopped at the Newell Avenue stoplight, and before she could turn, Kisi was out of the van. She hopped over a two-foot brick fence, squatted down, and peed. This started a laugh attack that lasted all the way back to the Maples Parking lot.

"I had to go when Fred got pulled over but I didn't think it would be a good idea."

Even Fred was laughing now, and asked us, "Should we tell Don?"

We all shook our heads. To this day, I don't know if Don knows why we crack up when we talk about Casa de Fruita. But every warmup after that, as I stood on one leg and touched my nose, I remembered Fred in the headlights, giving the most clutch performance of his entire volleyball career.

Kairos

When Kisi, Krush, Grits, and Stuey got into Kairos for the fall of 1981, the house became the volleyball hangout. Despite the foyer's smell of musty beer, the open kitchen and two sundecks kept us full and happy. The frequent visits of Eric Heiden, the 1980 Lake Placid Olympic Winter Games star, added to our joy. He had won the gold in all five speed-skating events, including sprint and distance, while setting four Olympic records and one world record. As a premedical transfer student to Stanford, he didn't know anyone and was more interested in getting into medical school than girls at the time.

We had a biology teaching assistant in our house named Steve, who was friends with Eric. One day I happened to be sitting on the sofa in the lounge, near the ping-pong table, reading. As a junior and the house food manager, I had a single room, so when I became lonely, I trudged downstairs to feel like I was part of something. We had a home match that night, so my afternoon was free from practice. When Steve walked in with Eric, I thought I recognized him but I couldn't place him. So many Stanford students were famous or had famous families, that it wasn't a big deal anymore.

Steve introduced me as one of the volleyball players in the house, and Eric nodded. They played some ping-pong, and after that, Eric stopped by once or twice a week to play. He became a fixture in the lounge on some late afternoons, smacking the ball expertly. Olympians often played ping-pong to pass the time and burn off steam, I learned. Eric wasn't done competing either. He told me he transferred to Stanford because of the opportunity to cycle in the hills. Apparently, speed skating and cycling are complementary sports, and he now competed in road races.

"Do you cycle at all, J.J?" he asked when I first met him.

I told him about my black Sears three-speed, and he laughed. Later I learned he had graduated from both Stanford and medical school. He proved it was possible to compete and succeed in sports and in the pre-med curriculum, if one had gold medal level focus.

We were approaching midterm week, and for once I wasn't panicked. I only had one actual test, a German grammar exam. My other classes just had take-home papers and in-class essays. I was reading every chance I had and even took a few notes about what I read. For some reason, I was afraid to write in the books I bought, which were already marked-up used books. When I entered the English building next to the church, I had no fear or anxiety. Instead, I was excited to hear what the professor thought and what my classmates would say. Gone were the lecture halls of 750 students and the HumBio classes of one hundred; now my largest class had thirty students, and my creative writing seminar had only eight. Teachers knew my name, and I laughed at least once during every lecture. Fuzzy studies were so fun and interesting that I felt guilty for not suffering.

I found I wrote better with a deadline, though I wish I could say I started my papers well in advance and revised my drafts before I turned them in. Actually, I wrote them all the night before, inspired by the impending doom of the deadline and exhilarated by how my mind seemed to write automatically under pressure. Shocked, I received some A-minuses on my first papers, and I thought I might actually show my family my grades over the holiday. But the sitting and reading for hours was taking a toll on my physical conditioning. I wasn't jumping as high or staying as strong at the end of a match. All the reading made my eyes light-sensitive, so in some away gyms I had to blink to track the ball under the hanging can lights. That messed up my timing a bit, but I was still a productive hitter. It was the blocking— or rather, closing the block—that began to be affected.

Still, our team was playing very well as we navigated the tough weeks of midterms. We knew we were going to qualify for the NCAA championships, for the format had been changed from the four-day tournament to something similar to the men's basketball Final Four. They would take thirty-two teams, rank them, and place them in regional championships; the regional winners would play the semis and finals at UCLA's Pauley Pavilion.

We had beaten UCLA at home. We lost to them on the road, but had seen the wizard of Westwood, John Wooden, in the stands. Coach Fred knew him a bit from his own UCLA days, and Coach Wooden was a volleyball fan.

We walked by his pyramid of excellence, which was stenciled on the hallway wall, and stepped onto that holy hardwood. This was a religious experience for me, a basketball
junkie, and I couldn't wait to leave a sweat streak on the
floor. We just had to figure out how to get back there in December.

The Women of Troy

In the meantime, USC was locked and loaded, even without the 1980 player of the year Paula Weishoff. Weishoff had
dislocated my thumb with one of her incredible spikes in a
pre-season tournament, then left to join our Olympic team
with the 1984 games in sight. She was the best athlete I'd
ever seen – with the same quick-twitch muscle group, awesome vertical leap, and fast armswing I was told I possessed.
We even shared the same middle name: Jo. But Paula was
6' 1", and would become a star for three Olympic games. I
loved playing against her, loved blocking her and loved
knowing I belonged on the court with the best, even though
I had to wear a plastic brace to keep my thumb in its socket
the rest of the year. I learned respecting our opponents
didn't mean being intimidated by them; it meant knowing
we had to bring our "A" game. Coach Fred always warned
us about playing at the level of our opponents. He meant
playing down, but I reinterpreted this maxim when we had
USC in our sights. To beat them, we'd have to play up. When
playing the Trojans, I realized that I played my best when
we played the best teams. I also knew why Coach Erbe
never had a rebuilding year. So many players wanted to be
a woman of Troy that he simply picked the best and re-
loaded. When I felt frustrated about never being allowed to

set again, I reminded myself I'd be on the bench at USC. At Stanford, I had a chance to play. I had coaches who preached constant improvement, and I believed them.

We ended with a solid record, received a top-twelve seed to the tournament, but had an additional hill to conquer on the way to the first women's NCAA national championships. That November, we learned most of the other teams were allowed to take their finals in January, which afforded them extra study time during December and no looming deadlines during the championship tournament. Not so for us. We were students first, and Stanford student athletes were given no special treatment. Jan had huge and complicated macro- and micro- economics finals to conquer. Krush and Grits were in the HumBio core and had a massive amount of information to memorize. I had take-home essays I would have twenty-four hours to complete. But much of those twenty-four hours needed to be spent in practice, or in the training room nursing a sore back, icing my thumb and my toe and my ankle, then finishing the reading. I really had about two hours for each test. First draft = final draft. We had a lot on our minds, but most of us just dealt with the workload. Being mentally tired was a familiar burden.

Even with time management, no time was left for anything besides reading, eating, sleeping, and volleyball. I did go to one Thursday night frat party. During the second or third pogo song, I realized my legs were exhausted. Our practice hadn't been that hard, but we had another round of play-offs starting Saturday, so I sat down for a while. I didn't know how my superb conditioning had degraded during the academic term, but I knew it was too late to get it back. If I rested and saved my legs for practice and playing, I should make it through. We know now that cross-training, stretching, and rest days are necessary to balance the demands of a physically brutal sport like volleyball. But "rest" was not listed in the dictionary of a Stanford student.

We slogged through our tests, papers, big exams, and little take-homes until we faced UCLA across the net in the regional final match. The winner would be at UCLA the next weekend, vying for the first real NCAA championship trophy. The loser would be going home and staying home. Either way, we had finals to take, and the Bruins had the option to wait. There was no sense whining about it: we had work to complete before we left.

Much of the results of a volleyball match between two highly skilled and motivated teams occurs not on the court but between the ears. Fred's game plans were epic, perhaps too detailed for December. I studied shot charts and defensive shifts and servers' tendencies and hitters' favorite shots, but my mind was far from photographic. We had a few videos of our opponents, and we sat in a small viewing room and tried to see what the coaches saw. Looking at the plays from the view of the stands, I couldn't translate everything I was supposed to execute, couldn't visualize what I'd see during game time. Maybe something useful would come from the time spent in the film room.

UCLA's Court

The rituals of volleyball warfare started with my hair. I untangled my curls, slanted my part slightly off-center, and began to French-braid a pigtail. I embedded red-and-white ribbons into the three strands as I twisted and flipped them over and around, smoothing the ribbon so it lay flat on my carefully portioned hair. I attached the two pigtails together at the bottom with another hair band, which had a bow tied in double knots; my braids wouldn't budge the whole match, for my mom had taught me well.

I heard pain in her voice on the phone before the match. I knew if I made a mistake, I would think of Mom's tenacity and toughen up. I was so excited I could hardly breathe. We were going to be on TV!

I tried to conquer my queasiness. I could tell if I was going to barf based on how well I could concentrate on my music. I used ritual lip-syncing as a relaxation tool. *Biofeedback is the thing for me*, I sang to the tune of "Green Acres." I chanted to the rhythm of "We Will Rock You": *Stanford got poise, make a big noise / playing in the gym, gonna be All American babe / We'll spike ones in their face / hit service ace / Kick UCLA all over the place.* Teammates joined me in the locker room. I hummed "Hands Across the Net" as I put on my socks and missed Paula. She would make me laugh, but why sing "Bench City" her senior year? She had left the team to focus on school, leaving the back-up setter duties to DD.

Someone cranked up a mix tape with the Go-Gos, Talking Heads, Blondie, and The Pretenders as we dressed and danced. We wore my favorite uniform: white Adidas short-sleeved shirts with red stripes down the sleeves, and red Adidas shorts. I smacked a volleyball between my hands as I waited for my Stanford volleyball teammates to finish getting dressed before we played in the first Women's NCAA Volleyball regional final.

Then it was showtime, and basketball coaching legend John Wooden was in the stands. He waved to our coach Fred. I saw the beautiful and glamorous UCLA players, with their long, bleached hair, waxed legs, mani-pedis, and memberships at private beach clubs. I used to be jealous of their look, but now I wasted no energy on something that wouldn't help me win this match. Sure, they delayed their finals. Yes, they looked like models in their uniforms. All of us were hard-working women who wanted to win. We just wanted it more, I kept telling myself.

First, I had to scout this court. I skipped and karaoke twisted on the floor, testing its surface. Would I slide when I dived after balls? Would I stick and jam my wrist and peel skin off the heel of my hand as I saved another ball from hitting the floor? The court had not been freshly varnished, thank God, as aldehydes gave me headaches. It wasn't end-of-season slippery either, which meant a diving sweat mark made while sprawling on the court wouldn't automatically make us lose our footing during a long rally. I dove after an imaginary ball, and my hand slid easily along the sideline. The lines weren't too sticky either. They were painted, not taped on.

I looked up at the hanging can lights, at the packed stands, and took a moment to absorb the noise. These people were here to watch women battle. We had fought for access, attention, and recognition. We were going to scream our joy and sorrow after every point. Did they have any idea how we burned inside for this; how brutal our competitive instincts were? Or did they think we were invading the world of men? Or did they simply watch and wait for a glimpse of T&A slipping out from underwear not designed for athletes? I showed off my handstand, let the blood run into my head, then cartwheeled on the sideline and finished like gymnast Nadia Comăneci. It was my ritual.

Our warmup of stretching, balance, and core work was as rhythmic as the music on the Bruins' sound system started.

When Foreigner's song "Hot Blooded" came on, we smiled and laughed and started playing pepper—a one-on-one game with a teammate that allowed us to bump, set, and spike the ball at each other without using the net. Boom-Boom and I kept the ball alive for most of that section of the warmup. She was intimidating with her six-feet of long legs and arms, her shoulders as broad as a linebacker's, her scowl that could scare a referee into doubting his call. She was the best server in college volleyball, and serving could be the difference in the game.

In what seemed like ten minutes, we had won two games, and the Bruins had won two games. The stands were buzzing: nobody thought we could take any games from UCLA, yet here we were, in the huddle drinking Gatorade and waiting for Coach Fred to tell us the lineup for the fifth and deciding game. There was nothing left inside my stomach except bile. The familiar churning began as the Gatorade descended down my esophagus and I tried to force the acidic juice to stay down while I let out the *burrrrp*. Everybody laughed, and a bit of tension lifted.

We had forced UCLA to make errors, and I hoped they would make more under the pressure of high expectations. We had nothing to lose going into game five. We'd already overperformed. And we could win.

All match long, the coaches had been playing chess, trying to line up their better hitters against the weaker blockers on the other side. Fred never started me in the front row, as our other middle blocker was 6' 2". Also, he often substituted me out of the back row so Kisi could play spectacular defense. By the fifth game, I needed this rest. I hoped I would get to serve before Kisi came in, but Fred made a switch. I started in middle front. This meant Boom-Boom would start in right front and be our first server when we sided out and got the ball. I liked the game plan. I would play three rotations in the front row, be subbed out in the back row where Kisi would take over for three rotations, and together we'd keep a lot of energy in our position.

Jan was next to me, as we'd had a great deal of success blocking. Now we were matched against their best hitter. UCLA's setter shot the ball quickly to the outside red-and-white antenna, and Jan watched her hitter, set her feet in front of her angle of approach, jumped after the hitter, and put her left hand in front of the ball, taking away the line shot with her right hand. I exploded to the right, planted my right foot next to Jan's and closed the block. My left hand was a little late to stuff block the hit, but I was strong enough to deflect the ball to our defense. I was a little slower in game five, but I still kept the ball in play. I liked our matchup.

I landed, turned, and looked back into our side of the court, where I saw Tina make a perfect dig just right of the center of the court. I took three choreographed steps to get off the net, then watched the ball head toward Krush's waiting hands and timed my jump to lift before she touched the ball. Off the net in three steps, back on and up in a three step-close. I was waltzing on the Bruins' Blue Danube. I was in the air, with my arm cocked and ready, and checked the block and the backcourt defense in the microsecond before Krush set the ball.

Deep angle was open, and I swung as she released the ball. The other middle blocker jumped with me, for my timing had forced her to commit to block my hit. Krush knew this, knew that when I was early, she could shoot the ball past me to our outside hitter, Boom-Boom, who was unstoppable when she faced only one blocker. She converted the point, and I high-fived Krush and Boom for their connection. In the box score, Boom-Boom would get a kill, Krush would get an assist, and I would get nothing. But I knew I'd done my job. I accepted that only once in every four or five times I jumped early in our offensive scheme would I get the chance to actually hit the ball.

That was my new role: I ran the fake.

My explosive jump, arm speed, and accurate shot selection meant I had a high hitting percentage even though I didn't get set often, and I helped our superstars succeed as well. UCLA had a hard time stopping us and we scored many points because our timing was so good. I jumped, loaded, and exploded before the blocker had reached her full jump. Boom-Boom jumped, hung, hit high and hard after the blocker was coming down. From the bench, I saw Kisi and our defenders were exhausted, and I cheered their great efforts.

"C'mon!" Kisi yelled after every point, pumping up the team with her energy.

We were dragging. They were dragging. It was a battle royale, with the score now ten-ten when I substituted back in the front row. Krush was my setter. Their hitter hit a medium-speed shot, which my block channeled to the defense. Kisi's dig was perfect again. I waltzed away, then back to the net, my arm cocked and ready, and to my surprise, Krush fed me the ball.

At the peak of the set was a huge full moon suspended in motionless time. I orbited out of my body, saw my arm swing through the ball, forcing waves and tides to change, parting the sea to reveal the short angle where the defender was back on her heels, a little too deep in the court. My wrist snapped over the top of the ball before the blocker's hands were over the top of the net. The sweat from my arm drenched Krush's face as she ducked to avoid it. The ball bounced in front of the defender, clocked her in the chin, and knocked her backward. As I landed, I felt guilty for the sweat and for the pummeled player. But our bench erupted, screaming "six-pack" and slapping hands.

Wham bam thank you ma'am, I thought, high-fiving Boom-Boom and Krush in the air.

Now that I'd had a momentum-stealing kill, I expected the set, but the next connection was not as solid. I was late, the set was leading me away from the angle of my approach, and I knew I couldn't swing hard. I did the best I could with the set I had and carefully targeted my off-speed shot toward the backcourt, where the setter had to play defense. I flung the ball to that area, landed awkwardly, felt a sharp dagger in my lower back, and resumed my defensive ready position. My "rally ball" kept us alive.

My hands were above my head, ready to block the quick middle set or ready to pull me to the outside. I felt tingling down my right hip, and the pain brought me back inside my brain. I exited the "zone" top athletes describe when we are mindless beings operating on animal instinct. I, the adrenaline junkie, didn't have any endorphins left to block this new pain.

We rallied on, losing the point after a Tina mis-hit. I had sweated through my shirt, which was now see-through. Since I was flat-chested, nobody noticed. Every time I hit the ball, my sweat dowsed Krush. She couldn't always wipe her hands on her shorts between plays, so when her next set was ruled a double-hit, it made sense.

But that missed set was truly a subjective call.

She protested to the referee, who waved her away. It was

eleven-eleven. She turned and looked at me, and I knew she was going to yell, "Fuuuuuuck," so I yelled "Craaaap" to prevent the referee from hearing her swear and giving her a red card. Our noses nearly touched, and we screeched until we were out of breath. All six players huddled for a second, and we inhaled collective belief, exhaled to begin again.

We rallied on, winning a point, then losing a point after another missed hit. I was running back and forth across the net to close the block on defense, transitioning on offense to jump, then swung fast. But the set went past me, and I was back on defense. I stuff blocked their middle hitter, but their setter covered the block, sending the ball back over the net. Jan dove after their mis-hit, popping up the ball with her fist. Krush set Tina, who wasn't quite ready but managed to make a great shot. UCLA scrambled, then gave us a lollipop over the net. I got excited, seeing a hole in their defense. I was up early, with my arm ready, but the ball was set past me again, and the rage I felt matched the bayonet in my back.

If I could just get a chance to hit the ball, I was going to kill it. It was twelve-all, and if we won the point, I would be substituted out of the game and wouldn't be on the floor for the end of the match.

I screamed, "I'm up!" but the set I got was not the set I wanted.

All the frustration of my hard work without reward made me mindless. I swung as hard as I could, with no thought of the block or the defense or where to take my shot. None of my teammates knew how this would end. But I knew the rally would be over after I got my palm on that ball. I was hitting a "one and done."

I saw my hit touch the tips of the blocker's fingers, a tool off the block, but the linesman didn't call the touch. The down referee didn't call it. My coaches were yelling at the refs, but they were signaling for UCLA to serve again. They were ahead thirteen-twelve, and quick served so that we weren't ready and made an error. They served for the match at fourteen-twelve, and the rally was short. They won the match on another hitting error.

I ran the fake.

To have the match riding on my shoulders, to have the opportunity to make the play as an undersized five-foot-nine middle blocker with an oversized work ethic: this was a rare chance at glory that I craved and didn't get. Every time I jumped, I yelled, "Set me!" I wanted to destroy that fucking ball, and I played my designated role to the best of my ability. But we lost, and I didn't get the chance for that golden spike.

After battling for almost four hours, we were not going to the Final Four. UCLA was favored to win the national championship. Don was ranting about the referees; they were unfair at the end, he claimed, as if they expected UCLA to win and helped them by calling Krush's set a double hit and my hit off the block an error.

Coach Fred's head was curled over his ever-present yellow legal notepad, undoubtedly taking notes for next year. Nerding out probably hid his tears. He rarely yelled at refs, but he screamed at them that night. Everyone was frustrated. I never liked losing, but knew there were gradations in a loss. Losing because of our own mistakes sucked; losing due to an opponent's superior play was tough, but digestible. The worst thing? Losing due to a referee's bad or missed call. Sure, we should have shaken off two bad calls in a row, but everything happened so fast we were left in shock as the Bruins celebrated.

I took stock: my skin was salt-crusty and dry. My knee-pads were stench-stiff with solidified sweat. My back was sending pins and needles down my hips and sciatic nerves. As I entered the locker room, the others were furious. But I loved playing in this tight match. I loved performing on this stage. We gave them everything they could handle, and we barely lost. Next time, we'd win. I just knew it.

I saw a million little hairs sticking out of my braids in the mirror and I smiled at myself: I was so good at being a dork. But I couldn't ignore the slow realization that I'd lost my cool, the growing recognition that I didn't use my head at a crucial time in the match. I could have played it safe with a rally ball, but instead I went for the kill. Coming down from competition's high, I couldn't help wondering: was I fearless or was I mindless? Either way, the box score would read "error" on my last hitting attempt.

Like Coach Fred, I was a volleyball nerd going into analytic mode. I thought we'd be back the next year. I saw chinks in their armor. They were not as cohesive as we were; they had a lot of stars, and we had each other. Our returning players would be mentally tough, and I would be one of the senior leaders.

I took off my shirt in the locker room and wrung it out over the shower drain. My adrenaline depleted, I noticed the tingling from my right hip was now throbbing and continued down my leg. This was more than sciatica, as the pain shot down both legs. I took a cold shower after the postgame meeting, and my muscles went into spasm. I asked for an ice pack. I couldn't tell the difference between the internal fire of a compressed disk and the external cold: how could both burn my skin?

Patty was very concerned. "J.J., I know your pain toler-ance. This isn't good."

I nodded and let her shove the ice pack down the back of my sweatpants. I couldn't get comfortable on my stom-ach, so I paced the locker room, as my teammates dressed, and held up the ice pack with alternating hands. Once again, I had ended the season with an injury.

CHAPTER 12
Swimming in Winter

Volleyball season was over, and I had to face some hard truths. Studying for finals was going to be difficult if I couldn't sit down, although I could stand and type my papers just like Hemingway did. Even though I still dreamed of healing my mother, I needed to accept that I wouldn't be going to medical school. My volleyball obsession had allowed me to avoid this hard reality.

Losing a match is hard; losing the opportunity to cure my mother's mysterious disease by underperforming in Stanford's premed curriculum was like clinging to the crumbling ledge on El Capitan, unable to climb up or down, barely able to think. I was not sure how I was going to hang on, but I didn't have time for a crisis. I leaned against the wall and hoped I would get admitted to creative writing so I could finish in the five quarters I had left before my full scholarship ended.

The phone was going to be available for me to call my mom when Kisi was done, and I had to decide what I was going to say to her about the match. She had gone to every high school game and many of my college matches. While she couldn't be at this game, I could imagine her difficult day; her pain was so different from my backache, caused by doing something I love. Until I was 20 and in pain myself, I don't think I truly empathized with her struggles. I avoided the old theodicy question: if He were omnipotent, why did

God let bad things happen to good people?

Whenever I heard my mother's voice, I knew so much about her current state of mind. I knew if she was in pain, feeling depressed, tired, angry at her bad luck, and bitter that she was stuck at home without a car to drive around, or stuck in the body that had betrayed her. Or if she was feeling okay, which was rare for her, she was full of questions and interest and wisdom. Perhaps she'd display her incredible sense of humor and timing, perhaps she'd need a pick-up, kind words, support, and encouragement. Since the age of ten, I'd measured my mom's voice to know how her pain was treating her and how to meet her needs.

After our UCLA loss, I knew I would tell her about the game. I would admit my frustrations, and wait to see how she responded. I hoped I could also tell her about my academic difficulties, something I'd withheld from her since I began college. My parents still hadn't asked to see a report card, for they assumed my perfectionism, my planning, and my achievements during my first eighteen years were helping me in college. They chose to let me succeed on my own terms.

The problem was I wasn't succeeding; I was failing at my dream of being an Olympian and a doctor. Like my mom's body, my body had not been up to the brutal beating I gave it every day in volleyball practice. The difference was I abused my body on purpose; my mom's autoimmune disease attacked hers, with little warning or mercy. When we talked, I'd know if I could tell her what really happened last summer at the Stanford Hospital, or if that needed to remain a secret. I knew how to carry my own burdens, but it would be nice if I could share the real reason I lost my drive in my premed studies. Who would want to be a colleague with the male chauvinist pigs who ran the old boy network in a hospital? What female doctor with a pinch of self-respect would want to be told by another doctor to make the coffee during grand rounds? And, what if I couldn't avoid sexual assault in the on-call room? Watching a slim, female resident wrestle out of the grasp of a male attending doctor had opened my eyes to the true power dynamic in the medical world: getting an MD didn't end misogyny; in fact, that status could make a woman a target.

When it was my turn to talk, I dialed home on the rotary phone in UCLA's locker room.

Mom picked up. "Jenyth Jo, how did it go?"

"We lost in five, Mom."

"I know. I heard the match on the radio. Was your last hit a touch? I had a feeling it was. How's your head? Are you dizzy tonight?" These were always her first questions, for she couldn't forget waking me up every hour to make sure I could regain consciousness after my first two childhood concussions. She was by my side after the third concussion, the serious headbanger at sixteen that produced a week-long coma and left my memory a mess. She believed I was concussed after my bike wreck too, but I didn't go to the doctor then.

"No, Mom, I didn't hit my head. I did dive and pick up a few balls though. I wish you could have been there to see us play. We battled and really scared them, and Mom, we can beat them next year. I know we can."

"How is your ankle? How is your back?" she continued her interrogation.

"My ankle is sore, and my back is killing me. No pain, no gain. I have an ice-pack on right now."

Mom sounded pretty good, like she could handle a lot.

"How do you think you played? Dad wants to know."

I looked around to see if any teammates were listening to me, but most had left the locker room. "I left it all on the court, but I didn't get as many sets as I wanted. My head started pounding in the fourth game, but I didn't feel much in the fifth. It was sooo exciting. We were sooo close, Mom. I've never had this much fun playing. It was a scene! So many people in the stands, and the oohs and aahs! I'm kinda happy, even though we lost. We beat ourselves with our hitting errors, Mom. They weren't better than us: points were won and lost on our side of the net. And everyone is talking about our defense. We were scrappy. We kept so many balls alive that those UCLA sweat-wipe boys were always busy. And UCLA's cheerleaders were there! Did you ever think we'd see that?"

"What did Fred and Don say?" I heard the disrespect in my mom's voice. She would forever claim the coaches had changed my playing position and ruined my chance at making the Olympic team.

"They were really upset at the two calls the refs made at the end, but in the locker room they were high-fiving us and telling us we did a great job."

"Are you going to talk to them about being the starting setter next year? Jan will be graduating, and it's your turn."

I knew there was no point asking the coaches to let me play my favorite position, but I chose to keep my mom's hopes alive. "Yep. As soon as I'm done with finals, I'm going to meet with them. And Mom, I don't think I'm going to be a doctor." I blurted it out without thinking, and sucked in some air, waiting for her response.

"Well, Jenyth Jo, you don't have to decide anything right now. You're always planning so far in the future. Settle down and study. Studying all night doesn't work. You know that, right? Please promise me you'll sleep this week. You need to rest your brain."

"Mom, I have so much to relearn. Biochem is really hard. But I'll get some sleep. Love you."

"I can't wait to see you next week. The refrigerator is full. Let me do your dirty laundry. Love you. Dad too." Mom hung up, and I sighed.

If she knew what the next week was going to be like, she'd say I was crazy, especially now that I was not going to be a doctor. I placed the phone's handle back in the cradle and shuffled back to the bench, where my travel bag lay. The jersey was still wet and filthy, with horizontal dirt lines that matched my rib cage. I couldn't find an extra plastic bag for my jersey and my knee pads, so I rolled them up and set them at the bottom of my bag. I picked up one knee pad, and a chunk of talcum powder and skin fell out from the inside, just below a bloodstain. I should probably buy a new pair for spring season, but these two stink bombs would forever be my favorites.

Execution

The protocol after a back injury was simple: daily therapy in the training room. I was familiar with the heat packs pulled out from the steel hydrocollator, the ice bags, and the electronic stimulation machine with an ice pack on top of it, but the intense pressure in my lower back and the zaps going down both legs were beyond anything I had experienced before. I could tell the staff was concerned, for I never had the relief of heat, only inflammation-reducing ice. In the early 1980s, we learned about nuclear magnetic resonance in physical chemistry, as our professors were really excited about using it for imaging. This morphed into magnetic resonance imaging, or MRI, which became available after 1986. I didn't have the benefit of that. The best X-ray available in 1981 revealed a bulging disk, which was probably pinching my spinal cord and causing nerve pain to radiate down my legs. The Stanford sports trainers were very careful, as they feared making the injury worse, so they sent me to a back specialist at my favorite place: Stanford Hospital.

It's hard to limp when both your hamstrings have electrical currents pulsing through them, but I favored my right foot with the broken ankle (freshman year) and broken toe (sophomore). My lower back hurt when I stood; when I tried to sit (couldn't); when I lay down on my bed on either side, with a pillow propped between my legs. Some positions hurt more than others. I yearned to be still, comfortably in one place, but I had to keep shifting positions. Maybe this doctor had a quick fix that would take the pain away before my last final exam.

I limped into the dull brown entrance of the hospital, checked in at the brightly lit information desk, and followed the red signs to the spinal clinic. Inside some avocado green therapy rooms, I saw patients strapped to machines, on black gravity boards, suspended upside down for traction, and wondered what was in store for me. I remembered Brody Lockhart, a member of the men's gymnastics team, who had started Stanford with me. He had a life-threatening neck/spinal cord injury at the beginning of our freshman year and probably had been strapped to one of these contraptions. I hadn't seen him since then and wondered if he had been able to continue school since he couldn't compete and was severely paralyzed. What would I do without my scholarship? I was trying not to get anxious, but pain made that unavoidable.

Keep calm, I told myself. I knew traction might help decompress my spine but wasn't so sure about the other options. *Stay calm.*

At the door of the clinic, an X-ray tech greeted me and told me to sit down in a blue wheelchair. "This is our procedure for new patients," he explained, as he wheeled me down a blazing white hallway smelling of isopropyl alcohol. I wondered if he saw my nauseated face, for he grabbed a towel and put it on my lap, saying, "You're going to see our top doc, so don't worry about a thing."

The wheelchair's donut padding, which had a hole for my tailbone to sink into, helped relieve the pressure on my S-1 joint. This was new. And encouraging. I waited in the gray and stainless examination room, curling and uncurling my toes to keep my circulation going. Instruments of torture hung from the ceiling, and my imagination started ramping up when a white-coated, gray-haired man with those half-glasses smart people liked to wear walked in. I sighed, recognizing the type from my summer internship at the hospital: older, white, chauvinistic male doc who never makes eye contact, whose arrogance supersedes any personal warmth or empathy.

He read some reports out loud to me, as if I were a child and not a Stanford student, peering over his half-rims to look once toward my left shoulder. He never checked my range of motion or asked me any specific questions about what made my pain better or worse. He put my file down on the counter and pulled an old-fashioned rubber reflex hammer out of his white-coat pocket. He tapped each knee, and my legs jumped in the usual way, proving my reflexes were intact. Then he proclaimed, "Miss Gearhart, you are going to need back surgery. The question is which one."

I jolted from this shock. "What do you mean? Can't I keep doing physical therapy?" I begged.

Doc pointed at the X-ray on the light board. "You're going to need to have your L5 and S1 joints fused or you're going to need a partial resection of your disk, which is probably bulging. Either way, there are many risks involved. I don't really know what it's going to be like until I go in, and I may go in through your stomach instead of your back. Then I'll decide what the best course will be. You'll have to sign release papers verifying you are willing to have invasive back surgery. I'm the only doctor in the country who knows how to do this surgery, and you're lucky I had room in my schedule to see you today. Do you understand the risks involved?"

"Sort of, but which procedure will get me back onto the volleyball court the soonest?"

"You're not going to be playing volleyball anymore."

No more volleyball? I couldn't believe it. I tried to talk, but my throat choked any noise I could make. My whole body flooded with a fever, an anger that after all I've been through, this guy was telling me I wouldn't have a senior season. I knew my face was red—blushing had given away my poker face many times. I tried to talk again, but the doc droned on.

"Let's see. Today's Wednesday. I can get you into surgery Friday. You'll be done with finals, right? Then you'll need to rest for a month. Are you ready to schedule? I can do you first thing in the morning. You'll have to be here at 5:00 a.m. for pre-op," he said, shoving the clipboard of release forms toward me.

A different emotion pushed the shock out of my system. Now I was very suspicious. *What's the rush?* He had made up his mind about my spine without really examining me. But I hadn't made up my mind. I felt like I was hearing the sales pitch for a once-in-a-lifetime opportunity, but this was not an opportunity I wanted. I needed time to think; this was a huge deal. I couldn't let this guy touch my back until I had more information. Then I had a better idea. "Doctor, I'll need to discuss this with my mom."

"You're twenty. You can make this decision as the responsible adult."

Not over my mom's dead body, I thought.

"The Friday appointment might be taken later today," he declared. He looked me in the eye, and I remembered Dr. Zimbardo hypnotizing me on stage my freshman year, making me wave a white flag.

Since I had been involved in experiments by the Psychology Department in which they were not actually studying what they told you they were studying, I was able to meet his stare with the defiance of a skeptic. "I'll definitely need to discuss this with my mom," I concluded, gathering up my bag.

He shrugged his shoulders, and I shuffled out of the examination room, leaving the wheelchair behind. *No way is that hack going to touch my back*, I thought, as I found the exit door and gimped outside to the campus bus. Just the thought of needing my mom to rescue me inspired me to rescue myself. I could say no to a male power figure.

By the time I left for home that weekend, I could hardly walk for the pain. I didn't have the time to get treatment at the training room, but I did well on all my tests. When I turned in an English exam, the department secretary had a letter for me. She smiled as she handed it to me, for inside was my acceptance letter from the Creative Writing Department. I'd gone from hard science to psychology to a subject about as fuzzy as a study could get. But I realized the connection where others did not: these courses were all about creating combinations until the art emerged from the science. Writing about humans was a deep dive into the psychobiology of love and caring, human connections and conflicts. I looked forward to learning more about the craft of writing so my hyper-analytical brain could relax and let my imagination spin some stories. I vowed to stop turning in first drafts, to learn to revise and prune and plump. And if that didn't work, I'd just make up a stunt or two, watch how it played in real life, and write it.

Not a Fiction

"There's no hurry," my mom said, for the thousandth time in my life during Christmas break.

The second-opinion doctor disagreed with the Stanford doc about the best treatment for my back, and Mom wanted to take the least invasive action. "You have a chance to heal, so why not wait? Stanford just wants their doctor to operate on your back because they feel guilty. They didn't take care of you during the volleyball season. I'll make sure they honor your scholarship next year. Now tell me about your period. We'll need to take care of that right away."

Over the course of a few months, my menses had become completely irregular, probably from the eight-pound weight gain over the summer before my sophomore year, then the trailer housing diet of Top Ramen and broccoli over the summer before my junior year. I had consciously become a vegetarian: why would I eat the animals I loved?

A quick trip to the obstetrician revealed severe anemia and an admonition to start eating at least fish and chicken again. I didn't see a connection between protein, menses, and weight, but we know a lot more about balancing diets for vegetarians and athletes now. The kind doc put me on birth control pills and said to double up during my period.

When I told my mom about this, she shrugged her shoulders and said, "How about cast-iron chicken-fried steak for dinner? That will help your anemia. I wish I could get you to eat chicken livers. Organ meats might help."

"Gross, Mom. Let's stick to chicken-fried steak."

The night before we returned to campus in January of 1982, I sat in my bedroom, remembering the last time Mom had gone to bat for me to make sure Stanford honored the coach's promise to raise my eighty percent scholarship to a hundred percent. Two years later, Mom only needed a phone call to confirm that I would keep my full ride, whether or not I could play my final season. If I wanted another chance at UCLA, I needed to be as strong as my mom.

Just getting out of bed was difficult for Mom now. If she could grab the combed cotton sheet (likely drenched with her night sweats) with her swollen right hand, she could sit up and get out of bed without waking my snoring dad. But benign positional vertigo would swoop the room over her head, as if she were on the tilt-a-whirl at the county fair. The first step of the day was the other measure of her physical status: hopefully she was able to pick up her feet, for "shuffling is what old people do," she once told me. Mom was forty-four.

By the time Mom had awakened my dad, made his breakfast and lunch, started the stew in the crockpot, cleaned the kitchen, put the sheets in the washer, packed him off in the Monte Carlo for his commute to McClellan AFB, and vacuumed the house, she was exhausted. Still, at 7:00 a.m., she took her two-mile daily walk, no matter how hard she had to struggle to complete it. Then, she walked to the family den, arranged a pillow on the couch, and collapsed on top of it. She sorted through her pile of library books, perhaps picking out one of my Chekhov plays or a Dickens novel. If she was really hurting, she'd pass on the Modern Library Classics and pick up a Harlequin Romance. Sometimes, she told me, she needed to look forward to a happy ending.

Every day was a battle for her. She probably had the chills by mid-day and was wrapped in the crocheted blanket my nasty great Aunt Mildred—who told me I was ugly in front of our entire family reunion—had made me. Was she looking up at the disco ball she installed for my sixteenth birthday party? Was she studying her carefully curated wall of honor: shelves of her bowling and softball trophies from the days in Alabama before she got sick; shelves of Dad's athletic and career awards, including a prized picture with the Air Force Base commander and a four-star general of the Army? Did she get up to dust Stan's shelf of baseball, basketball, and football trophies? Or was she looking at my rainbow of 4-H horse show ribbons, dog training plaques, public speaking trophies, and presidents' gavels? Did she ever wonder if I missed my animal world, or if I truly loved performing as a girl jock in the spotlight? After three seasons as a collegiate athlete, I was physically and mentally stronger and I could see the reality of her life: she was getting weaker and weaker.

I did love playing volleyball. I didn't love playing through pain. I did love playing for Mom. I didn't love the pain that plagued her. When she asked me how many sets I received in a game, I always said: "Not enough, Mom, not enough." I had a hunger for something that only volleyball could give me, but my career might be over before I could understand what that something was.

Olympic Pool

At campus in that winter of 1982, a winter covered in tulle fog and slanting rain, I began therapeutic swimming. The team doctors thought the right side of my back was overdeveloped from spiking, and swimming would equalize my left side, helping my spine stay in alignment. By the end of January, the tingling down my right leg had stopped, I could sit for more than fifteen minutes at a time, and the relentless ping-ponging of my mind had paused to a single focus: getting to the pool by 6:00 a.m. so I could be in the slow lane.

Now that I had an early morning swimming schedule, my whole mental state began to change. I looked forward to the daily DJ discussions, where the All-American swimmers argued over whether AC/DC, the Talking Heads, or Bruce Springsteen should be played over the new in-pool speakers. I silently rooted for the Talking Heads' "Life During Wartime," as the beat matched my slow kicks.

I met the swim coach, who helped me with my stroke and greeted me every day, telling my volleyball coaches I was working really hard in the pool. I'd always loved the feeling of diving into a pool, into a womb of comforting, caressing warmth, but I remembered to look at the number on the pool wall every time I dove in. I had knocked out my front teeth the summer before my senior year in high school, when I thought a three-foot marker said five feet in Carmichael Park's new pool. My senior portraits reveal yellowish fake teeth that didn't match the others. One tooth needed a root canal after I returned from Oregon.

In this brand-new pool, I felt no fear when I dove in, just the predictable pressure when, at about twenty meters into a fifty-meter pool, the wake waves from the lanes on either side of me created so much resistance I felt like I might drown—gulping water instead of air. Then the other wall came into sight. I caught my breath, then pushed off. Even though the swim coach said flip turns would decrease my time during my morning mile, I couldn't do them. The dizziness made me surface too soon, and I'd veer into the line divider, gasping for air. I kept the tedious push-turning.

As boring as I found swimming to be, the workout forced me inward. One of my housemates had recommended Alan Sillitoe's *The Loneliness of the Long Distance Runner* that winter, and I wondered what it would be like to run through physical and mental walls in order to become a marathoner. With no coach or teammates to encourage you, and no one to determine if your pain was helping or hurting you, your aloneness must pose another problem. As I swam laps, I was grateful I wasn't trying to make an Olympic swimming team, even though I was swimming in the lanes next to some future stars of the 1984 LA Olympic Games. I tried not to think of my own Olympic dreams, crushed between my L-5 and S-1 vertebrae. I missed the chatter of my volleyball teammates and feared I would never be part of the team again.

My morning mile gave me time to consider a lot of things I'd done. I felt shame for some of them, such as the infamous Milk Farm cow scene. I reviewed many events of my life and realized I was pretty immature. I had a list of achievements, but was I a good person? I liked to think I was a good friend and teammate, but I still didn't know anybody like me. At Stanford, which selected its student body based on diversity of geographic location and areas of excellence, my fellow students were fascinating in unique ways. Many were simply weird for weirdness's sake; others were gripped with social anxiety; and still more were flattened by internal and external pressures. I understood much of this, but wallowing in unhappiness wasn't something I was interested in. Still, I thought I should be more grateful that I was attending a school that accepted everybody on their own terms. We were a proud Nerd Nation.

As I jumped into the pool on January 31, 1982, my twenty-first birthday, I happily remembered I'd be talking with my mom in an hour or so. Then I remembered how much I missed being with my team. Singing in my head helped me balance my emotions. When the swimming got really tough, I dug deeper for better memories. I channeled the toughest coach I knew: my high school coach, Ted, who was an ex-Marine working as a probation officer by day and a volleyball coach at night. He had become a college coach at Weber State in Utah, after winning a community college championship at Mesa College in Arizona. Ted would say, "You're tougher than you think you are, so toughen up." I missed him but wished him well and wondered how his son "J.J." was doing, as I swam lap after lap.

Thinking back about the months in the pool and how my body changed from a bottom-heavy jumper's to a muscled v-backed swimmer's, I wonder why I didn't recognize how anxious I'd become at Stanford. I didn't realize my headaches were decreasing at the same time my thinking was clarifying. Yet, the moment I left the pool; rinsed off in the locker room; waved to my teammates, who had another hour of morning practice in the gym; and hopped on my bike to ride back to Kairos for breakfast, something switched on. Anxiety fueled my peddling, and my only relief was finding something completely nonacademic or nonathletic to look forward to.

Viennese Ball 2

In the midwinter of 1982, I'd begun writing a few columns for the *Stanford Daily*, when I was assigned club sports to cover. One particular oarsman, JP, and I became friends. When I told him about the annual Viennese Ball, he was interested. "I'll have my mom send my tux out," he told me, and I started to get a sense he had a different background from mine. "I hope it still fits. I haven't worn it since I was eighteen. Will we be able to get wine or champagne at the ball?" he wanted to know. "I'm not twenty-one yet."

"They don't card once you're inside the Roble Complex, and anyway, I'm twenty-one. I'll figure it out."

We walked the half mile to Roble in our formal wear. White gloves weren't required then, but I felt more like the glamorous Countess Elsa Shrader than awkward Maria von Trapp. As we entered the gates of Roble, the music was just beginning. It was a polka. The year before, we polkaed in the gym where I'd fainted sophomore year during a game. Then we waltzed in the dance studio. This year, they set up refreshments in the gym, and dances rotated from waltzes to polkas in the enlarged studio. As it grew darker, soft lighting around the potted plants created the most romantic scene ever at Stanford. Gone were all my worries and questions about my future. For once, I was in the present.

After an hour of dancing, we ate some cookies at the gym and I took him to a little table next to the fountain. I grabbed a hidden bottle of champagne from the water and some glasses I'd hidden in a camellia bush after dance class. JP shot the cork straight into the air, and we began toasting again.

"May we be the last dancers standing at the end of the night!" JP toasted. We laughed, had some chocolate truffles, butter pecan cookies, and more champagne. With JP, I didn't worry about bumping into anyone. They needed to worry about us: two tall athletes drunk-galloping around the room.

As the committee turned up the lights and started sweeping the debris from the hardwood floors, JP's red bow tie was missing, the bottom red ruffle of my skirt was torn and tripping me, but we made it to the last dance—waltzing to Chopin's "Minute Waltz" playing on the sound system, while the orchestra packed up.

Most of my time in college was spent in gyms, training rooms, the library and class. I worked in food service all four years. I missed only one class in four years. So, these little detours into the fantasy land of a ball or late night climbing through steam tunnels just because there was an open manhole cover gave me a diversion necessary to my sanity. Thinking about these beautiful balls now reminds me how much I yearned to go overseas to study. Even if Austria was just imagined in the Roble dance studio, I knew I would waltz to Strauss in Vienna someday, and I did, in 1984 and again in 1993.

CHAPTER 13
White Punks on Dope

While Stanford had no real mascot and no official motto, by my junior year, it was clear to me the mantra was "Work hard, party harder." From my first year, when some senior athletes from other sports emerged with bloody noses from the bathroom after doing lines of cocaine, to the 'shrooming trips with the SLE gang in front of the Washington Square church in San Francisco, to dropping acid and Ecstasy and lying around the third floor sun deck, to making pot brownies in the chemistry lab—drugs were as large a part of the campus landscape as alcohol.

Notably, the best chemistry lecture ever occurred during my freshman year when we learned about lipid solubles at 9:00 a.m. A Nobel-winning professor turned on his Bunsen-burner, dropped in a quarter cup of butter, and started sautéing pot leaves. He explained that real chefs created psychoactive butter for brownies this way, as he strained the leaves from the butter. "You'll eliminate the bitter taste of the leaves and enjoy the effects of the THC molecules that are bound to the fats," he said in his best Galloping Gourmet style. "Only dopes don't strain the leaves from the butter. Don't be a dope." He picked up a plate of previously made brownies from behind the dais and started munching. I couldn't believe it. Now I knew why the Stanford band loved to play the song "White Punks on Dope," which we translated to "White Dopes on Punk" when we sang with them.

But I was never tempted (or never brave enough) to try anything other than alcohol. When I was fourteen, a teenager at my high school whose Coca-Cola had been laced with a combination of acid and meth by someone he didn't know died at a Fourth of July party. His parents' shock and my parents' anger were enough of a deterrent. This, and my multiple concussions made me choose to be the designated driver on excursions with my friends. The entertainment value of those trips satisfied me, especially when they asked me the next day what had happened. I enjoyed telling (and embellishing) the stories.

I had no doubt in my mind that my closest friends and I were the straightest girls on the entire campus. It wasn't necessarily our choice; it was partly for lack of opportunity, due to our hectic schedules. I liked being different in this way, for my high school was full of partiers, and I had avoided that identity then. In college, however, I lost my judgmental superiority about recreational drugs, because I had already accomplished my goal of playing sports in college. With a sore back and the strong possibility of being unable to play my senior season, curiosity got the better of me. I went in search of pot.

White Punks on Dope

I didn't have to go far. Many of the guys in our house had stashes, and when I approached a housemate about my find, she too was game to try. What else was there to do when all our guy friends were busy with beginning of spring quarter projects, studying, cramming, etc.? We couldn't get any attention, and we were tired of their teasing us for being so straight. "Why don't you just loosen up a bit?" was the question we always got.

I bought a baggie of pot for five bucks, then rode my bike two miles down El Camino Real to buy Zig-Zag papers at a convenience store, which was terrifying to me. What if someone I knew walked in, or another volleyball player? I completely overdramatized the situation, but that's how straight I was.

Back at Kairos, I waited for my friend to return from her late-afternoon lab. "Did you get it?" she asked.

I nodded.

We went to the wooden picnic table out back, as we knew everyone was out front, throwing the frisbee in preparation for our intramural sports match. We were the defending coed ultimate Frisbee champions and also in the running for the coed field hockey title, probably due to our plaid skirts from thrift stores. All the non-players were in the library. There would be no witnesses. I put my precious bag down, laid out the Zig-Zag papers, and asked, "Do you have any idea how to roll a joint?"

She shook her head but held down the top paper. I opened the fold-over top baggie and started to gently sprinkle the pot onto the paper. It resembled oregano. Just as I had distributed the weed evenly onto a couple of papers, a huge gust of wind blew everything around us. We were Antigone burying her brother with the gods' help, or the victims of the Aeolian winds meant to push us away from our terrible path and out to sea in the wrong direction. Actually, we were Kairos sisters without any pot. Leaves swirled in circles above our heads, then mixed with the eucalyptus branches and bulbous seeds above us; leaves floated away toward the rain gutters.

I couldn't stop laughing at the shock on her face; in fact, I had the most epic laugh attack of my life, rolling on the ground next to the picnic table. When I could finally talk again, I told my friend I had a bottle of Blue Nun. She didn't think that was funny, but my laugh attack began again as I told her: "Get thee to a nunnery!"

A few weeks later, Splendor on the Grass weekend arrived. Nobody was studying. The band lineup was posted all over campus, and the first band started at noon on Saturday. The usual 'shrooming and tripping began; you could tell by the style of the dancing which drug had been consumed. The uplifted faces of acid-induced visions, the slow and stumbling moves of pot-brownie consumers or beer-bong-hit wonders, the rapid pogoing of the coke-heads, and the mellow moves of those of us who were waiting a little longer to pop the first beer can. I just didn't have much interest in getting wasted anymore, not since I started swimming every day. After mellow dancing for a few hours, I was starving. I walked back to Kairos to make some healthier food than corn dogs.

During my Stanford years, I was in love with yearning: wanting to be a doctor and cure my mother, wanting to be a starting volleyball player, wanting to learn everything put before me, and wanting to someday satisfy my insatiable curiosity. I wish I could say I had insatiable intellectual curiosity, but many of my questions had to do with people, not ideas. The pain I felt any time I thought of losing my mother would be worse if I had a lover and lost him, I believed.

It wasn't until the next morning, when I woke up happy after dancing to two more great bands the prior evening, that I noticed my back wasn't hurting for the first time in six months. I stretched, did ab crunches, swam my mile in the afternoon, and felt no pain. I wondered if I had pogoed the joints back into place on the dance floor.

If I could get through finals by standing up when I studied and sitting only when I wrote or took a test, I might make it back to preseason training camp in August. Buoyed by this realization, I looked forward to writing about Anthony Trollope's use of humor and satire in his novels. I loved Professor Polhemus's class, and I hoped to impress him. Maybe I could earn some A's at last. And, I had my Theta formal dance to look forward to.

Volleyball Is Your Metaphor

In spring quarter, I finally slowed down a bit and started to think about my future. I made some decisions while swimming my morning mile. The first was to stop beating myself up for failing to climb the pre-med mountain. Watching my pre-med friends cram every night and stress out and have absolutely no fun made me sad. Sad for me, for I didn't get to spend as much time in their company. I was happy, though, with my fellow creative writing and literature students, who were so articulate and engaging and willing to spend hours talking about ideas. I wished I'd met them sooner.

The SLE gang had instilled the idea of learning for learning's sake, and I began to differentiate between this course of study and the career preparation of prelaw, premed, prebusiness. I wasn't arrogant enough to create a hierarchy of meaning or needs, but I did understand I was very lucky. Without my scholarship, I would have had to study for a profession. Now, I could slow down and soak in every experience as the date of my graduation loomed, just one year away. I took classes that interested me, not classes necessary for graduate school applications. This didn't help my GPA, but I was constantly stimulated and engaged with ideas. I met so many people who were different from me. I stopped hating my pre-med failures, as I realized we were all struggling, albeit in our individual ways.

My second decision in the pool was born of necessity. I decided not to decide my career post-Stanford. With a ton of units in English requiring hours of reading and the writing demands of the creative writing major, I had no time, so I abdicated the decision. If I could graduate in June 1983, that would be enough. This meant I didn't have to study for the MCAT or the LSAT or the GRE. I just completed the assigned work and focused on reducing my back pain. From my mother's experience of illness, I had an example of how to deal with chronic pain, and I tried to be as stoic as she. And my back kept improving.

Spring quarter at Stanford blossomed as a hopeful time. Our Theta formal was held at the Tonga Room in San Francisco. It had a Tiki raft that silently appeared from behind a curtain, then lit up the house band, who played Polynesian-inspired music. While we were eating dinner, a fake thunder-and-lightning show filled the lagoon, so hokey it was cool. After this delightful 24-hour detour, it was back to work. The dinner dance inspired an incredibly schmaltzy short story.

My professor was not impressed.

Professor Gilbert Sorrentino arrived at Stanford's Creative Writing Department via many other East Coast schools, and with an impressive list of experimental publications.

I heard a rumor he never actually graduated from college. Originally from Brooklyn, his thick accent enhanced an erudition beyond the average professor, however. An elegant man with a salt-and-pepper goatee, he liked to wear black turtlenecks under a houndstooth plaid jacket to the fiction writing workshop. When we read our stories, we knew his raised eyebrow was not a positive sign. When he asked me to stop by during his office hours, I was terrified.

"Jenyth, I understand you are on the volleyball team. Is that right?"

I nodded, disappointed that he had found out I was a dumb jock—even though I changed out of my sweats and into my plaid skirt or camo pants before every class.

"I don't understand what you are writing about here. These stories read like sentimental domestic fiction from the nineteenth century, and they don't jive with what I'm hearing you talk about in class. What's the deal?" He lifted up my latest submission, then let the pile slide off his desk onto the floor. I wondered if he would retrieve the story or drop it in the wastebasket.

"I know. I just don't know what to write about, so I write about my life." As the words tumbled out, I turned bright red. I had just admitted to living in the realm of a Harlequin Romance, a genre with predictable plots, flat characters, and satisfying, happy endings. Here was the author of *Mulligan Stew*, a "brilliant work of comic subterfuge"—a teacher and a book beyond my comprehension. I felt myself shrink into my chair. "Fake it until you make it" was not going to work for Gil, the first name he wanted us to use. My story remained on the floor.

"Being an undergraduate creative writer is very difficult, Jenyth. You don't have much experience in the world, and your worldview is limited. You won't have much to say until you're at least thirty, and by the time you are fifty, you won't have enough time to say everything you want to. Still, you are here, and I think you're missing a terrific opportunity with your writing."

Great, the guilt trip was about to begin. I couldn't meet his eyes, let alone call him Gil. I stared at my story.

"Jenyth, you already have your metaphor."

I realized he must like my name, because he kept saying it. I was no longer the volleyball player "J.J." in his world, and he pronounced Jenyth perfectly. A peculiar feeling began, and my curiosity increased as he picked up my story. "I do?"

"Yes, Jenyth, you do." Sorrentino sat up, crossed his arms over my paper, and waited for me to respond.

I had no idea what he was talking about. I knew he was a master of "wait time" in class, and he certainly waited a long time, until I finally admitted my ignorance. "I'm sorry, professor, I have no ideas for you. I just get through the day, really. I'm nothing special." I started getting emotional and squirmed to relieve the pressure on my back. "Here, I'm surrounded by superstars. I've tried a lot of majors. I love to write, but I'm so far behind everyone else. I'm sorry. I just want to graduate before my scholarship runs out." I tried to stuff the tears, barely managing. No way could I call him "Gil."

"Volleyball, Jenyth. Your metaphor is volleyball. Think about that and try to use it in your next piece. I think you'll be amazed at what will happen." Sorrentino appeared a bit uncomfortable and stood up, ending the conference.

I nodded as I walked out. I started to think: *He said volleyball is my metaphor. I know volleyball, I know metaphor, but how can I connect the two? How is volleyball my metaphor?*

The pieces I wrote for his class did change, but they were weak compared with what my fellow creative writing majors wrote. All of us were struggling to meet his standard, yet I was happy to be any kind of writer, posting weekly sports articles to the *Stanford Daily* and occasionally going to Antonio's Nut House for the Tuesday night hangout for English professors and majors. A pitcher of beer was two dollars and fifty cents, the peanuts were free, and it was great fun to spend a few hours drinking and tossing peanut shells on the floor. I felt like I had found my people, even if I wasn't the best writer. I had finally found something to study that made me feel alive. I began to differentiate between journalism's five questions to ask and answer, and literature's question without the answer (thanks for that, Barthes). What should remain objective and two-dimensional as opposed to what needed judgments, symbolism, and implied meaning to round out a character? Best of all, being able to appreciate the work of others, while receiving their compliments and suggestions, seemed to be what college was all about. I viewed our workshop group as another kind of team. Even if I was the weakest one, I could learn from them and they from me.

Unfortunately, I had only one year left—one year with three quarters with twenty-plus units, one year with a chance to make the NCAA Final Four, one year of freedom before I had to decide what to do with the rest of my life. It would be years of back and forth, plus a stint at graduate school (thanks to Sorrentino's letter of recommendation), before I understood what Gil meant. The winter and spring of 1982 were full of painful compromises and reconciliations with my physical and mental uncertainties. Fortunately, whenever I had a down moment, I relived the most glorious volleyball game of my life: the regional finals of the NCAA tournament against the Lady Bruins of UCLA. I yearned for a rematch.

CHAPTER 14
Last Summer Home

The return to Carmichael for my last summer as a college student began the usual way: several days of sleeping, as my dear mother laundered all my stinky clothes and waited for me to emerge from my teenage bedroom.

As I crawled out from under the spring green comforter and stepped onto the grass-green shag carpet I loved, I caressed the wrought-iron bed my mother had bought at a flea market in New Orleans. Dad wanted to leave the heavy bed in Alabama when we moved to California in 1965, but mom insisted we keep it. While pregnant with me, she had sandblasted the rust and discovered a smelting date of 1855 on the frame. She painted it pink when I was born, federal blue when we arrived in California, then antique white when they bought their first California house after renting for twelve years. Even though I was too tall for a full-sized mattress, I loved curling my toes around the iron scrolls of the footboard. It was good to be home.

Mom was fully in charge of my summer activities. Both parents insisted I shouldn't work, and I was very grateful to skip the summer job. After my freshman year, I was jealous of my teammates who traveled or played beach volleyball at their private clubs all summer. The summer after my sophomore year, I learned how harsh the world of medicine could be for women. After my junior year, I ran summer camps for my old school district, then directed the UC Davis volleyball camp for a third time. A job-free summer left me with a lot of mental energy for reading and writing. I needed to read as many novels in preparation for my graduation requirements as I could. Fifty-eight units over three quarters was going to make for some wham-bam-thank-you-ma'am classes. I hoped something about what I read would stick in my sieve-like brain or at least inform my writing.

Meanwhile, Mom had signed me up for the Carmichael Athletic Club, a sports club just down the street from our Hackberry Lane house. I continued swimming, and Mom fed me her custom-designed anti-inflammatory diet. Western medicine had given Mom a diagnosis of multiple kinds of autoimmune diseases, a diagnosis that had never been given to anyone and was likely incorrect. When she had a flare, they gave her massive doses of prednisone. Mom turned to Eastern medicine and found relief through diet, exercise, and acupuncture. I went to her acupuncturist, who was also an MD/OB-GYN. He had many ideas for my healing and my excessive monthly bleeding. He had trained at the London School of Chinese Medicine and loved difficult cases such as my mother's. A regimen of needle therapy, moxibustion, meditation, a complete diet overhaul, and herbal teas really helped my pain level.

Mom's research into foods that helped decrease inflammation was later validated in *Heal Yourself* (1984) and *Dr. Berger's Immune Power Diet* (1986). Those books are considered pseudoscience today, but some of the principles really helped us. Mom steamed the superfoods, fed me clean grains and proteins, and upped her level of Mom-spoiling.

Every night at the dinner table, we discussed the books and plays I had brought home for her to read. Chekhov's

The Cherry Orchard and Ibsen's *A Doll's House* were two of her favorites. She nearly cried when we read Nora's thoughts: "Free. To be free, absolutely free...To have a clean, beautiful house..." and "From now on, forget happiness. Now it's just about saving the remains, the wreckage, the appearance." She told me how much she related to that play, but I didn't connect her confinement in her home to Nora's. Her spotless house brought her joy.

We read *Phineas Finn* aloud together after I told her about brilliant Professor Polhemus's Anthony Trollope course. I was looking forward to taking the second course in the series. I shared my favorite quote with her:

There is nothing in the world so difficult as that task of making up one's mind. Who is there that has not longed that the power and privilege of selection among alternatives should be taken away from him in some important crisis of his life, and that his conduct should be arranged for him, either this way or that, by some divine power if it were possible, — by some patriarchal power in the absence of divinity, — or by chance, even, if nothing better than chance could be found to do it?

When Mom asked why I liked it, I told her I felt comforted that over a hundred years ago, somebody else had trouble making decisions and realized decisions could be based on class limitations, financial necessity, God's will, or just plain dumb luck. The desire to abdicate the decision sometimes overcame the desire to determine one's own experience. "Mom, sometimes I think luck might be the most important force of all. But I'd still procrastinate until I looked at every angle."

"That's the best rationalization of your procrastination I've ever heard. But you're getting much better at follow through, aren't you?" she responded.

We read *Macbeth*, and I told her about Professor Ron Rebholz's incredible memory for Shakespeare's sonnets and key lines in all the plays. I didn't tell her about my obsession with the three witches—where did Shakespeare dig up those creatures? —and the occult section, or my reading of Wiccan brews that might help alleviate her pain.

Even though Mom was a biology major before she left college to marry Dad, she developed well-formed opinions about all the literature we discussed and surprised me with her insights into human nature. Our relationship transformed from mother-daughter to two adults with much in common. Nothing pleased my dad more than to hear our laugh attacks.

Once Mom starting laughing, she often snorted, making a hilarious baby-pig-like noise that made everybody in the room laugh. On many occasions, our cheeks cramped up from laughing too much. Mom found the silly and the absurd in so many things. When I shared Dr. Who with her, she had an epic laugh attack. "People watch this stuff? It looks like they're filming in a gravel pit. Where's their budget? Is it part of London's sanitation system?" Snort, snort.

I spent a lot of time reading in a chaise lounge I had pulled from a dumpster and topped with a Hawaiian pillow from Pic-a-Dilly. Mom had found a round redwood picnic table with four curved bench seats at a garage sale. She always had a craft project going, and the smell of Modge Podge, the multi-purpose découpage glue she used to make pictures look like antiques, permeated my elementary school years. Then there was the American colonial-style buffet with a missing leg. She sawed off the other three, sanded down the stubs so the top could sit level on the floor, and created the world's longest coffee table in American Colonial Blue, the same shade as the aventurine and alabaster chess set proudly displayed on top of it. This was the color she wanted to paint the redwood table and chairs, but the redwood didn't take the paint as well as the oak buffet. As I read Chekhov's "The Name Day Party" to her, she sanded and painted different shades of blue on the old roof shakes the Norway roof rats were chewing up and dumping on the lawn that summer. Mom repurposed the shingles for her paint samples.

One afternoon, as I walked up the driveway, having returned from my therapeutic swim and weightlifting routine, I heard a *thunk, thunk* I'd never heard before. *Thunk, thunk, thunk* as I walked into the front door and past the colonial blue buffet and harvest gold furniture of our living room and called out for my mom.

"*Thunk, thunk, yeoww!* I got 'em!" rang from the backyard.

I pushed open the screen door to see my mom jumping up and down. "Mom, what are you doing? What was that noise?"

She sat down on her rounded redwood bench, huffing and puffing, then started laughing hysterically. "I got him. I shot one of the Norway roof rats."

"Ooh, mom, you killed him? You shot your BB-gun in suburbia?"

"No, with this." She held up a strange yellow and black metal contraption. "During the school year, I found a slingshot at a garage sale, but the rubber bands kept breaking. Dad bought me this wrist rocket with surgical strength yellow tubes. It's hard to pull back very far. But I'm getting stronger. Black walnuts are my ammunition."

"Huh? You killed a rat with a black walnut?"

"I don't think I killed him, but when I hit him, he fell off of the power line and into Bill's yard. Bill's good about collecting and returning my walnuts. He just dumps them over the back fence, and I reload. You're looking at me funny."

"No, I, uh, well, I don't know what to say. How long have you been shooting at rats on the wire?"

"Dad brought the wrist rocket home for Mother's Day. While you were swimming, I saw the big rat with the white streak on his chin in the garden. Dad will be furious when he hears Rat Fink was trying to climb the mammoth Kansas sunflower. I had to shoot him. Oh, I'd better get the walnuts out of the garden before he gets home. He doesn't need to see my misses, does he?"

I walked to the back fence in my flip-flops, wondering why my mom named the rat she wanted to kill. I said hello to Bill's dog and looked for a body. No rat, but dozens of walnuts sprinkled Bill's dead lawn. The dog jumped up on the privacy fence, and it started to lean a bit. I looked at the slats, saw dozens of pockmarks, and realized those were Mom's misses. If a walnut could dent redwood, it could kill a rat. I walked over to Dad's garden, a square plot of the back lawn he'd rototilled into a master garden. In late June, the roses were at their peak, the dahlias were about three inches across, and the sunflowers' heads were still green and growing. "Mom, have you read Katherine Mansfield's short stories yet? There's one about a garden party. She says something about roses being the only flowers that impress people. Do you think Mansfield would be impressed with Dad's?"

Looking back toward my mom, I saw her organizing the walnuts in a small box. "She would love them. He spends so much time pruning. Like you, he loves to be outside."

I noticed a painted target in the north corner of the yard, a canvas white circle with red and blue painted areas, sitting on top of an old sawhorse. Mom was taking her target practice quite seriously. "Mom, when did you get that target? Can you hit it consistently?"

"Dad gave it to me for Mother's Day, along with the wrist rocket. There's something I didn't tell you, Jenyth Jo. I started smoking again after you left for school in January. I must've smoked a pack a day until Valentine's Day. Then I started eating chocolate. In March, the Girl Scout cookies. I couldn't stop. Eat, eat, smoke. My monthly blood tests showed an increased sugar level, and my heart rate was much faster. So, I had to stop smoking and find another way to relax. Shooting at the rats did it. Whenever I want to come outside and smoke, I have my wrist rocket and I count my walnuts and walk a lap or two, then sit on your chaise and wait for them to run around in the afternoon. They like to run over our maple tree to the house, which is a harder shot than when they run on the wire. Want to try and hit the target?"

Of course I did.

It was harder to pull the tubing back than it appeared, and my walnut sailed over the target and into another neighbor's backyard. My round black bomb thunked their metal storage unit.

"Don't worry. Delores hates the rats too. She drops off the walnuts on the front porch during her morning walk."

It took me eight or ten tries to hit the target, and it wasn't moving. How did she hit a rat running on the phone line? My dad had a case full of marksmen medals from World War II, but my mom never said anything about being a dead-eye shot. Wrist rocket in place, a pile of old walnuts at the ready, her shots on Rat Fink either nicked him or barely missed. One time, she hit him squarely in the head, but his front claws stayed clamped on the wire, while his momentum made his back legs flip and spin him sideways. He hung, swinging. Dazed. Then he popped back on the wire and took off in the same direction. Rat Fink was as stubborn as my mom.

For the rest of the summer, I watched and looked around for cigarette butts or tell-tale ashes, but the patio was swept clean. I couldn't remember not smelling smoke on either or both of my parents, and I was grateful for the pure air when we hugged. Dad had kicked the habit a year before, but Mom struggled when she was in pain. I couldn't imagine how to live life waiting for another flare, another kidney failure, another trip to the hospital. For now, Mom had a new way to forget about her festering skin and degrading organs. Shooting at the rats disrupted the tedium of her chronic pain.

Still, my dad had to climb on the roof and repair the rat-damaged shingles a couple of times that summer. The sunflowers grew, their heads bloomed, and I watched their faces follow the sun on the long, hot Sacramento summer afternoons. I never hit a rat, but I did see my mom knock the fat one off the wire. We whooped and high-fived, then saw Rat Fink climb up the neighbor's tree.

When I think of that summer, my last one home, I think of the rats and the sunflowers. I see sunlight reflecting off of my dad's silver temples and my mom's golden pixie haircut, as they try to pull dandelions out of their lawn without letting the seeds escape.

Playing With Pain

I couldn't remember a time when I had been as relaxed as I was when I started driving to UC Davis to attend the twice-weekly volleyball open gyms. Afraid to jump and compress my spine, I returned to setting and directing the traffic of the court. I enjoyed quarterbacking and making my coed teammates look better. By mid-July, I was started to jump set and block a bit.

At the end of July, I visited my Sacramento spine doctor, with mixed expectations. Mom had contacted the athletic department to double-check I would have my full scholarship if I was not cleared to play. I fully expected I would not be able to play, but worked out anyway. The doctor was shocked at my lack of pain and my range of motion. I could put my palms flat on the floor. I weighed only 153, and my back muscles were perfectly balanced due to the swimming. He measured my height. It was still 69.5 inches, although he had said I would shrink, and my legs were aligned and the same length. He presented me with a paper saying I could play as long as I was honest about my pain.

I didn't laugh in front of him, but later on that afternoon, when I had the back patio and chaise lounge to myself during Mom's nap time, I had a private chuckle. Playing without pain. Really? Hadn't that doc ever driven up Highway 50 to South Lake Tahoe and stopped at the Burger King in Placerville, the one where Oakland Raider Jim Otto displayed all the photos of his injuries on the walls? Cauliflower ear, torn ACL, back fusions, knee surgeries, and neck braces, and more?

After three years of college volleyball, my list was not as

long but was as serious. Seven concussions in ten years, and the recurring headaches that accompanied traumatic brain injuries. A sprained ankle that more advanced technology in the future would reveal was actually broken. Yes, I had played on a broken ankle the year before I played on a broken toe. At least three of my fingers were broken as I tried to block monstrous hits, but I simply taped the broken one next to a healthy one and stayed in the game. Plantar fasciitis in both flat feet meant orthotics in my shoes and foot cramps that woke me up at night. Neck pain from looking up at the ball and carrying the weight of my world had compressed my Atlas joint (or atlantoaxial joint, to confirm I did learn something in anatomy). I had hyperextended each elbow at different times while sprawling for the ball on defense. Both big toes had been jammed so hard into my shoes that their toenails had fallen off. During season, my knees were as bruised as they were in my kindergarten tomboy picture, despite wearing knee pads. Then there was my right thumb, whose metacarpal ligaments were ripped from the trapezius bone when the future starter of the 1984 Olympic team crushed a ball through my block. My back was the latest of these injuries. An MRI years later, after I broke my tailbone and had to have the dreaded tailbone exam, showed I didn't have cartilage or a disk between my L-5 and S-1 joint. Was I born this way, or did my grinding through season after season wear out what cartilage I had? Forty years later, at a non-volleyball Stanford women's team reunion, seven out of fourteen legs had hip or knee replacements. When we took our opportunity to play, we truly did not know the physical costs. We feel them now.

At the end of July 1982, I simply had permission to play. My parents were against it. That afternoon, for about ten seconds, I thought, *fuhgeddaboudit. I could have a senior year at Stanford, study hard, raise my GPA, write the Great American Novel, and graduate on time.* Around the eleventh or twelfth second, I started getting excited. *Hell with the book, I could be on the team again.* We were going to have a great year, and I yearned to compete. The desire to take out UCLA on the way to the national championship would eliminate any pain I felt, or so I believed. I couldn't remember the last time I had played pain free, so as long as I avoided sciatica, I was willing to play. I wanted to play. I waited to play. I was going to play.

The one month of total relaxation morphed into the usual sense of urgency that had infused my life since middle school. I had one year left. I was going to live each day as if it were my last, and make the most of everything.

When I left home to direct the UC Davis camp, I met my future coaching mentor, John Kessel, who served as head camp coach for two weeks. A future USA Volleyball Hall of Famer, John has an incredible mind and memory. Once he said, "Give them what they don't want," referring to serving strategies. I became a wiser, more careful volleyball player after working with John.

"Keep it simple, J.J. You're getting paralysis through analysis. Stop worrying and start reading what's happening right in front of you on the court." I often repeated those words to my own teams. "Stop worrying about losing. You'll learn more after a loss than a win. Just make sure you think about how you lost." I overheard him gently tell a camper she was trying too hard. "Effort and outcome aren't always the same thing." I nodded to myself: how many times had I tried my hardest and still failed? Success creates confidence, failure creates fear. I wondered if this explained my test anxiety in the sciences at Stanford, but I didn't have to worry about that any more.

John said, "Don't try. Just do it," years before Nike branded themselves with that slogan. He once wrote "Why?" in permanent Sharpie on the net pole pads of the championship high school team I coached. Every year, I had my senior captains explain the growth mindset to the incoming freshmen. I used positive psychology in my coaching (instead of using the fear of losing) to make a better team. I created new statistics to reinforce my players' efforts, like counting the number of times my middle blockers closed the block, or ran the fake. These were not included in the box score, but measuring these kinds of performance goals demonstrated my intent to appreciate effort over outcome. Even with my first high school team, who went 0-14 in league, we measured so many different performance goals that they knew exactly how much they had improved after the first seven matches. We had a successful season for that reason, and all those eligible came back for another year. John's most riveting tip? Never be a player's last volleyball coach.

Preseason at Lake Arrowhead

My generous parents were still leery of me returning to play for my senior season, and decided the drive to Lake Arrowhead would put too much stress on my lower back. We were going to train at Hoss Ranch again, and I was looking forward to seeing Krush's parents and the rest of the team. My parents gifted me with a plane ticket to the Ontario airport, where Coach Fred would pick me up.

When I contacted him and said I was cleared to play and

was coming to camp, genuine joy came through the telephone lines: "I'm so happy you're going to have your senior
season, J.J. After all you've been through, you deserve it."
Of all our players, Fred knew I was the one who understood
his pre-match preparation and stellar strength and conditioning regimen. He also must have known that sophomore
Fly-shit – Kisi gave her the nickname, but I'll call her Fly because she could - Fly's vast improvement as a middle
blocker would challenge his tradition of playing seniors
over underclassmen if both players were equal.

Fly was a true specimen, an elite athlete who was as fast,
as strong, as quick, and as determined as I was. She was also
six feet tall, and the national high school record holder in
the high jump. I had not attended spring workouts so I did
not know how much she had improved and how well she
fit into the scheme, but from the moment we began our
warmups without the ball, it was obvious she was incredibly
talented and in fabulous shape.

Our highly touted recruit, KimO, wasn't on the All-
American list at the beginning of her freshman year but she
was near the top by the end of it. She and Fly would control
the middle and allow the backcourt defense latitude to pick
up junk, as the block would always be closed. Krush was a
junior, team floor captain, and doing everything in her
typically fearless style. I could match her during conditioning for only the first half now, as the altitude and lack of real
wind sprints for six months had left me short of breath for
the second half of conditioning.

From the sidelines at the end of the day, I could already
tell the starting lineup. DD, sister of an All American from
USC, would set, along with Krush. Boom-Boom would hit
in one outside hitter spot, and Bakes and Comp would battle

for the other. Our serving, passing, blocking, and hitting
were going to be technically sound and tactically demoral-
izing. We were going to compete for the national championship, and I'd be on the bench, singing songs with Grits
and cheering on Kisi.

Still, the joy of practicing a sport I loved was enough. I
loved being back with my team. By the time our preseason
training was over, I was on the second team and had learned
how to hit around the big block of KimO or Fly. A better
blocker than I, Fly's hitting was still inconsistent, and I saw
her landing on one foot quite a bit. That was exactly how I
hurt my back over time: sometimes my approach was off,
sometimes the set was to the side, but too many unsteady
landings compressed my spine and misaligned my hips.
Now I was mindful of these issues and careful to land with
two feet as often as I could.

While I wasn't in the starting lineup, during our preseason matches Fred made sure to insert me into every match.
Sometimes it was a starting position in the second set, sometimes I played the entire third set during mop-up time. He
was very true to his seniors, and he and Don coached me as
meticulously as ever.

As my strength and endurance improved, I started con-
necting with Krush and DD during hitting drills. Fly and
KimO had a hard time blocking me during practice, and I
made sure to torture the backcourt with tips and a variety
of shots to keep them on their toes. We strove to make each
other better, and everyone on the team was getting along.
Strangely, I didn't resent sitting the bench, because we were
winning and I was getting into every match.

Then I started sharing more court time with Fly, and I
thought there was a slight chance my hitting could help me

take over that middle position. She started the match, I started the second set, then whoever was playing better was put into the third. In my head, I was earning this court time, but the reality was—and this knowledge was not shared with the team—Fly's back was starting to break down. All of a sudden, she was sidelined with excruciating pain. My emotions were conflicted as I wanted to play, but she was from the Sacramento area like me, a terrific person, and had an Olympic track career in high jump ahead of her. Yet once I was back in the starting lineup, I thought only of staying on the court. I wanted that rematch with UCLA.

Fred and Don came up with the scheme of playing Kim and me at the two middle blocker spots. Kim started in middle front, and I went in for Kisi when KimO went back to serve. Kim and I gave other teams fits, for our playing styles were opposite. When KimO arrived, she was six-foot-two and weighed less than I. Her long arms and legs meant she didn't have to take as many steps to close the block and to get off the net for transition hitting. It took a while for her arm to get all the way up to full extension, and the setters had to learn to set high enough to take advantage of her reach. In addition, she was still growing and had to eat a lot more than she was used to in order to stay strong.

Fred never subbed Kim out. She burned thousands of calories during a match, as the other teams served at her and hit at her block. I, on the other hand, sat for three rotations, and when I came into the game from the bench, I was fired up and ready. Apparently, I had what is known as fast-twitch muscles. I popped off the floor very quickly, reaching the top of my jump well before the blocker was in the air. If I had a good set, I could swing and hit before the blocker was ready. Sometimes I hit the ball on the way up and sometimes at the peak of my jump. Other times, I jumped, hung, then hit when the blocker was on the way down.

My vertical leap caught the eye of a professor researcher in the HumBio Department who came to watch us play. Lots of faculty members were volleyball fans, and our crowds were full of university employee supporters. This man measured my tibia and fibula, put it in his data processor, and told me I jumped so high because I had a lot of African in me.

Since I sunburned and freckled easily, I thought this was pretty ironic. "We're all from Africa, aren't we?" I asked.

"You're about as white as it gets, J.J.," he replied.

I was more aware of skin color than ever before. In Sacramento, I played basketball with a number of Black girls, but the volleyball world was very white. I wanted to make sure everyone treated KimO well, and like Krush the year before, I felt very protective. However, she had no need for a savior. Her warmth, humor, and unselfish personality were instantly loved by all, and the fact she could block and hit at a level far above the rest of us meant she had our respect as well. Many of us felt KimO was our game changer, especially on offense, and we entered the league full of high spirits. Our incredible preseason work was paying off, and we didn't see any limits. I wanted that rematch with UCLA.

Air Supply

Preseason continued back on The Farm. We were in the dorms with the water polo and soccer players again. Backgammon and Buds rules were explained to our freshmen, who were all great people and players. Kisi and I, as senior captains, made sure everyone felt welcome on campus. Krush, as floor captain, cheered on the new players. We were attracting incredible volleyball recruits with tremendous personalities, so once again the volleyball floor was full of buzzing boy-bees.

Murph, a sophomore middle blocker with lightning quick reflexes and Paula's sarcastic sense of humor, was assigned to be my roommate. Murph's quick wit and SoCal tan were too much for the soccer team. None of them would leave her alone. It was funny at first but became tiresome when I returned from lunch to find one or another of them trying to get her to join him in an "afternoon delight." She played it cool with them all.

I tried to be nice about it, but I needed that afternoon nap. At Kairos, we employed a variety of devices to let roommates know they should not enter due to "research activities." I had a single room, so I didn't need to have Mardi Gras beads or a "Do Not Disturb" hotel sign or even a dirty sock on the door knob. But my gal pals in the house often knocked on my door with a sleeping bag in hand and asked if they could sleep on my floor while their roommates got laid.

When I finally got the nerve to talk to Murph about the constant visitors, we came up with a plan. We would play Air Supply if one of us needed privacy or a nap. Whenever I hear "Lost in Love," "Making Love Out of Nothing at All," and "The One That I Love," visions of those soccer boys flirting with Murph still make me laugh.

As our record improved, the bleachers became fuller for every home game. We averaged more people per match than either the men's or women's basketball teams, for the women's volleyball team was considered to be quite "cool" now. I recognized a lot of area high school and club coaches at our games, knew all our referees, and generally soaked up the atmosphere and relished it when the fans came up to me before and after games.

I had never enjoyed attention as much as I did my senior year. I loved our uniforms; our training staff; our fans; our sports information people; our bouncy floor; our pregame mix tapes, which played classical music as our opponents hit and the GoGos when we hit in warmups; and my long hair. Everyone was involved in team hair-braiding sessions and a few other secret rituals, including dancing in our locker room before the coaches arrived to review the game plan. The dancing helped us blow off steam and jitters, and the French braids meant I didn't have to brush bangs out of my face in between plays. And I was playing well.

Everything on the court was coming together. KimO became stronger in the back row, and her serve had become a weapon. Team chemistry was effortless, as we understood each other's little quirks and needs. I tried to be the glue that kept us together, with well-timed jokes and occasional philosophical speeches.

I kept Boom-Boom involved. We needed her brains and power on the court. She had had her own Stanford nightmare: a departure to train during winter quarter with national champion USC after our first season, with a promise to play there on scholarship, before realizing the academics were not at Stanford's level for premed. Like me, Boom-Boom wanted to be an Olympian and a doctor and didn't think Stanford would get her to the national team. I thought she'd succeed wherever she went, as her focus and determination were incredible. And she didn't need any sleep, unlike me. She was as sharp after four hours' sleep as after seven or eight. By the time we were seniors, she had managed to channel all her energy when she was on the court and to focus her brains on premed studies when she was off the court. Boom-Boom's serve became the best in the country. I wish we'd had radar guns back then, for I know it topped 40 m.p.h.

CHAPTER 15
The Play

M y new writing courses were challenging and delightful. Most wonderful was the opportunity to meet the new crop of Stegner fellows. These writers were from all over the country, and one seemed most interesting: Neil McMahon from Montana. As Kairos food manager and guest speaker coordinator, I had invited several faculty members over for Sunday dinners my junior year, so it felt natural to invite Neil over for Sunday dinner. In a laconic cowboy drawl, he accepted.

Our five-day-a-week chef prepared a wonderful Sunday dinner. I kept peeking out the window until a 1966 red Ford Mustang with a blue star on the hood parked in front of Kairos. I could see the Montana license plate. As Neil stepped out of the car, I could see he had shined his dark-brown cowboy boots. I met him at the door, shook hands with him, and led him into the dining room.

Neil had prepared a short reading from his novel in progress, and the Kairosians filtered in to listen. He had an eye for detailed descriptions and stuck to storytelling, not abstract, experimental language that obscured easy meaning. When he finished, the spell was broken and we let him go through the buffet line first. Several of us gathered at the best table in the house, near the front windows. He talked with everyone, and the more we laughed, the more normal he seemed, reminding me of my 4-H friends back in Sacramento

County when he told us he missed riding. When Neil signaled it was time to end the night, we all stood up.

After he left, I thought about public readings. Wouldn't it be cool to be invited to read a chapter of a book to a group of college students, or bookstore patrons, or anybody? Would I ever write something I felt worthy of public view? Instead of the inspirational speeches I gave as senior class or 4-H president, or the clichés I yelled during a time-out huddle, I could read something of my own. Did I have enough talent? Did I have the perseverance?

Something about Neil's cowboy boots made me feel grounded and near a barn—opposite of the crazy theater that was Maples Gym when our crowds screamed in the stands as we kept the rally alive. We won nearly all our home matches.

The Play

Campus was abuzz all week with activities surrounding the eighty-seventh Big Game. The rival game between Stanford and California-Berkeley had begun in 1892. The Big Splash between the top two nationally ranked water polo teams attracted a large crowd. The Stanford Gaieties, a vaudeville-style satire of California's Oski Bear and Berkeley as a whole, were scheduled for the Friday night before the football game at Cal's Memorial Stadium on November 20. But I wouldn't be there.

Once again, I was disappointed that, for four years in a row, we had a Southern California road trip on our schedule. This year, we had back-to-back matches with UCLA and USC. I pouted off and on all week: we didn't even have a mascot; we were now the Cardinal. While the students voted to replace the Indian with the Robber Barons or the Sequoia, our Harvard Crimson alum president said we'd be the Cardinal. At first, we thought we were red birds that didn't even live in the Bay Area, then we thought we were one level below the pope. Once we knew we were a color, I thought, *Where's the fun in that?*

As the week of rival silliness continued with pranks, such as the giant football teed up under the hand of Junipero Serra's statue standing above Highway 280, I learned I had a serious opportunity. With two games left in regular season play, I'd accidentally seen Coach Fred's weekly statistics printout and learned I was tied with USC's Tracy Clark for best hitting percentage in the country. Our team didn't focus on individual stats, but learning I ranked at the top in something meant the world to me. This stat was an objective measure of my worth to the team, and vindication for wanting more opportunities to hit the ball. If I played well against two of the top five teams in the country this week, I could win an award at last.

Volleyball hitting percentage is very similar to a baseball batter's average, and Tracy and I were over .300 going into this last weekend. She was an outside hitter, a position that usually received more sets and therefore more opportunities to notch kills. As a middle, I didn't see the ball unless our pass was good enough to run the middle, so I would have approximately a third of the sets Tracy would see. I would never get the chance to have the most kills for this reason, so I envied that hitting percentage crown. I didn't know if such an award actually existed but hoped my name might go down in history in some way.

At Stanford, volleyball was gaining momentum as an intercollegiate and high-status sport on campus. Thanks to

Title IX, no longer did we have long van rides to LA; instead, we flew on Delta Airlines. We stayed in Marriott properties instead of roadside motels. I really looked forward to staying in the Marina del Rey Marriott, the nicest hotel I'd ever been in. It was near where Fred had grown up in Pacific Palisades. On the plane ride down, we wondered if USC still didn't have a library for us to study in. Because they were so good, we had to mock them down to size: The University of Spoiled Children.

I've never understood why I can remember the tiniest detail of just one rally of volleyball but can't recall if we beat UCLA on Thursday night. I do know my hitting percentage was higher than Tracy's after that game. Going into the match with USC, I just needed to hit my shots and help my team win, and I would wear a crown nobody else cared about.

As the defending national champion coached by the strategic Chuck Erbe, USC gave us more than we could handle. We were a little tired after UCLA, and USC was relentless. I was keeping a different score in my head, and as the match neared the final point, Tracy rotated to the front row. One-on-one, I'd be blocking her. When Kim Ruddins, the fabulous USC setter, set a fast set to the outside, I ran right to close the block. I saw Tracy take an inside approach. If I stayed in front of her, I could block her. My mind wanted to go one-on-one and stuff her, but years of training made my feet and hands close the block so the defense behind me would know what to do. In the air, I pressed my left hand forward, hoping to stop her shot, but I didn't touch anything. Her hard angle shot was so good, so authoritative, that nobody on our team could touch it. She had made The Play. And that was it. We lost the match, and I finished number two. Nobody remembers second place.

The Big Game

After we shook their hands and had our postgame discussion, Fred called over the very glum seniors. "Girls, Don and I have been thinking. There's an 11:00 p.m. mail plane to San Francisco on Delta. Do you want me to change your flights so you can go to the Big Game tomorrow? We'll have to go to the airport in just a few minutes. Patty said she'd fly back with you. J.J., I know what a football fan you are. Do you want to go? Kisi, Boom-Boom, are you in? I can have game tickets at Will Call for you."

Did I want to go? Heck, yes. I wanted to watch John Elway have the game of his life and win the Heisman Trophy. I wanted to yell, "Beat the Weenies," with other Stanford students, even though I didn't know why we called the Cal Bears the Weenies. I wanted to shower too, but there was no time for that. Kisi, Boom, Patty, and I shoved our gear into our bags, and Fred dropped us off, while everyone else went back to Marina del Rey. We found seats on a plane that literally had mailbags in the back. It was so cool. Boom-Boom had to study on Saturday, so she drove back to campus with Patty and said I could have her ticket to the game.

I had time to call my brother and tell him I had tickets for us. He said he'd meet me at the stadium and drive me home for the night. By the time we landed in San Francisco, it was well after midnight. Some Kairos friends had a hotel room at the Holiday Inn Fisherman's Wharf, so Kisi and I took a taxi there.

As I paid the driver, Kisi disappeared. It was 1:30 a.m., and she had become part of the cold fog sitting on top of Russian Hill. I walked around the high rise, tried to get into the locked doors, but had no luck. I couldn't find a security guard or a house phone on the outside. I recognized a Kairosian's car in the lot, and while the doors were locked, I knew Sam's hatch didn't shut all the way. With one last look for Kisi, I climbed in and pulled down the hatch. Curled in a little sausage roll, I fell right to sleep.

I woke to Kisi and Sam and a bunch of other Kairosians rocking the car. "J.J., wake up! Why didn't you come into the hotel? We never went to sleep!"

I uncurled my sore legs and tried to get the kink out of my neck. "Where's breakfast?" I wanted to know.

"We're going to take BART to Berkeley. We can find something to eat there."

My first Bay Area Rapid Transit train ride was uneventful and I tried not to think about going under the bay. We got out at Shattuck Avenue and started walking up the hill, past some frats. I had a friend from high school in the SAE house, so I wandered over there, still in my red Stanford volleyball sweats and carrying my travel bag.

"Hey Stanford girl, take off that red shirt!" chanted a bunch of guys drinking beer out of plastic cups.

I laughed and asked if JB was there.

They said he'd already gone to the stadium. "Here's a beer. Take off that red shirt!"

I chugged with them, then asked if they had any food.

"Nope. Who needs food?"

I walked up the hill to the south entrance, where my brother was standing. "Hey, J., you just missed JB. He's covering the game for the *Daily Californian*. Let's go inside!"

Eighty-five thousand screaming fans would fill the stadium for the Big Game. Anyone in Cal clothing told me to take off my red shirt. I thought about flashing them, but not in my Stanford uniform with my brother next to me. We were early to the Stanford student section, and moved as close to the center of the field out of our endzone corner area as we could, which was about the five-yard line.

Four hours later, a field goal gave us a twenty-eighteen lead, with a few seconds to play. After our final kickoff, the Cal returner caught the ball, then weaved left and right, and lateraled the ball to a player behind him. Our band was in our endzone, ready to storm the field. After the third lateral, I saw the sideline referee to the left of the Cal bench wave the play dead, but Cal's players kept running forward. There was chaos right below us as a Cal player ran over our trombone player Gary Tyrell and crossed into the end zone. The referee there signaled touchdown, and the Cal fans stormed the fields to stand below us and taunt. After a brief discussion on the center logo, the referees gave the game to Cal.

I didn't know why the guy who signaled the play dead didn't speak up. My brother and I were confused, until a lacrosse player fired an orange that hit me in the shoulder. With lacrosse sticks and surgical tubing launchers, they started shooting hard apples and oranges at us from the field. My brother caught one, stared the lacrosse guy right in the face, and buzzed a ninety-mph fastball right over his head. "Run, J.J., run!" I did, realizing Bub could have hit him if he wanted to.

Stanford students were brawling on the field, and the crowd was completely out of control. Instead of running down to the field, we ran up and out the entrance, down fraternity row, and all the way to the BART station before we stopped. While we waited for a train to Concord, I was the only one wearing red. Old Blues from the Sacramento Valley arrived and boarded, heading to the same station. For that short ride, they razzed me, and I couldn't decide what was worse: losing to USC, losing my mythical hitting percentage crown, or watching Elway lose his chance at the Heisman because a field judge missed his call.

By Sunday afternoon, we'd seen the replay a dozen times during the NFL games, but I didn't see the view of the opposite sidelines I had. No shot of the umpire waving the play dead. And now I knew I was part of history. This famous football event would forever be known as "The Play."

But Stanford had the last laugh. A select group of senior editors gathered on Sunday afternoon and convinced our faculty advisor to fund a different version of the *Daily Californian's* cover page with the caption "NCAA Awards Big Game to Stanford." Starting at 3:00 a.m. Wednesday, our editors tailed the *Daily Californian* delivery truck, switched the covers, and went back home to sleep. Confused radio talk show hosts, even Joe Starkey of KGO, tried to find out who in the NCAA had overturned the outcome. Several hours passed before they realized our joke. The editors of *The Stanford Daily* became nationally famous and heroes on campus.

Elite Eight

Despite our loss to USC, our volleyball team was on fire. I was stoking the flame with more passion and energy than I'd ever felt for anything. We earned a seed to the second NCAA national championship bracket, and our first two rounds would be played at home. If we could make it to the final four, we'd be playing near my hometown, in UOP's new Alex Spanos Gymnasium in Stockton. Before that round, we had to travel to Alabama, and if the bracket seedings held, play UCLA again in the regional finals for a chance at the national championship.

I was born in Mobile, Alabama, but had not been back since we left in 1965. Before my brother and I were born, my parents left Topeka, Kansas, to get out of the range of my dad's overbearing mother. Grandma was an operative in the Kansas Public Employee Retirement System, a treasurer of the county Republican party, a delegate during election years, incredible with numbers, and very bigoted. She also hated my mother. Grandma called my dad "Junior," as he was named for his dad Leland Stanford Gearhart, Sr.

Grandma told a story of George Gearhart, our ancestor who worked on Leland Stanford's transcontinental railroad as an engineer and who was present at Promontory Point when the drunk Big Four arrived to pound in the last railroad spike, the famous Golden Spike. She also claimed George was the one who dug up the spike the next day, when a sober Leland Stanford wanted it back. In the grand picture of the moment that resided in the Sacramento State Capitol during her only visit to California, she pointed him out in the crowd. I'm not sure about the accuracy of her claim, but I do know George named his son after politician Stephen Douglas, and Stephen Douglas named his son after Leland Stanford.

After six months of wedded bliss, tempered with six months of grandma's resentment, my parents left for the South. At Brickley AFB in Mobile, they lived in base housing, played in the base bowling leagues, and socialized with Air Force enlisted men and officers. Outside the base, beaches were segregated, and water fountains were labeled "White Only." When my brother was born, they had to move across the street from the hospital because Leland

Stanford Gearhart, III, was a blue baby, with sleep apnea and asthma that stopped his breathing. After my birth by hypnosis eighteen months later, my mother, exhausted from postpartum hemorrhaging, hired Prunella, a nanny who cleaned and cooked and forced my mother to rest.

When the Pentagon decided to close the Air Force base after the Cuban missile crisis, my parents were financially ruined for a decade. They lost all the money they had put into their brand-new house when they had to sell it to a bank for one dollar. Fortunately, Dad was transferred to sunny California, where he could play golf and my mom could play tennis at the public facilities, while they scrimped and saved to buy another house.

Eighteen years later, I was returning to the homeland. The NCAA bracket had been favorable for us, as we had won our two home matches during the first round. I looked forward to visiting the University of Alabama in Tuscaloosa. My family were diehard Alabama football fans, and I was excited to see the campus; perhaps see the elephant mascot; and reconnect with Stephanie Schlueter, the Alabama coach who had recruited me to play there. I was both nervous and excited to see what life was like there now.

We won our Sweet Sixteen round match and were ready to face UCLA in the round of the Elite Eight. The winner would stamp a ticket to UOP in Stockton and have a chance to play for the national championship. The previous year, UCLA had broken our hearts during this match and had gone on to win the semis but lose the national championship to USC. This year, I liked our chances to reach the Final Four.

A copy of *Volleyball Magazine* was floating around, and I read the paragraph that described our remarkable rise near the top of the volleyball world, our incredible defense, pinpoint serving, and smart shot selection. "Stanford is a very dangerous squad," the writer concluded. We were by far the most entertaining team to watch as we scraped and scrapped until the other team tired. Problem was, we weren't the tallest or the most athletic, we were just the most tenacious. Would that be enough to beat UCLA?

Once again, I resented that other volleyball teams got to take their finals after Christmas but we would be on the same schedule as other Stanford students. I had books to finish reading and papers to conceive but still had some creative thinking time. The faculty club dining room at 'Bama reminded me a bit of *Gone with the Wind*, with white-columned brick-faced buildings and white-painted wood-framed windows. We dressed up, excited to hear who would be selected for All American, Coach of the Year, etc. at the big banquet between the semis and the finals. The UCLA girls brought some Hollywood, sitting at their table with perfect tans, perfect skin, and perfect hair. Most of us had books on our laps, reading glasses on, and little or no makeup. Even though we weren't paying complete attention, I knew we would show up when it counted. And our KimO was named All American.

The pregame pep talk and game plan were unlike any Fred had ever conducted. We had heard rumors about him dating the star outside hitter of UCLA, the lovely Linda, during the summer as he played on the Association of Volleyball Professionals beach tour. But we didn't know he had inside information on her, information he had ignored during league and reserved for the playoffs. Instead of showing us slide after slide of hitting charts and defensive positioning, he kept repeating, "Do not play her sharp cross-court hit.

It is always out. It might look like it's going to drop in, but it isn't. J.J., you'll be blocking her two of three rotations. Take the line and give her cross-court. Left backs, play rally defense and shift in for the tip or roll, but do not reach back for the hit. It will be out." He probably repeated these instructions three times. No specific plans for any of the other hitters, just for Linda.

We had been serving and playing well, and I was happy to have a simple game plan. I knew I would have to work hard to get all the way outside to the line and would have to resist the temptation to drop my left hand to try to stop the cross-court shot, but we had come this far by having a closed block and incredibly quick backcourt movement on defense. If we could trust each other on this new strategy, maybe we would have enough to win. As the national anthem played and I looked across the court at the Bruins, I saw Linda staring at Fred. Pen in mouth, clipboard in hand, a sweat bead forming on his nose, Fred was studiously avoiding anything but his statistical chart. I became suspicious. What happened between those two? Were we about to enact his revenge?

During the first set, we were forming our block correctly but still playing any ball we could get our hands on. With Boom-Boom and Comp on the outside and digging left back, we had solid defenders and excellent serve receivers. Kisi came in the back row for me when KimO went to the front, and Krush and DD were setting solidly. Both of them took away the line on the block, forcing their left-side hitters to hit crosscourt or roll shot, and Boom-Boom and Comp picked up everything. The first set was tight, but we won.

During the changeover, Fred drilled down again: "Those crosscourt shots are out. You have to let them go."

Boom-Boom rolled her eyes. On the first Linda-cross-court shot, she stood up and didn't make a move for the ball. It looked in, but it was out by about two inches. The lines-man's flag rose, and Fred leaned back in his chair, his clipboard covering a smile. Boom-Boom glanced at him, raised her eyebrows, and camped out in the rally defensive position, playing only tips. Boom-Boom and Comp could hit that crosscourt shot and keep it in, and they did. KimO showed why she was an All American and had an outstanding game. I hit well and put a lot of energy into cheerleading. Our bench was noisy the entire match.

But Linda went into the tank. By the time the match was over, she had multiple hitting errors and only a few kills. We won in four sets and couldn't stop jumping on top of each other on the humid, sweaty court. In a surreal moment, we saw Linda at the airport bar the next day, wearing an impeccable white tennis outfit, drinking some umbrella drink at 9:00 a.m. and looking down her nose at several Southern gentlemen who were fighting to get her attention.

But we were going to UOP, to face Hawaii in the semifinal of the national championships. Krush was already talking about their offense, for we hadn't played them this year and she had played club volleyball with three of their starters in high school. For the entire plane ride home, we tried to concentrate on homework and cram for finals, but the prospect of another match with inside knowledge was too tempting to ignore. Inevitably, we dropped the books and huddled around Krush as she described the hitting tendencies of the Pulaski twins. I worried about Robyn Ah Mow, the twenty-six-year-old setter who'd had a kid and was back running the offense with a warrior mentality. Her hand position made her sets impossible to guess, and I'd have to simply react to where the ball went. This was going to be a battle.

Final Four

Walking into the Alex Spanos Center, with my gym bag across my shoulder, I saw UOP's coach by the door. He congratulated me and said he was rooting for our team. Inside the gym, I ran into Debbie and Gary Colberg, my high school club coaches and UC Davis volleyball camp employers.

"Jenyth, where's your mom? She invited us to a pregame party."

Of course Mom would be having a party. "I'd look upstairs in a corner, if there's an empty space. I'm sure she wanted to plug in her Crock-Pot."

We laughed, and they walked up the stairs, as I headed down to the locker room. I saw my UC Davis friend Max, who was dressed in a referee's uniform but holding a linesman's flag.

"Max, are you working our game?!" I hoped.

"Just the USC-San Diego State game. I can't wait to see yours." Max had officiated many of our home matches, brought his guitar to volleyball camp, and was one of my strongest allies. I would play USA club volleyball on his teams after I graduated.

I looked up to the stands and saw my mom and dad, surrounded by friends. Just like my first Stanford tournament at UC Davis as a freshman, Mom had commandeered the best spot and brought her card table, red-checked tablecloths, and sunflowers. I wondered if I'd be able to hear her screeching at the ref during this match. I waved at the group, and one of my club teammate's parents grabbed my mom and pointed at me. We waved, and she blew me a kiss.

I walked by the announcer's table and saw Chris Marlowe talking into a radio mic. Cameras were all over the gym, and the thought we'd be broadcast live sent shivers down my shoulders and arms. What little girls might be at home with their parents, watching volleyball for the first time? Would they see how much we loved the game, how much fun it was to keep the ball alive, and how we never, ever quit? Would some of them fall in love with the game I loved and dream of playing in a national tournament? I grew up watching women's professional tennis players and women's team sports only every four years in the Olympics. Would this match ignite interest in our sport? Would I be able to watch other professional women's sports on TV some day? Off in LaLa land, I didn't see Marlowe stand up until he pulled one of my braids.

"Well, J.J., what do you think?"

"I think I got an A on the paper I turned in at 8:00 this morning," I said, winking at him.

"How will you beat Hawaii?"

"I can't tell you our game plan, but I can tell you they are going to have to play their best to beat us. Who do you think will win the USC-SDSU match?"

"Journalistic objectivity, J.J., I can't tell you what I think. But I have a hunch." He nodded toward Chuck Erbe, who was running a warmup drill with his USC team. Tracy Clark, now an All American, was pounding the ball. I nodded in agreement. Erbe was a master coach, and any team he coached would be tough to beat. I stretched my right thumb, a thumb whose ligaments USC's Paula Weishoff ripped during one of her vicious hits last year. I had worn a large plastic brace taped in place for much of my junior season and had to show it to the referees before each match so that they would approve its legality. If we played USC for the championship, I might tape it on again. Patty had already triple-taped my ankles, applied a heat pack to my back, and helped me stretch my neck.

I stayed a bit longer to witness the stands filling up and the noise level increasing in the gym. A snack-bar line snaked past my mom and her friends, and I caught my brother's eye. We waved. Everything was in place. Time to watch the first set of the other semifinal before we went into the locker room for our pregame chalk talk.

As we stood at the end line, facing number one Hawaii across the net, and listened to the introduction of the starting lineups, the reality of our situation finally struck: we had no chance in the world of beating them. I remembered the words of Atticus Finch when he described Miz Dubose's courageous attempts to quit her morphine addiction: "It's when you know you're licked before you begin but you begin anyway and you see it through no matter what. You rarely win, but sometimes you do." They had only one loss for a reason: nobody could score any points on them, because their serve receive was so incredible. A team might side out, but Hawaii never lost two rallies in a row. Most of the media had written us off. Jayne Gibson from UOP, now an assistant coach, had sat at my lunch table earlier in the day, telling whoever would listen that UOP was the real Ivy of the West. I was tired of the disrespect.

I was tired for another reason. Determined to do well on all my finals before the Final Four, I had stayed up all night to complete a long paper for Professor Polhemus. He promised to meet me in his office at 8:00 a.m., when I'd drop off the typed paper (a first draft) and ride my bike over to catch the team van to Stockton for the pregame luncheon. Krush insisted on driving me over, probably remembering a different bike ride, and we joined the team for the hour drive. No time for a nap and right now, I had enough adrenaline for the entire team.

Fred and Don had positioned KimO as starting middle, which meant I would face off with eventual national player of the year, Deitre Collins. Kim and Deitre were the two strongest middle hitters and blockers on their respective teams, but our coaches decided to put the taller Kim against six-foot Lisa Strand, another sophomore, and me against the five-foot-eleven Deitre, a junior. I knew she jumped, hung in the air, then hit, so we put up a triple block, hoping to force her to tip. It took me a few plays to get the timing down. But I did. Our match became a battle for the few openings we saw in their defense and were able to exploit.

Krush's high school club teammates Kris and Kori Pulaski were passing machines. Missy Yomes went in the front row for one of them and had an amazing match. We didn't expect that. We knew crafty Robin Ah Mow would run an offense that would work us middle blockers. I tried to exhale every time she set the ball. I tried not to guess where the ball was going, and my reaction time was working. I got fooled once, but not twice, closing the block again and again. Boom-Boom and Comp and Bakes were passing and digging well, and I was thrilled when Fred left me in the back row to serve and play defense for a few rotations, reserving Kisi for later. Seeing KimO close the block time and again allowed me to roam the back line and finally make a few digs. My serve was effective and we scored some points. When Kisi subbed in for me, both Don and Fred had determined looks in their eyes. They truly believed we could beat this team. So did I. We knew Hawaii would play rally ball until they wore us down, but we were not going away. We had nothing to fear.

Three-and-a-half hours later, we were still on the court. We had started strong, taking the first and third sets. We were up two games to one, but the momentum shifted, and Hawaii took the fourth set. We had broken the record for the longest match in the short history of the NCAA and still had a set to play. Tied at two games apiece, we were entering the fifteen-point final game. With a change to rally scoring instead of side-out scoring, every play mattered. Every play would result in a point. Every mistake would cost us.

As I warmed up at the end of the bench, my legs started to feel heavy, and the familiar tingle of sciatica was creeping down my right leg. But I would fight on, humming USC's fight song in my mind. *Bah ba buh bah bah bah…* USC had already defeated San Diego State and was in the stands waiting to see who their opponent would be, hoping to repeat their national championship from the previous year. When I subbed in the front row and cross-stepped to close the block on the strong side hitter, I realized my legs had lost their pop. We didn't score many points on my trip across the front line. While I did have a kill, Robin's sets were now too fast for me, and I was getting in the way of the backcourt defense since I didn't consistently close the block. Should my teammates step into the hole I was leaving? Should they have faith I would make it, and stay deep?

When I came out, I saw Fred and Don whispering. My backup, Murph, the lightning-quick middle blocker who had been my preseason roommate, was warming up at the end of the bench. Air Supply. That's exactly what we needed.

The coach in me knew what was coming, but when I sat down on the bench after high-fiving everyone, I tried not to cry. I had never felt so tired in my entire life. I had nothing left in the tank, but I cheered hard for Murph when she subbed in for my position. She actually stuff-blocked Kori one time. A picture of Murph from this set was featured on the cover of *Volleyball Magazine* next summer, as part of their preview article. Stanford was preseason number one.

But here, in Stanford's first and my only Final Four, we lost the fifth and final set by 15–8. We battled until the bitter end, but I didn't feel right about the outcome. If I hadn't stayed up all night to finish my paper, maybe I could have kept up with Robin's sets. The letdown I felt was physical and emotional: I had to watch the last half of the final set from the bench. Murph rose to the moment, and I knew she would be great next year. Once it became clear we would have no miracle comeback, around 13–6, I took my eyes off of the court and took a look around. I found my parents, blew Mom a kiss, and leaned forward to high-five my teammates once Hawaii had won the match. Deitre Collins would be MVP and the solo block record (fifteen) she set for the tournament still stands forty years later.

KimO, Kisi, and I were asked to meet the press in a back room, and I was thrilled to be a part of it. When a reporter asked Kim a question, she turned to me and said, "What do you think, J.J.?" She was too exhausted to talk, and Kisi was too shy. I provided all the answers, explained what we had achieved as a team and as a school, and expressed my happiness that we had made Hawaii beat us.

They asked me if I thought Hawaii could beat USC, and I said, "Yes. It's going to be close, because USC has had experience in championship settings before, but serving and passing will win. The Pulaski twins can pass any serve. They are machines and will wear out the Trojans."

Broadcaster Chris Marlowe nodded, took a final pull on my braids and said, "J.J., have you ever thought of being a broadcaster?"

I giggled, flattered he liked my commentary.

Back in the locker room, utter exhaustion had taken over the team. We had to play SDSU tomorrow night for the third-place trophy, and nobody wanted to play. We had lived our motto: Leave it all on the court. What else was there to do?

Mama Jo's Brunch

Fortunately, we had something to look forward to the next day. My mom had invited the entire team to our house for brunch. I knew her food, love, and care would be the balm we needed. I tried not to think how our tract home would compare with Hoss Ranch and took comfort that everyone would have a good time.

The next morning, Fred and Don said they weren't going to come over, that they had to do pre-match preparation. I felt so bad for my mom. Making food for others was her calling card, and she would wonder if the coaches thought she was good enough. Mom had organized the parents' section at every home game, had traveled to the away games with Comp's family, and had invited them and Kisi's parents from Hawaii to stay at our house during the national championships. The parents helped her prepare the pre-match food at UOP and would help at our team brunch. Mom would be in her element, although she probably had exhausted herself with the preparations. I tried not to worry about her physical condition, and I planned to make sure she sat and rested part of the time. We both loved the culture of volleyball: intense competition on the court and loyal friendship off the court. Play first, party later, both teams together.

When I walked through our front door, my mom was full of smiles.

"You girls were awesome! You were on TV! You gave those Rainbow Wahines all that they could handle." Her unbridled joy put everyone in a good mood. I observed Mom wasn't wearing her wedding rings.

I showed off the disco ball in our family room after everyone grabbed a plate of food. Without a true dining room, we ended up sitting on the living room floor and stuffing ourselves. Our trainer, Patty, kept saying, "Don't worry about the calories! You're going to need them tonight." We stuffed ourselves with Aunt Joan's ham, super-duper potatoes, Uncle Bob's green bean casserole, red-hot Jell-O salad, orange beets, Aunt Louise's cinnamon rolls, Watergate salad, and of course, buttermilk brownies. Most of us slept on the ride back to Stockton.

The pregame meeting was a bit of a shock: the seniors were told we weren't going to start; next year's potential starting lineup was going to be playing. As I warmed up, I couldn't believe it. Had I played my last match for Stanford without even knowing it was my last match? We lost the first two sets, and the seniors were allowed to come in for the third set. We won. We battled back, and won the fourth set. When the fifth and final set began, the seniors were left on the bench. SDSU won that final set, and I was on the sidelines when the whistle blew the end of my Stanford volleyball career.

I was so mad. The seniors should have been on the court, not the bench. I believed we deserved one last chance to win.

Still, we female athletes had been *seen*. A nationally televised tournament, postgame interviews, and coverage in local and national newspapers were evidence that our sport had evolved from just another small Olympic sport to something entertaining and relevant. This was a far cry from my freshman year, playing in old army hangers or gyms with cement floors covered in Tartan coating. I'd left my sweat on the floor of many storied courts: UCLA's Pauley Pavilion, Hawaii's Klum Gym, USC's Memorial Gym, SDSU's Peterson Gym, Cal's Haas Pavilion, and Alabama's Coleman Gym.

I knew Stanford's commitment to implement Title IX had been sincere and effective. Our volleyball court lines were painted onto the floor of Maples Pavilion, a permanent reminder that we belonged in that gym just as much as the men's basketball team. There was no better university in the country to be a female athlete. And this was just the beginning of hundreds of matches won at Maples. Old Roble Gym would always have a strong pull on my heart, but mostly for the Viennese ball, not for the game where I fainted.

Stanford Volleyball has been in every NCAA tournament, beginning in 1981. But it is what our players do outside college that is really worth noting. Boom-Boom is a noted orthopedic surgeon. Kisi ran the Special Olympics for years in her native Hawaii and still teaches and coaches. KimO played on two Olympic teams and served as captain for one, then coached a high school team to the California State Volleyball Championship two years in a row. Krush trained killer whales at Sea World before becoming a teacher and coach. Jan and Paula broke through the glass ceilings of investment banks and created more opportunities for women in the Wall Street world. Grits worked as a physical therapist for three decades. Comp became a lawyer and raised four kids. Murph taught and coached for decades. Bakes published photographs and designed art displays, along with teaching and running a business. And I? Well, that needs a bit more explanation.

CHAPTER 16
The Almost Ending

Returning to campus in January of 1983, I knew I had an incredible task before me. To graduate on time with a degree in creative writing, I had to take twenty-two units in the winter and twenty-one in the spring. I had to get special permission from the dean to do this, so I explained my financial situation, and he signed off on the schedule. Busy was my middle name, and winter quarter flew by.

At the beginning of spring quarter, I signed up for my senior advising session with Nancy Packer, the director of the Creative Writing Department, and showed up in my best plaid skirt and twinset sweaters. Little did I know I was about to get kicked out of the literati of Stanford.

"Well, Jenyth, I have your academic record here. It looks like you're doing well in your literature classes. Both Michael Koch and Gilbert Sorrentino gave you solid recommendations for the major and said your writing is improving. What are your plans next year? Do you have an advisor for the honors thesis?"

"Uh, Professor Packer, I won't be here next year."

"Why not? You've only been in the major for a few quarters. You need another year to boost your GPA and write an honors thesis so you can get into graduate school, get funding, and write novels."

"I can't stay. My volleyball scholarship expires in June.

I have a student loan from my freshman year, and my mom is sick. I need to graduate on time."

"That's not what I want to hear. You need to stay another year and work on your writing. You're really just getting into the best courses we offer, and I'll be teaching the workshop in the fall. You need more work."

"I'm sorry, professor. I just can't."

At that, she slammed shut a red Pee-Chee folder with my name on front and slapped a disgusted look on her face. "Well, then the only thing you're fit for is to be a high school teacher." She stood up, shook my hand, tossed my folder into a file drawer and led me out of her office. I was dismissed.

As I walked downstairs and out the English Department door, I headed left toward the entrance to the Stanford Church. In times of trouble, a magnet dragged me into the cavernous expanse of what my architecture professor had called "The ugliest cathedral on the planet." The church had served its purpose for me. I went to my favorite pew toward the front, slouched down on the hard bench, and looked skyward to the windows in the dome. They were dirtier than they were when I had arrived—a greenhorn hoping to become a world-famous Olympic star who would become an auto-immune doctor and could cure her mother. So many discarded dreams, so many prayers for guidance in this space.

My 1983 at Stanford felt full of loss: no study abroad opportunity, no Viennese Ball or spring formal, no intramurals, no sorority rush parties. I had no time for fun. I was still filled with imposter syndrome—until I learned that many of my varsity athlete classmates would not be able to graduate in June. None of us had known how hard this student-athlete gig would be at a pressure-cooker place like Stanford. Still, I was determined to graduate on time.

Nancy Packer's words started to sink in. Not the words that were so like Eliza Doolittle's in *Pygmalion*—when she says, "What am I fit for?"—but the phrase "honors thesis." Professor Packer thought I had come in to select an honors adviser, and was actually encouraging me to continue writing, to continue studying the authors I loved. My literary life was full of crushes: Mr. Darcy, Kafka, Rilke, Coleridge, Byron, Keats, and Shelley. O to have dinner with Anthony Trollope – what a lark that would be. I wanted to be a sister scribe with Jane Austen, Emily Dickinson, the Brontës, and Elizabeth Barrett Browning. I wanted to rewrite Shakespeare plays from a female perspective. I was good enough, in Packer's very critical mind, to continue. As I ruminated over that fabulous fact, I realized I had replaced "fake it until you make it," with "Face it until you ace it." No longer did I feel the creative writing department had been fooled, the English department duped, and my friends disappointed when I left the sciences for fuzzy studies. Sure, I didn't know what I was doing all of the time and had many gaps in my knowledge of English grammar, but I'd played to my strengths: my love of words and ideas and lively characters. No longer did I feel like an intellectual phony. Professor Packer's declaration that I'd never return to school once I started working, and my realization she was disappointed in that certainty, fueled my ambitions. Then and there, I made a vow: someday I would go to graduate school and write a book.

First, I had to graduate on time and get a job and a life. Financial independence was available to me only if I could get that diploma. How I was going to make money was not

as important. I'd never had a problem finding work. I just
needed to start somewhere.

Paradise Lost

Most of my classmates were winding down their academic lives with an easy final spring quarter. In May, when
the pool and Lake Lagunita beckoned, however, I couldn't
accept the temptation of any gatherings. I'd left Professor
Evans's demanding class in Milton for the last quarter. The
class everyone said was so difficult I found fascinating and
overwhelming. It describes my entire Stanford experience:
Paradise Lost. Reading this and Milton's poetry took up
hours every day. I tried to imagine myself in Milton's story
but didn't find any relatable women in it. I didn't want any
of the sacred feminine roles. I was not the virgin, was not
equipped to be a seductress, hoped to be a mother someday,
and was willing to wait a long time for the old crone
moniker.

I kept returning to two passages and wondering how
Milton was so wise to know "A mind not to be changed by
place of time. / The mind is its own place, and in itself / Can
make a heav'n of hell, a hell of heav'n." I thought that line
was the epitome of volleyball—the back and forth; the rep-
resentation of how one's attitude influences the mind, the
body. I connected this to Hamlet, who said, "There is nothing either good or bad but thinking makes it so."

As I read and read near a favorite tree so I could be outside for at least part of the day, I was jealous that friends
were playing volleyball on the sand every afternoon. I
wished I had more time at Stanford. I wished I could stay
for another year. I knew cramming was not learning, and

now that I had found something I wanted to learn, I had to cram it all in to graduate on time.

The question that had haunted me for my whole life came back again: Would I ever find someone like me, someone who lived a lot of life in his head, who had an uncomfortable mind but the willingness to live with it? Milton offered one out: "Solitude sometimes is the best society." But a lifetime of loneliness had no appeal at all. As I read and read and wrote literary analyses and submitted first drafts of stories all spring, I was forced into solitude to complete my studies. Friends came by to check on me, or borrow my dresses for dances and formals, but I stayed home to read and write. I was determined not to miss any classes or skip any of the assigned reading. While I slept as little as I had as a premed, I remembered the German and forgot only my Milton. As finals approached, I worried that I might not be studying the right books and lines. Would I choke on this final instead of graduating? I couldn't drop the class on the day of the final to avoid a bad grade. Milton was required reading.

The Spy

I did emerge for one unforgettable party. My first-year volleyball teammate Tucker was about to earn her MRS degree and was celebrating her engagement at her fiancé's Atherton home. We'd met him freshman year while watching his band, and I hadn't seen much of Tucker since. My parents were coming to the party, and I knew they had never seen a home like this one. Mom was a little nervous, but Dad looked great in his impeccable blue suit and tie. I wore a lightweight shift with a matching bolero jacket, my new shoes matching one of Mom's old handbags. Mom's shoes and handbag perfectly coordinated with this year's church suit, a lovely aqua blue that matched her eyes. I adored the aqua pearl choker and earrings she wore.

We drove the Monte Carlo up the long driveway, and a valet took our keys, gave my dad a ticket, and pulled the car out of sight behind a black Lincoln town car. When we walked past the Italian fountain and onto the expansive porch, a few people were ahead of us. Tucker and Rich were greeting everyone and introducing them to their parents. My folks shook hands with Tucker's family, and I observed them with pleasure. They had sent us an incredible Texas steak for Christmas one year. Then Rich introduced us to his parents, and his mom held onto my mom's hand for a bit.

"I'm sure we've met somewhere before," she said "It's a pleasure to see you again."

Mom smiled and didn't say anything. I thought how pretty she looked in her church suit, her large pearls encircling her neck, and her eyes popping with shy delight. Rich's dad said the same thing to my dad, whose ramrod posture, firm grip, and fearless gaze hid the true jokester he was.

All Dad said was, "It's possible," and turned to wink at me.

We walked into a massive room with food around the perimeter and lots of important people mingling. Mom and I were given some champagne, and my dad found a brandy.

A little later, Rich's dad came back to us. "I remembered, Lee. We met at the Pentagon, didn't we?"

Dad smiled, and I thought about the times my brother and I pretended Dad was a spy. "Oh, of course, Lee," he said, "you can't discuss what we talked about. I'm so sorry. Let me introduce you…" And off my parents went, taken around the room like honored guests. They meeted and greeted, and I stood near the bar and watched the entire room move in a counterclockwise circle. The ceiling had a fresco of angels, and I thought Milton would approve of this heavenly room. My parents had no money, no social connections, no importance in a place like the Stanford community, yet they could navigate through it all with their charming manners. They had class, I thought, and was so proud of the way they handled themselves. I hoped I would have my mom's poise and my dad's distinguished air someday.

After we picked up the car, Mom turned to me in the back seat and said, "Wasn't that a hoot, Jenyth Jo? Do you know everyone thinks your dad is in the top-secret part of the military, and he never told them otherwise? Isn't that a kick?"

Dad nodded, smiling broadly, and as usual, kept silent. Unlike me, he never interrupted. Maybe that's why the Atherton folks were drawn to him: he let them talk and talk their way into their opinions, without ever giving his. I loved watching my parents enjoy themselves even more than I loved the real champagne at the bar.

Diploma Blues

After running through most of the fountains the night before... after leaving bottles of Andre "champagne" in the fountains by Roble Hall, Memorial Auditorium, and the bookstore... after meeting up with the SLE gang so we could drink them at 7:00 a.m... after letting John Elway grab my bubbles and blow them in Frost Amphitheatre, as Donald Kennedy told us to choose service over profits, I found myself with the English majors sitting in Memorial Church around noon. I looked at the arches, the gold leaf, the altar reconstructed after the 1906 earthquake (gone after the 1989 earthquake), the organ behind us, and the pew where I had prayed before every chemistry test. My head was starting to ache, not from the champagne, which was still providing a numbing high, but from lack of sleep and fear that I might not actually graduate.

Memories flooded in—of telling my parents I wouldn't be making the sophomore year road trip, so they could see me play; of telling my mom I wouldn't be able to be a doctor and cure her disease, because I fainted when the anatomy professor revealed our cadaver Leon; of telling my parents about dropping inorganic chem on the day of the final, or the four other science courses I dropped sophomore and junior year when I panicked at getting a C. I remembered telling them I had changed my major to creative writing because I could finish it in the five quarters I had remaining, not realizing twenty-one units in the final quarter of senior year is a bad idea. Yet, my Milton final was an essay exam, and I felt much more confident in forming an analysis and backing it up with quotes from the text than I did using the process of elimination on a multiple-guess test. I knew I had filled an entire blue book with ideas. Would that be enough?

The pressure in my head was building, as I looked back at my mom, dad Leland Stanford Gearhart, Jr., brother Leland Stanford Gearhart, III, Grandma and Grandpa Kottong, all sitting up tall and proud and waiting for me to graduate.

When Professor Polhemus walked up to the podium, placed a stack of notes on the lectern, let his mortar board tassel fall in his face so he could puff it up with air from his lower lip, I knew I would be fine. Whether the diploma case actually held a diploma or not, I knew I was about to be entertained one last time by the best nineteenth-century English literature professor I'd had. He filled his Trollope class with hilarity, yet we knew we had to be on top of our games, as he never hesitated to call us by our first names and banter with us. Polhemus's wit was so subtle and intertwined with the material that I found myself shaking with laughter through most of the class. I knew he recognized that I recognized his efforts, and every time I caught one of his oblique references, he'd glance over to make sure I was giggling.

Today, he pulled a typical Polhemus stunt and dropped most of the papers on the church floor. Yes, he could have stapled them together, in order, but this gave him the opportunity to say, "Welcome to the architectural nightmare Leland Stanford's wife gave us. While I prepared copious notes about the solemnity of this occasion, I don't need to read from them to tell you what you need to hear." At this, he glanced at me, winked, puffed up his tassel again, and pretended to read from his reorganized but upside-down notes. My dad was chuckling, while the rest of my family looked concerned.

As Professor Polhemus continued to "read" the university-required script, it became clear to me he had been drinking something stronger than coffee. His nose became redder, the puffs more frequent, and his cadence more Irish. "What, me worry?" he mimed, like the cover of *Mad* magazine. He told us we were about to enter the time of our lives, and some more *blah, blah, blah* that he didn't believe. Finally, other professors came forward for the reading of the names, but I knew I didn't have to be anxious about whether my first name would be pronounced correctly. Polhemus loved saying Jenyth.

Sitting there in the church with my family at my back and favorite teachers standing in a line to shake my hand up front, I realized no one would know if I had a diploma or not. If all the praying didn't result in a passing grade, and I had to retake Professor Evans's Milton 373 to graduate, at least I knew where all the occult books were located in the undergraduate library. Perhaps my alchemical skills could produce a spell as potent as lipid-soluble pot brownies. I could navigate any place in the Green Graduate Library—the best places to sleep; the dusty tomes downstairs in the stacks, where any question could be answered, next to the cubby where I had hidden one last bottle of Andre champagne for the future. I knew how to get there via the steam tunnels and which manhole cover was loose. I could talk to any Stanford student about their major, was unafraid of the university president or any person in power. I could stand up to a volleyball coach or a teammate, could wrench a suicidal friend off the roof of the third-floor sundeck and stay with her until she was checked into a mental health facility. I could waltz like an angel and polka like a bulldozer, and best of all, I could type seventy-five words a minute on my Sears electric typewriter. Once again, I had been assured by the CPPC office that I could get a job.

On the other hand, my back and ankle hurt all of the time. I was not qualified to apply to medical school, and would never make the Olympic Volleyball team. I had come to Stanford full of hope, but nobody would remember me at this school. I had ruined my body in pursuit of my dreams, and I wondered if it was worth it. I refuted myself at this thought. Every spike, every dive, every play was worth it. I helped create a new dynasty in sports, even if I wasn't an All-American.

As I waited to receive my diploma cover, I took stock of my financial situation. I had twelve hundred dollars in the bank, the exact amount of my student loan from my first year. Many friends would graduate with enormous debt that would take decades to pay off. Some of these signed on with high-paying, soul-crushing jobs that would allow them to make their debt payments. As I was in the black, I didn't need to go to work right away. I'd use my student loan to establish credit. I could sleep for a week, knowing I had a mature mind that could analyze and solve most problems. I knew I was the most thankful girl in church.

As Professor Polhemus called, "Jenyth Jo Gearhart, AB Creative Writing," I held up my gown and walked up the steps. I caught a glance of a piece of paper sticking out of the diploma case as Polhemus handed the folder to me. As I shook his hand, he grinned and I giggled: paradise regained. I looked up at the cupola, then out at my mom, and completed a different degree in my mind: "Jenyth Jo Gearhart, Stanford Woman." Thanks to funding from Title IX, I had learned how to manage a multi-potential life. Now I could decide how to spend the rest of it.

Purpose

After the postgraduation glow faded, I thought about our university president's call to service during his commencement address. I felt free to explore my options as long as I could pay my bills and be financially independent. Like my spontaneous and creative classmates, for whom thinking outside the box was a mindful decision, I became part of the thousands of Stanford graduates who tried to make the world a better (and more colorful) place. While some in the

1980s were "finding themselves," we Stanford graduates were creating ourselves. We took a shot at something to see if the idea worked; "ready, fire, aim" described us well. Thus began the dot-com boom and dozens of patents for a wide variety of devices and intellectual property.

For many years, I did regret skipping a fifth year and working on an honors thesis. Professor Packer had quoted Thomas Wolfe's title *You Can't Go Home Again* when she told me I was making a mistake. I didn't believe her. Home was home with my family, not Stanford. Still, I thought I would return to school someday. I began my working years as a breakfast chef at the Stanford Sierra Camp on Fallen Leaf Lake, moved to a corporate job in San Francisco, left for the grand tour of Europe I'd missed in college, and returned to coach men's and women's volleyball at UC Davis. I tried to win doubles tournaments in California's outdoor beach and grass circuits and had an undefeated season in the grass volleyball leagues.

My mom complained I was still marching to the beat of my own drummer as I strove to be a well-rounded person who was always curious, always learning, always kind. My volleyball doubles prowess caught the eye of the Italian pro leagues, and I enjoyed a brief spring stint playing with an indoor semi-pro A2 team. I had an offer to return in the following year to play for a true professional A1 team full of Italian Olympians, and I decided to teach high school and try to write a book while I trained. I could return to Italy as long as my mom's health was stable. Mom was in and out of the hospital and had started smoking on the sly again. I was worried.

In 1986, Mom was very sick, so I prayed, "God, give me her pain." He did.

CHAPTER 17
The Glint of Light on Broken Glass

My coed doubles partner and I had won thirteen tournaments in a row and were expected to win again at the season finale. On the University of California soccer field, I landed on a flat, six-inch sprinkler head, and my foot slipped sideways. The crack was so loud everyone in the tournament stopped. I had blown out my knee and broken my leg in three places. I don't remember the screaming, the ambulance, the shot, or the loss of consciousness, but I do remember waking up in the hospital and watching the 49ers play football, while I waited for the orthopedic surgeon to arrive.

Three weeks before, I had started a high school teaching job, which I already loved. Unfortunately, my new health insurance was not valid, and I was kicked out of the hospital. Once again, Mom came to my rescue and managed to get me into a surgeon a few days later. My parents took out a second loan on their house, paid for my surgery, hired a lawyer, won the case for health insurance, and got their money back. Meanwhile, I lived in my childhood bedroom for three months with my leg tied to the ceiling and my dad changing my bedpan. My parents took turns massaging lotion into my feet, as damaged nerves jolted pain down my leg. I returned to teach in a wheelchair, and my dad drove me to and from school for six months. I had a planned second surgery in the summer.

It was during these months that I started wondering why my mom went into remission whenever something happened to me. First, the concussions, then the coma when I was sixteen. Now this career-ending injury. I was told I might never walk again, and Mom told me not to believe them. She cooked anti-inflammatory foods and helped me with physical therapy, and I was walking in four months. Mom was such an inspiration.

I tried to do some writing, but the painkillers seemed to have affected my ability to concentrate. I put the first manuscript in a bottom drawer so I wouldn't have to look at my failure to complete it. This was Book Failure #1.

Book Failure #2

Some disaster happened every time I tried to write this story. In 1990, I went to grad school and began writing again. I was in my second year, when Boom-Boom got married at Lake Tahoe over Labor Day weekend in 1991. She made a point to ask about my mom. "J.J., she doesn't look good. Has she been checked out?"

Boom-Boom was now Dr. B., and over a glass of champagne at the reception, we discussed Mom's diagnostic tests, none of which showed anything.

After the wedding, my mom told my dad that they were selling the Carmichael house and moving back to Kansas. I was surprised, but the cost of living in California on a fixed income, plus the opportunity to help their parents in their old age, motivated them to move.

Just a week after they left for Kansas, the phone call I had dreaded for years occurred on a Sunday night. My aunt told me Dad had taken Mom to the ER. She was having a hard time breathing, and my parents told her not to call me. "I probably shouldn't be saying this, Jenyth Jo, but I'm worried. Just wanted you to know."

I did know, in the deep recesses of my amygdala. A bolt of adrenaline shot through me, as if I'd just hit a match-deciding spike. I called the ER in Topeka and asked to speak to the doctor. He came on the line and wouldn't give me any details. I said, "I just need a yes-no answer. If this were your mother, would you get on a plane and come to Kansas?"

"Yes, I would come as soon as possible. Tomorrow if you can."

Somehow, I swallowed my fears, packed a bag, jumped on a plane, and was in her hospital room by 4:00 p.m. the next day. She was on the sixth floor, in a colonial blue room, with a row of pin oaks turning color down the street filling up the view from her window. Mom was very gray but perked up when I walked in.

"Jenyth Jo, I'm so glad you've come. I've had an X-ray, and they've taken out one of my lymph nodes."

Dad gave me a hug and said he was going to go outside for a walk. He had quit smoking several years before but started again this day and would smoke for the rest of his life.

A large nurse came in, checked Mom's vitals, adjusted some knobs, and told her that dinner would arrive at 5:00. The doctor should be in soon. I looked around at two IV drips, read "saline" on one and "morphine" on the other. "Mom, are you in pain? What does it feel like?"

"I can't take a deep breath. Yesterday, I could hardly breathe, and my chest kind of cramped up when I did breathe. I'm more relaxed now, but I'm sure something's really wrong. I haven't felt good for months, but now... well, I guess we'll find out soon."

I adjusted her pillows and found some lotion. Time for a foot massage. I was rubbing her toes when the oncologist walked in with a stethoscope around his neck. My mom and I met eyes, and hers crinkled at the corner. I was terrified.

"Hi, Mrs. Gearhart. How are you feeling today?" He did the usual blood pressure and chest-listening drill, then sat back with a sad expression. "I have some results for you, and I'm afraid I have bad news. Is this your daughter?"

"Yes, and she needs to hear everything you have to say."

"The chest X-ray from yesterday shows a large tumor in your left lung. We took a biopsy of the tissue and also removed a lymph node. The results came back. You have non-small cell lung cancer, specifically squamous cell carcinoma. This morning's X-ray showed an additional tumor in your bronchi. It appears the cancer is spreading quickly, perhaps due to your autoimmune history. I'm afraid we can't do surgery or radiation or chemo to help you."

Mom's face showed complete acceptance. "Thank God. I can't think of anything worse than prolonging the agony with chemo. I'd lose my hair and my brain. What's the point? It is going to be quick, isn't it?"

I gaped at her, shocked that she was giving up so quickly. Couldn't we do something to prolong her life? I didn't want her to die, but she sounded like she didn't want to live. I couldn't wrap my brain around this. Life without my mom? I couldn't imagine the inevitable.

"I'm so sorry I don't have better news for you. It's a matter of weeks, no longer."

Mom nodded, then asked him where he'd trained for medicine

When he said "UCLA," we both laughed and told him about our volleyball rivalry. "My wife and I moved here so our kids could grow up on a farm. We really like the people here."

Mom nodded again. "I wanted to come back here for that reason."

They shook hands, and he closed the door. Tears started to flood my face, and my body began to shake. When I blubbered a bit, my mom said, "Jenyth Jo, stop it. We have work to do. Please get me the phonebook." I couldn't believe it: Mom had just been given her death sentence and she wanted to make phone calls? "Do you have a notepad in your book bag? Good, start taking notes."

For the next hour, I recorded Mom's wishes through blurry vision: which funeral home, which cemetery, which dress she wanted to be buried in. I kept thinking, *How can she do this? How can she consent to this without a fight?* So I finally asked her. "Mom, I can't believe we're doing this. Don't you want a second opinion?"

"Nope. I want the list done before my dinner arrives. I think we're in good shape. Now you are going to find your dad. Where has he been all this time? He can sit with me while I eat, and I want you to go to the store and buy enough Halloween decorations to cover this room, and several bags of Halloween candy. Be sure to get the chocolate ones, with Almond Joys and Mounds. I'm going to sort through the bag and eat them all. Why not?"

I shook my head. She wanted me to decorate her room?

Later, I put up the spiderwebs and witches and garish skeletons by the bathroom. The pumpkin banners said "Happy Halloween," but I couldn't imagine any happiness in that room.

A few days later, my brother and his bride of a year came and laughed at our decorations. Nurses came by all the time to eat from the candy bowl by Mom's bed, and she became friends with them all. We heard stories, such as the pepper on the pillow plot and the time my brother ate all the Christmas freezer cookie dough and blamed it on me. Instead of sadness, the room was filled with joy, as all my mom's cousins and family stopped by.

The nights were different. My brother told me how my mom cried and struggled with God. I was nervous when it was my turn to stay the night. October 12 was my mom's best friend's birthday. It was stormy, and our beloved pin oak and liquid amber leaves were blowing off the trees. Everyone went back to Dad's sister's house around 8:00 p.m., and the nurse brought me a pillow. Mom and I talked, but I sat next to her bed instead of on it with her. She said, "There's only one thing I'm afraid of, Jenyth Jo. It's you. Please don't get married just to get married."

I fingered the diamond ring her mother had given me for my birthday a year before. I wore it as a pendant. Grandma had said, "Here's my diamond ring. Every woman should have a diamond, whether or not she has a husband." Why were these two so concerned?

"Mom, I won't get married just to get married, but I do hope I meet someone who loves being part of a family as much as I do."

"I hope you do get to be a mom. Your children will be lucky. In the meantime, I want you to take care of my rings for me." They slid off her atrophied finger easily.

"You are the best Mama Jo anyone could have. I don't know how I…" I cried a bit then, realizing she would never get to be a grandma. She patted my hand, while looking out the window.

Mom's body seemed to shrink in a matter of hours, till it

looked like the skeletons hanging over the bathroom door. Cancer fed on her flesh, and the skin on her face stretched over her skull in a ghoulish way. Her blue eyes were huge below deeply grooved lines in her forehead. She began talking to other people I could not see, breaking the silence of the room, since all the machines had been turned off. Only the morphine pump remained connected to her.

I thought of my conversation with God when I'd been in a coma, and wondered if Mom could see something similar. There were no nuns in this hospital, and no witches in the flesh, just cardboard grinners. I wondered if the creepy visions I'd had at sixteen would be realized here, but her room remained quiet.

Around 2:00 a.m., she started seeing something with her eyes closed, either a real heaven or a reel of her life playing on the screen of her subconscious mind. She said hello to Daddy Tom, Aunt Hilda, and her dad Jim. Then Mom bolted awake, looked at me, and ordered, "Jenyth Jo, I need some morphine. Hit the button twice."

"Mom, you know I can't do that. You won't wake up. The nurses warned us."

"That's the point. I'm ready to go."

"I'm not going to do it."

"Okay, I will." She sat up, grabbed the safety bar, and pressed the button. Once. Then she slid back into bed, her tiny body disappearing under the hospital gown. "I'm cold. Can you pull up the blanket? Ahh, I love you so much, Jenyth Jo. You have my wedding rings, right?" She smiled at me and took my hand, looking at the rings. "Is it midnight yet?"

I looked at the clock and nodded. "It's 2:12 a.m."

"Good." She closed her eyes, and a slight smile tilted the

edges of her mouth. She would not die on her best friend's birthday. A little victory.

But she did die when the sun began to lighten the row of pin oaks. As I held her hand in mine, I couldn't understand how something so anticipated felt so unexpected when it actually happened. Her mouth gaped open, then she stopped gasping for air. I felt her pulse continue. I waited for the next breath, but she didn't breathe again. I kissed her cheek. Instead of transferring my warmth to her, I felt her cold throughout my body. I needed to move. I paced. I found the nurse. I called my dad.

When my dad and brother arrived to say goodbye, I went outside to shuffle my feet in the leaves. I spun Mom's wedding rings on my right hand and looked up, as the final leaf on a liquid amber tree twirled to join the earth, leaving an empty winter branch poking a hole in my sky.

Book Failure #3

For the first two years after Mama Jo died, I had to exit before the Milk Farm cow every day so I could cry in the exact same spot my mother had sobbed at my insensitivity. I fantasized about buying a bazooka and blowing that Holstein out of the sky and over the moon. My commute time increased by a half hour to allow for crying time, until I figured out I could take the back roads to Vacaville High. My nightmares returned, and I failed to save my mom again and again. I went to grief therapy, and it was worse than grieving on my own. Writer's block and self-doubt crippled me for years, but my love of teaching and of my students gave me purpose.

When I borrowed a colleague's three-legged stool after

my four-legged one broke, I noticed it didn't rock back and forth while I twitched, waiting for students to answer a question. It was balanced, stable, and I felt centered on it. I tried to share this serenity with my students, whose teenage stress was magnified by hormones and a world becoming too complicated to comprehend. I had been brought up to believe being well-rounded equated to striving for super-woman status; I must excel at everything I did, for all of the women before me who had had no opportunity to try. As I passed 30, I began to believe that my intense inward life was a blessing and I could stop comparing myself with others. When I told my students to focus on being the best person they could be without measuring themselves to a false standard of excellence, I began to practice what I preached. I focused on a new approach to goals. My 4th grade teacher had told me I was a writer, and I kept trying to deserve the moniker.

I met and married, had a daughter in 1995, and decided to write the book again in 1997 while I was pregnant with my second child. Competitive jock that I am, I wanted to see if I could have the second baby without medication for pain. I had played volleyball with a broken ankle and a broken toe and a damaged back. I believed I could conquer the pain of a natural birth through breathing techniques. I found a Native American birthing guide and hoped their method would work. Lo arrived right on time: a fat, full-term beauty. But at seven weeks of age, she stopped breathing.

It was moving day, a day I thought would be a simple two-mile move across town to a larger home. Everyone was unloading the truck at the new house while I stayed behind with Lo, waiting for her to wake up from her nap. While I was washing and packing the breakfast dishes, I distinctly heard the voice of my mother. "Jenyth Jo, go pick up your baby." For the six years I'd been without my mom, I'd yearned to hear her voice again; I reveled in the sound. "Jenyth Jo, go *now*." I obeyed. When I saw Lo sleeping face down in her crib as usual, something seemed wrong. I picked her up and there was no tension in her body. Her face was blue. I felt a pulse, but she wasn't breathing.

Holding her against my chest, I grabbed my purse, jumped into the front seat of the Volvo, banged her head on the wheel, started the car, held her with my right hand and forearm next to my heart and plowed down the street. I didn't take the time to put her in her car seat, and coaxed her as I drove. *C'mon Lo, breathe baby breathe.* We'd practiced going to the hospital during my pregnancies and I knew I could make it in two minutes, faster than an ambulance could reach my house.

Running through red lights, I screeched up to the emergency room door, left the car running, and bolted through the entrance. Nurses grabbed her from my arms, and I noticed a welt rising on her forehead. She started screaming, breathing, and I collapsed to the floor, sobbing.

A nurse helped me get up and seated me inside a room without a window. She gave me a clipboard, then left, locking the door behind her. I tried to breathe, in through my nose, out through my mouth, just like I'd done during preseason windsprints. I filled out the forms and kept waiting for the door to open when two policemen walked in.

"Mom, why did you hit your baby?" they asked me. What were they talking about? Why didn't the doctor arrive to tell me my baby was going to be OK? After several minutes of questioning, I remembered the lump on her forehead and the nurse who locked me into this waiting room. The thought of losing my beautiful baby girl terrified me, but when I realized they thought I was a child abuser, there were no words to describe my fear.

They left, unconvinced by my story, and I began crying again. I watched the second hand go around the clock. One minute. Two minutes. Five minutes. Ten. By the time 20 minutes had passed, I was furious. Then a group of people, including one of the officers, crowded into the room. I wanted to yell at them, "Where is my baby? What have you done with her?" But instead, I kept my cool.

"Mom, your baby is breathing. How did she get the lump on her head?" asked the doc in the white coat. I told him how I calculated the time it would take for an ambulance to arrive and felt I could drive her to the hospital faster. He shook his head, saying nobody in their right mind would have been able to behave as I did under such pressure.

I told him this: "I played volleyball at Stanford. I know how to fight. My baby had a pulse, but was not breathing. I swear I did not harm her." At this precise moment, a lab report was handed to the doctor. The doctor's face relaxed and he waved off the cop and everyone else, then sat down next to me with a kind look on his face.

"Look at this. Your baby's oxygen level when she arrived was barely measurable in her bloodwork. It's much better now. I don't know what happened when her head hit the steering wheel but I do know you saved her life. Have you heard of SIDS?"

I nodded and stared at him and remembered to take a deep, cleansing breath. Sudden Infant Death Syndrome did not steal my baby. A calm, a strength I'd never felt before, infused my body. What was the source? At the time, I believed my mom was still in my life, watching over us.

Now I realize four years of competitive athletics had prepared me for this moment. I'd learned enough pre-medical material to respond in a life or death crisis. Reliving this scene still makes me hyperventilate. I will always be convinced that sports both built and revealed my character. During this clutch time, I accessed the fierce determination I'd always possessed and made the play when it counted most.

Of course, writing a book after this was impossible. Lo had to be put on a monitor for two years and I became one of Pavlov's dogs, running when I heard her alarm. She slept under my arm for months, keeping time to my heart and breathing. I don't remember sleeping.

The local firemen became our friends, and they did Tuesday practice runs to our house. Captain Mike would knock on my door, tell me they were starting, then hit his stopwatch. They knew the names of our dogs, and how to get to her room through the front door or her second story bedroom window. I was glad to be part of this rescue team.

Eighteen years later, Lo would put on a San Diego State uniform to play Division I volleyball. She was a setter.

Book Failure #4

In 2004, I was a hundred pages into the story when another family member became seriously ill. *This story is cursed*, I thought. Now I had four unfinished versions. I put them into a binder, which I lost.

Fifteen years later, in 2019, I was granted a sabbatical from teaching in the California public schools and received a fellowship to study poetry in the MFA program with Brenda Hillman and Matthew Zapruder at St. Mary's College.

I enrolled in graduate school just as my two daughters finished playing college volleyball and started their own careers. As Poet Laureate of San Ramon, I was thrilled for the opportunity to focus on my own work instead of grading high school essays. I tried to write my way through my continuing grief for my mother in an elective creative nonfiction class. The incomparable Marilyn Abildskov built up my confidence and told me I needed to tell *my* story. I hadn't thought of a memoir; earlier drafts were fictionalized versions of the events. When the COVID-19 quarantine hit in 2020, I knew it was time to complete my Stanford story. The sense of impending doom made the writing inescapable. And I found the binder with the earlier versions. Marilyn invited me to stay for another year and earn a second MFA in creative non-fiction. What an incredible blessing is uninterrupted writing time. RIP Nancy Packer, I did return to college.

POST-GAME ANALYSIS

When I began thinking about the fiftieth anniversary of Title IX in 2022, I realized this story was not mine alone; it belonged to the women who came before me—including my mother, who was athlete of the year for the Topeka High School Trojans, winning the Miss Troy Jane title. She was one of three guards on the defensive half of her high school basketball team, because "girls couldn't run the full length of the court." The story belongs to all my peers at other colleges, who simply wanted hot water in their women's locker room and two referees instead of one. The story belongs to the three million young women playing high school sports now and the thousands who compete for their colleges

And their mothers? They deserve much of the credit. My mom fought for my scholarship, fought for my leg-saving surgery, and fought for my equal opportunity, even when she had no energy left to fight for herself. Because of my mom's brave activism, I vowed to hold the door Title IX unlocked for more generations of female athletes. Coaching them has been a highlight of my life.

Contemporary athletes may say we didn't push hard enough for perks and pay equity, but at the time we were thrilled with the opportunity to just play. It was fun. I fear the fun has left women's intercollegiate sports, and Name, Image, and License rules have increased income inequality and divisions within teams and between men's and women's athletics. I wonder how athletes handle demands to create content and be the brand of a sponsor, always in the public eye. When do they find any time to sleep, after they've taken care of class, homework, and practice? I wonder if they know how many of their non-scholarship teammates experience food insecurity, for the NCAA limits meal plans for teams. How could the NCAA allow some athletes to make millions and others to go hungry? No wonder athletes' mental health issues are on the rise. It was tough in the 1980's. I can't imagine how complicated the pressures are now.

Without Title IX, half of us wouldn't have been able to chase our dreams. I never did enjoy the glory of a golden spike that won the match, but I did learn when to swing hard and when to channel my lovely tenacity into the firm charm of an untouchable tip. That point, and the dazed expression of the opposing coach, still makes me smile.

My lifelong wish of writing a book was a dream deferred but not defeated. As I near the end of this story, I am now a multi-genre writer, with a play in the works and poetry chapbooks circulating the contest circuit. The loss of a beloved mother who didn't deserve to suffer suppressed my imagination for years, and then the fear of COVID ignited my creative energy.

My mom, so familiar with my procrastination, would have said, "No time like the present, Jenyth Jo. Get to work."

I did, Mom.

ACKNOWLEDGMENTS

In memory of Stanford female athletes who died while in school: Samantha Wopat, member of the volleyball team who died in 2012, and Katie Meyer, goalie of the national champion soccer team who died in 2021.

I'm grateful to St. Mary's College of California for scholarship and fellowship support. These funds allowed me to complete a dual designation MFA degree and fulfill my decades-long dream to write a book about Stanford volleyball. Special thanks to the Giacomo Leopardi Poetry Fellowship committee for the opportunity to write and perform in Recanati, Italy, as I revised this story.

To Marilyn Abildskov, who recruited me to the creative nonfiction cohort, then taught me how write through painful memories without losing the story.

For my poetry mentors Brenda Hillman, Matthew Zapruder, Cyrus Cassells, and Ada Limon, Poet Laureate of the United States.

For my creative nonfiction mentors Chris Feliciano Arnold, Brian Broome, Marcelo Hernandez Castillo, Jamil Jan Kochar, and Marie Matsuki Mockett.

To my SMC creative nonfiction cohort: your insight and specific attention to my work has left me in awe on many occasions. As I revise, I hear the voices of Hannah, Jo, Jon, Megan, Mike, Sam, Sanne, Emily, Faith, Lena, Christa, Carolyn, Emma, and Dakota. Your encouragement means so much.

To Susan Breen, my New York Pitch Conference instructor, and my fellow pitchers Sarah Andrews, Khara Brooks, Kathleen Furin, Sharain Hemingway, Angie Hoke, Shannon Holt, Eme McAnam, Pam McFarland, Jyoti Minocha, Melinda Olliver, Stacy Rogers, Emilee Struss, Peg Wiley, and Lisa Woolery.

To my fellow Poetry Crafters: Sandy Cross and Edith Friedman.

To all of the athletes I coached: thank you for helping me create a positive team culture. I learned so much from you.

To my editors and Beta readers Jude Berman, Laura Duggan, William P. Fisher, Jr., Barbara Magalnick, Margaret Grolle, Judy Jordan, Audrey Jo, and especially, Thomas Dunlap.

I'm grateful for the Faculty and Staff of Monte Vista High School, and the San Ramon Valley Unified School District for their support of my sabbatical.

I thank my teammates Boom-Boom, Kisi Haine, Kari Rush, Kim Oden, Margaret Grove, Tucker Ford, Paula Carmack, Jan Linden, Sandy Harris, Jane Bassett, Sherry Norman, Tammy Jernigan, Chris Anderson, Adrienne Duque, Sheila Godbold, Julie Baker, Brandace Hope, Bobbie Broer, Susan Compton, Karen Lysaght, Deidre Dvorak, Lisa Murphy, Terri Bryson, and Jodi Freeman.

I thank my Stanford friends for life: Deanna Boyette, MD; The Honorable John Guerra; Katy Hutt; Judy Jordan; Robin LeCount; David Montgomery, PhD; William Seavey, MD; Steve Schmidt; Lisa Watanabe, MD; Marty Yee, MD.

In honor of my mother, Jo Tindell Gearhart; my father, Leland Stanford Gearhart, Jr.; my brother, Leland Stanford Gearhart, III; my nephew, Leland Stanford Gearhart, IV; and my niece, Alexandra Joanne Gearhart.

And to Archer, my faithful spaniel who took me for long walks, then kept my feet warm.

ABOOKS

ALIVE Book Publishing and ALIVE Publishing Group
are imprints of Advanced Publishing LLC,
3200 A Danville Blvd., Suite 204, Alamo, California 94507

Telephone: 925.837.7303
alivebookpublishing.com